The
Scottish Rite
Papers

Revised Edition

A STUDY OF THE TROUBLED HISTORY OF THE
LOUISIANA AND US SCOTTISH RITE IN THE
EARLY TO MID 1800's

Michael R. Poll

The Scottish Rite Papers
by Michael R. Poll

A Cornerstone Book
Published by Cornerstone Book Publishers

Cornerstone Book Publishers
Hot Springs Village, AR

First Cornerstone Edition – 2020
Second Revised Cornerstone Edition – 2023

www.cornerstonepublishers.com

Table of Contents

Introduction

The peace and wellbeing of Masonry requires that long and undisturbed possession shall be universally accepted as equivalent to original title, in due form, and as conclusive proof of such title.
~ Albert Pike, 1877 [1]

When I was a boy, my reality was that there were monsters living under my bed. If I got up at night, I knew that I would be eaten alive and die a horrible death. As I grew older, I began to realize that my reality was faulty. There was nothing under my bed except dust and a few things that had rolled under to be forgotten. The monsters that I had so feared in my childhood simply did not exist. But as I grew into adulthood, I learned that other monsters did, indeed, exist. Ego, envy, jealously, lust for power, and titles, as well many other of the lesser qualities of man did exist. They found a home in more people, more Masons, than we might have expected. Like an infection, they could enter anyone at any time and destroy not only their lives but the lives of others. I believe that the Masonic phrase, "subdue your passions" applies to our quest to improve ourselves and fight these "monsters" within.

There is a common thought that before anyone can solve a problem, they must first acknowledge that a problem exists. This is true for the individual or a group. Because Freemasonry is composed of human beings, we must recognize that we can and do make mistakes. The whole premise of Freemasonry using symbolic tools to improve ourselves highlights the fact that we are not perfect and in need of improvement. We are human. We can't expect that we will always live up to the pure philosophy of Freemasonry. But, if we are sincere in our claim of being Seekers of Light, desiring, and working towards improvement, then we must acknowledge past failures. We must be honest with ourselves. We must know what is inside of us in need of improvement. We must grow. Once we acknowledge missteps, we can move past them and continue our path to improvement. If we refuse to acknowledge problems, or deny them, then we become bound to our flaws, and they will define us. Our path can change from difficult to impossible.

Insecurity plagues most all of us — even if we refuse to acknowledge it. We want to do good; we want to be successful, and yet we question our abilities and fear that whatever we do may not be enough to accomplish our goals. A deep concern seems to be that if we try and fail then we will open ourselves up to harsh criticism. Our reward for trying to be of service is to be attacked. On the surface, this seems to be a rational concern. But problems can often arise when insecurity overtakes us, and we fall out of balance. Ideally, insecurity and ego should play off each other to keep each other in check. Ego tells insecurity that we do have value, and insecurity tells ego that we are not perfection itself. In proper alignment, they create balance. When out of balance, reality becomes skewed, and we may see monsters where none exist.

I've been a Scottish Rite Mason over forty years now. I remember the day I joined like it was yesterday. To say that I was impressed with the philosophy and symbols of the Scottish Rite is about as great an understatement as possible. I knew instantly that I was home in the Scottish Rite. But as time passed, I began to see that something was amiss. The philosophy and the organization began to grow further and further apart. Good men joined, and some rose quickly in its ranks. While they appeared to be competent and even at times successful at running an organization, many also seemed woefully ignorant of the philosophy or teachings of the Scottish Rite. In time, it became clear that for some Scottish Rite leadership qualities seemed to be the ability to attend meetings, not give trouble, and be in the "inner circle." Understanding of the ritual and philosophy was not at all required nor did it even seem important. Like far too many lodges, the Scottish Rite had become a social cub with a breathtaking but mostly ignored, philosophy. The carrot that was so often dangled was, "Show up; make us look good; keep things going; and you too may get shiny rewards and one day be a *somebody* like us." Those who understood the philosophy found this environment disturbing. Attendance went on the decline. Very few were truly happy. The blame game followed with everyone pointing fingers. The situation was always the fault of someone else. This guy didn't do as he was told. That guy over there doesn't support us — on and on the excuses were made. Ego and insecurity were out of control. So, where did we go wrong? How did we go wrong? What can we do? Maybe we can start by looking at some of the less traveled roads of our history. Maybe a look at the past can help us today. With that in mind, this book is offered.

When I began the research that has led to this book, I was stunned at the various positions taken by the Masons on all sides of historical questions concerning the Scottish Rite. Some positions were accepted and declared "fact" with not a single scrap of evidence in support. They only offered opinion presented as fact. Other positions were pronounced "fact" and yet they are known today to be total fabrications. The ability to state so strongly and so officially something "as fact" with nothing at all in support of such statements caught me off guard. I thought we were better than that. Because I would see, time and again, known errors boldly proclaimed as fact, I began to treat everything written as suspect. It was clearly a time of great emotion, and while there was great passion for advancing fact, it also calls into question the ability to know fact from fiction. The foundation being laid was of clay not stone.

The Scottish Rite has always been a profound system of moral values, offered in a manner designed to infuse students with the desire for gaining more Light. But I believe that the organization stepped off on the wrong foot and has damaged or cracked the window from which Light enters. I don't believe it is an error that is impossible to fix, but it is one that will grow and remain as an impediment to our ultimate success. We need to repair the errors of the past. Bitter medicine may be necessary. I believe with all my heart that the Scottish Rite needs to rediscover its true purpose in Freemasonry by taking a good, long look at itself in the mirror. Only by embracing those on the same path, clearly identifying fact from opinion, and ceasing to throw rocks at kindred spirits will the Scottish Rite become what it always should have become.

The Scottish Rite was never designed to be a club to make "big shots." It is a profound philosophy that teaches us the path to becoming better Masons and better human beings. Monsters may, indeed, live under our bed. But knowledge destroys them.

I hope this book proves to be of some value to you.

Michael R. Poll
April, 2020

Notes:

1. James D. Carter, *History of the Supreme Council, 33° SJ USA* (1861-1891) (Washington, D.C.: The Supreme Council 33°, 1967) 149. Grand Commander Pike was speaking of charges that had been made against the Supreme Council of Scotland in regard to an opinion that they were irregular. The Supreme Council of Scotland was created in 1846 and was, at the time Pike wrote this opinion, 31 years old.

The Scottish Rite Papers

The Scottish Rite Dilemma
The Grand Constitutions of 1786 & Joseph Cerneau

Let's take a look at the creation and early years of the Scottish Rite. But before we do so, I must start off by saying that doing a subject like this is complex and often difficult to follow. I've tried to keep things as basic and straightforward as possible, but this paper does assume that the reader has, at least, some basic knowledge of early Scottish Rite history. Another problem is that when I do a paper like this, some get the idea that I am attacking the Scottish Rite. That's wholly untrue. My life is far richer because of the teachings of the Scottish Rite. As I have said before in papers and videos, my joining the Scottish Rite was like coming home for me. It is because of my deep love of the teachings of the Scottish Rite that I am compelled to point out and hopefully assist in the correcting of what I view as errors from the past. I'd like to contribute in some small way to making the Scottish Rite more of what it always should have been. I view it as a responsibility. So, let's take a walk through a most controversial subject.

Few Masonic documents have been debated, praised, maligned, studied, and misunderstood more than the "Grand Constitutions of 1786." There are actually two recognized collections with that name, one commonly known as the French version and the other the Latin version. The Latin version is far more detailed and complete looking. The French version is bare-bones and minimal. But we need to ask — what are these Grand Constitutions? Why are they important? And why all the fuss about them throughout Scottish Rite history? Let's try to look at a very complicated and contentious history and hopefully make things a little bit clearer.

The Grand Constitutions of 1786 are directly associated with the creation of the 33 degree Ancient and Accepted Scottish Rite and are its original rules and regulations. These Grand Constitutions contain 18 Articles, or rules, which were claimed to be approved and signed in Berlin by King Frederic the Great on May 1, 1786. The idea was to create a new Masonic system of 33 degrees. It was to be well-organized and workable. There is no question that they were successful in that goal. While this new system was built on and expanded the degrees of the older Order of the Royal Secret, it's fair to say that it was a new and very beneficial system.

Without getting into a lengthy side discussion of its history, the older Order of the Royal Secret was problematic in its manner of organization and government. The new system did bring order to the chaos of the old one. In addition, this new system reportedly had the blessing of European royalty. But the dilemma was and always has been that the entire story of the Grand Constitutions, as well as any approval by Frederic the Great, is unproven and dubious by any objective study. No original Grand Constitutions have ever been discovered. In fact, nothing of an original has ever been proven to have been in the possession of anyone from any known supreme council. In other words, there is not a scrap of clear evidence that they ever actually existed. Today, we are hard-pressed to find any serious historian who will claim that the Grand Constitutions of 1786 are anything but a fabricated story. There may be some debate about *who* fabricated the story, but most agree it is a made-up tale.

The first Supreme Council of this new 33 degree system, which we can prove, was created in Charleston, South Carolina, on May 31, 1801. It announced its existence in a document known as the "Circular throughout the two Hemispheres" and is published on pages 319-325 of Ray Baker Harris and James

D. Carter's *History of the Supreme Council, 33° (1801-1861)*. Today, this supreme council is commonly known as the Southern Jurisdiction or the *Mother Supreme Council*, as it was the first one created.[1]

The Southern Jurisdiction is located today at the House of the Temple in Washington, DC. But, if you noticed, I said this is the first supreme council, *which we can prove*. I said that because while the early Southern Jurisdiction, or Charleston Supreme Council, can rightfully claim to be the first supreme council of the 33rd Degree, a brand-new system, that's *not* what is written in the copies that we have of the Grand Constitutions of 1786. Remember, these constitutions were claimed to be the rule and law of the early Charleston Council. In those very constitutions it states that they were:

> *Made and approved in the Supreme Council of the 33rd duly and lawfully established and Congregated in the Grand East of Berlin on the 1st of May Anno Lucis 5786 and of the Christian Era 1786.*[2]

The fact is that no such "Supreme Council" has never been known or shown to exist in 1786 in Berlin or anywhere. The 1801 Charleston Supreme Council initially claimed their handwritten copy of the Grand Constitutions as their authority to exist and laws for their governance. The Grand Constitutions of 1786 contain 18 Articles, or rules, which were reported to be approved and signed in Berlin by Frederic the Great on May 1, 1786. The Grand Constitutions provided the first Supreme Council with a blueprint of sorts, which guided them in the organization, structure, and management of this new system.

In the early days of the new 33 degree Scottish Rite, the Grand Constitutions were perceived to be of great importance to the young Supreme Council, but they were really of no value to Grand Lodges. This new system was mostly viewed as side degrees by Grand Lodges. But for the Scottish Rite, they were central to the system's government and could also be used as evidence of legitimacy.

Interestingly enough, the Northern Masonic Jurisdiction and the Southern Jurisdiction have historically differed regarding which *version* of the Grand Constitutions they acknowledged (yes, there are several). The Northern Jurisdiction accepted the *French Version,* and the Southern Jurisdiction the *Latin Version*. I should also point out that they are not the same in style or content. But why should there be different versions of a document that is crucial to the Scottish Rite? What and where is the original? Well, the common claim was that the original was lost at sea when it was being transported to the United States. Copies were produced based on, I guess, what others remembered as being contained in these Constitutions. Of course, to remember something, you would have had to have seen it. I have never seen a clear explanation of how one would know what was contained in these Grand Constitutions if they had never seen them. I've also never seen an account of someone claiming to have actually held these constitutions in their hands and read them. If anyone saw it and copied it, then all others should be an exact copy of that copy. Logic dictates that either memories differed as to the contents (which would require several seeing the original) or it was a work in progress, in other words, a forgery that evolved and changed over time.

John Mitchell was the first Grand Commander of the Charleston Council (or "Southern Jurisdiction"). Mitchell had been a Deputy Inspector General for the older 25 degree

Masonic system known as the Order of the Royal Secret, but more commonly known as the Rite of Perfection. A Deputy Inspector General was one who had received the 25th Degree of this older system. This was the highest degree in this system and gave them defined rights and privileges.

John Mitchell

In 1807, another Deputy Inspector General of the Order of the Royal Secret, Joseph Cerneau, created bodies in New York that would evolve into a second Supreme Council of the Scottish Rite in the US. The Charleston Council did not approve of or apparently even initially know about the creation of this second US supreme council in New York. When they learned of this new council, the Charleston Council would use the Grand Constitutions in their argument that this second supreme council was illegal and irregular.

Joseph Cerneau

In 1813, Emanuel De La Motta, an Active Member of the Charleston Council, traveled to New York and — with or without the knowledge or authorization of the Charleston Council — created a supreme council in New York on August 23, 1813. The intention seems to have been to replace the Cerneau creation with this new one. This 1813 council would become the Northern Masonic Jurisdiction. I should note that some confusion seems to have existed for some time regarding the exact year that the Northern Jurisdiction was created. In a few places, Albert Pike noted that the creation was in "1813 or

1815." Regardless of any confusion, the existing documents show that it was in 1813.

When the Charleston Supreme Council demanded that Cerneau produce documentation showing it was authorized to exist, the Cerneau Council produced nothing. The Charleston Council labeled the Cerneau Council as irregular and Cerneau a fraud. When the Cerneau Council demanded that the Charleston Council give proof that they were authorized to exist, the Charleston Council pointed to its *copy* of the Grand Constitutions. The Cerneau Council dismissed this copy as a forgery and accused the rival group of hypocrisy. The Cerneau Council claimed it had the same right and authority to exist as did the Charleston Council. They demanded that the standards for legitimacy should be the same for everyone. But why would Cerneau have the same rights, and how? Then again, why would he not have the same rights?

Another claim made by the Charleston Council was that any additional supreme council created in the United States needed its approval, which it did *not* give to Cerneau. This requirement, or right, appears nowhere in the Grand Constitutions when speaking of the United States. But we might note that communications between De La Motta and the Charleston Council did suggest that the Charleston Council considered itself *the* supreme council for the United States. But it also exposes a problem in just how many supreme councils were allowed by these constitutions and where. We'll talk more about this shortly.

So, who, if anyone, was correct? Is it possible that the Grand Constitutions of 1786 *were* forged and never approved by Frederic? Let's look at what some have said about the two versions of the Grand Constitutions. Of the French version (the version historically accepted by the Northern Jurisdiction), Albert Pike says:

> *If I were satisfied that there never were any other Constitutions than those contained in the French version, I should not hesitate to admit that they were a clumsy forgery and that there was nothing in the world to prove them authentic.*[3]

Those are powerful words! But why would Pike write such a powerful denunciation of this French version? Past Southern Jurisdiction Sovereign Grand Commander Henry Clausen explains:

> *Pike's [Latin] version is obviously a truer copy of the original because it supplies omissions and corrections that were apparent in the French version.*[4]

Of course, the first question that comes to mind is, without the original, how would Ill. Bro. Clausen *know* which version was the "truer" copy or anything about "omissions" or "corrections"? It is pure opinion or guesswork. Regardless, Albert Pike would go on to provide a lengthy, rational, and categorical reproof of the French version, making it difficult to understand how one could, with any understanding of Pike's argument and its implications, reasonably defend the French version as legitimate. Yet, this is the very version that the Northern Jurisdiction accepted. Why? Even more interesting is the fact that Pike *himself* used the French version to support his position in a Masonic debate.

In the 1860s, the Supreme Councils of the Northern Jurisdiction and Southern Jurisdiction entered into a debate over territory. The Northern Jurisdiction wanted certain states,

Josiah Drummond

and the Southern Jurisdiction basically said, "No, you can't have them." Josiah Drummond, the Grand Commander of the Northern Masonic Jurisdiction, and Albert Pike, the Grand Commander of the Southern Jurisdiction, debated jurisdictional questions over these states and who would control which states. In 1868, Drummond wrote to Pike:

I hold that under the Constitutions of 1786, the Northern Jurisdiction and the Southern Jurisdiction are, in every respect and for all purposes, as distinct as if they were separate nations: that we, as well as you, derive our rights of jurisdiction from those Constitutions; that those Constitutions create two separate Jurisdictions. On the other hand, I perceive, that you have held that your Supreme Council had jurisdiction throughout North America, and that we get our territory by cession from you; and if by cession, consequently we get only such territory as you choose to cede: and as necessary, that there could have been no Supreme Council in this Jurisdiction unless you had chosen to cede us territory.[5]

How did Pike answer Drummond? Well, he answered by arguing the meaning of certain phrases in the French version. Pike wrote:

I do not agree that the Constitutions created the two Jurisdictions. For the United States composed a single Jurisdiction until 1813 or 1815 and might have continued to be as such until today. The provision is restrictive — that there shall not be more than two Supreme Councils established in the United States. That is the real meaning of it; not that there shall be two. But the point is of no practical importance, and I pass it…. If Illustrious Brother Drummond were right in holding that the Northern part of the United States did not belong to the Jurisdiction of the Southern Council, prior to 1813 or 1815, but was to vest, whether it willed it or not, in a Northern Council, whenever one should be created there, a consequence which he does not foresee might follow. That hypothesis would make the Northern states to have been unoccupied territory, in which any Inspector General could establish a Supreme Council; and it might thus make legitimate the Cerneau Council and annihilate that created in 1813 or 1815 by De la Motta. It certainly would destroy the principal ground on which the legitimacy of Cerneau's Council was always impeached; to-wit, that the Council at Charleston had jurisdiction over the whole United States, and that no other Council could be created anywhere in them, except with its consent.[6]

Interesting! Pike and Drummond debated, in part, the meaning of Article V of *the French version* of the Grand Constitutions of 1786, which determined the number of Supreme Councils allowed or required in various parts of the world. This debate resulted in Pike producing lengthy arguments concerning French and English grammar and the reasons for his position concerning the meaning of Article V of the French version. Pike even changed a portion of the English translation in his 1872 Grand Constitutions to reflect his opinion of the rendition.[7] In his 1868 Allocution, Pike very skillfully debated this interpretation of Article V of the French version at length, and he did likewise in his book, *The Grand Constitutions.*

But why should Pike bother to painstakingly argue a point specifically concerning a version of a document that he had soundly dismissed as a "clumsy forgery"? For the sake of clearly explaining his position, Pike should have debated the Latin version — which he claimed to be legitimate. Why didn't he? Aren't they the same? No, they are *not* the same. There *are* differences and some of them are significant.

Simply put, Albert Pike *could not* debate this portion of the Latin version — the very version that Pike claimed to be legitimate. And the reason is very interesting! The same portion of Article V of the Latin version (the version Pike refers to as the "law of the Rite"[8]) reads:

> *In each great nation of Europe, and in each Kingdom or Empire, there shall be but one single Supreme Council of this Degree. In all those States and Provinces, as well of the mainland as of the islands, whereof North America is composed, there shall be two Councils, one at as great a distance as may be from the other.*[9]

Pike strongly contended that *the meaning* of Article V (of the French version) was that the US was *not required* to be divided into two jurisdictions, yet that is precisely what the Latin version said — which Pike had himself published in 1859. Pike used the French version in his debate with Drummond because it was more open to individual interpretation. The undesired "consequence" Pike claimed if Drummond's interpretation was accepted is present in the Latin version — which Pike avoided using. Cerneau, it seems, might have had every reason, based on either version of the Grand Constitutions, to *believe* that he had every right to establish his creation.

The problem for Drummond was that Pike had skillfully painted him into a tight corner with his masterful use of

Drummond's French version. Drummond was not going to do something that might damage the existence of the Northern Jurisdiction. The territorial debate ended with Drummond yielding to Pike's demands.

The view held by Drummond, however, was *not only* based on his interpretation of Article V of the French version but also on the "birth certificate" of the Northern Council itself, which reads in part:

> *And whereas the Grand Constitutions of the 33°*
> *specifies particularly that there shall be two Grand &*
> *Supreme Councils of the 33d Degree for the Jurisdiction of*
> *the United States of America, one for the South and the other*
> *for the North.*[10]

It's obvious why Drummond interpreted Article V of the French version as he did. The Northern Jurisdiction *was* created with the position that there *shall be two* supreme councils in the United States. Drummond's view was that the Northern and Southern portions of the United States should be treated as if they were two separate nations. This was also clearly how De La Motta viewed the situation. That position is supported by the Grand Constitutions and the "Birth Certificate" of the Northern Council. Its only contention could have been if Cerneau was not a legitimate Sovereign Grand Inspector General. If he *were* legitimate, then the Cerneau Council would seem to be perfectly legal, and the Northern Jurisdiction was — by its own stated reason for being created — unauthorized! But … Emanuel De La Motta, upon meeting Cerneau, did *not* believe him to be a legitimate 33rd. De La Motta asked to see Cerneau's 33rd degree patent, and Cerneau didn't provide it. He didn't seem to have one. And nothing has ever been shown to prove that he did. So, for De La Motta, that was it. Cerneau didn't show his patent because he didn't have one. He didn't have one because he was lying about being a 33rd. End of story. Well, maybe not. Let's look closer at this situation.

Pike's opinions concerning the meaning of the French versions of the Grand Constitutions and their implications were clearly *not* shared by Emanuel De La Motta, who created the Northern Jurisdiction and was an active Member of the original Charleston Council. It is, likewise, evident why Pike's unspoken "threats" might well have been taken seriously. Drummond did yield to Pike. The only available attack that could reasonably be made on Cerneau, from the Northern Jurisdiction's perspective, was to discredit his legitimacy as a 33rd. To discredit Cerneau by saying that there was only one supreme council allowed in the US put the Northern Jurisdiction in a bad position. And it was *not* something in their known copy of the Grand Constitutions. But, as amazing as it may sound today, we can see that *both* Joseph Cerneau and John Mitchell (Charleston's first Grand Commander) were, in one aspect, in the very same boat. No 33rd degree patent *for either one of them* has ever been discovered. To discredit Cerneau's 33° by *only* pointing out that he did not have a patent could also discredit Mitchell. But that brings us to the $10,000 question. How did *both* Mitchell and Cerneau receive the 33rd degree? Who gave it to them? Where are their patents?

The short answer is that I have never seen a word written in any classical Scottish Rite history book that provided definitive proof of how either received the 33rd degree. We usually see what turns out to be convoluted and mostly long-winded opinions disguised as facts. But there are some clues. One thing that we must never do is judge past events by today's standards. What is normal and common practice today may have been very different in the past. We also must remember that we are talking about the creation of a brand-new system. So, let's look at it.

First off, the first *known* 33rd degree patent given to anyone that we know about was the one given by John Mitchell to Frederick Dalcho on May 25, 1801 — that's just six days before the creation of the first Supreme Council in Charleston. No earlier 33rd patent is known to exist. The question of how John Mitchell received the 33rd Degree did not escape early Scottish Rite historians. It is often claimed that Mitchell received the 33rd from some older 25th degree Mason. Several names have been suggested in various books. But if Mitchell received the 33rd from an old 25th degree Mason, who gave the 25th degree Mason the 33rd? We also see in Harris & Carter that in 1829, Moses Holbrook, the then Grand Commander of the Southern Jurisdiction, wrote to J.J.J. Gourgas of the Northern Jurisdiction about how Mitchell might have received the 33rd degree. Holbrook wrote:

> *"I took the opportunity in mentioning it to Br. Dalcho, to ask how Mitchell got the 33d. He replied that he could not ... recollect; But he [Mitchell] had signed some obligation in French for it. He thinks it came from some Prussian who was in Charleston, who was authorized to communicate it to him."*[11]

Why would a Prussian give an obligation to an Irishman in the United States written in French? Well, regardless, no proof has ever been produced that either Cerneau or Mitchell ever received the 33rd degree from anyone. But John Mitchell was the first Grand Commander of the first Supreme Council! He had to be a 33rd, right? Well, before we say that either one did or did not have something, let's see if there is another explanation.

When we look through old Masonic books to try and discover hidden gems, we find that sometimes more than one book is necessary for an answer, even if it is only a possible answer. But before I take another step, let me clearly explain something. Not for a moment do I believe or suggest that any aspect of Freemasonry was created by the Almighty kissing his fingers and *boom* creating some part of Masonry. Human beings created Freemasonry. They created it with all their flaws, geniuses, and insecurities. The 33rd degree, as well as the whole of the new 33 degree system, was created by one or more individuals, thinking it up, writing it down, and then going through all the steps to take it from an idea to a working new system. The inspiration may have been divine, but the action was human.

So, let's look at the period around 1801. John Mitchell and Joseph Cerneau came to hold the 25th degree of the older Order of the Royal Secret, often called the "Rite of Perfection." This system is often traced back to Stephen Morin, but it was in a troubled situation. It just wasn't working. The Masons who gathered in Charleston knew that the old system was a major problem, and they were trying to figure out a way to save or reorganize this beautiful system. And they did. By any objective examination, the 33 degree system is more workable and organized than the old 25 degree system. But these guys didn't have the internet, telephones, planes, or cars to spread the word. It was a slower process. However, word did start to get out, and when given the choice between the two systems, a significant number in the older system decided to move to the newer one. It was clearly a better system. So, how did they do it? They had to have thought about a process to move from one system to the other. It makes no sense to create a new Masonic Rite which builds on and improves an older one but does not have the means to bring in those interested from the older system.

With little trouble, we can find accounts of moving from the old 25 degree system to the new 33 degree one. As an example, under the heading of Joseph Cerneau, *Coil's Masonic Encyclopedia* tells us:

> *"Meanhile in Charleston, S.C., in 1801, the 32 degree system had been perfected and, in the process, the old 25th Degree, Prince Mason, or Prince of the Royal Secret, had been shifted to 32nd place. Since Cerneau held the Prince Mason Degree, he conceived that he should shift with it and, as it went to the head of the list, so did he. Perhaps he was entitled to do that; perhaps others did so, especially, those who belonged to the Rite at Charleston. But he was not entitled under any authority or by any interpretation of power to establish bodies of any rite in New York."[12]*

OK, so what are we talking about here? Cerneau held the 25th degree of the older system. The 33rd degree is not mentioned, but there is mention of the 32nd. If we look closely at this statement, what is being said here is that the 25th degree of the old system *became* the 32nd degree of the new system. Cerneau learned of this new system and liked it. As a 25th degree Mason, he moved over to this new system and, with that, held the 32nd degree. It also says, "perhaps he was entitled to do that; perhaps others did so, especially, those who belonged to the Rite at Charleston." He's clearly talking about Mitchell and the other 25th degrees Masons in the area. But then is added, "But he [Cerneau] was not entitled under any authority or by any interpretation of power to establish bodies of any rite in New York." Well, yeah, I've never known or heard of any 32nd who was entitled to create a supreme council. At least, I don't think so. But Albert Pike did say something very interesting. In his *Grand Constitutons* under *"Extract from the Collection of Constitutional Balustres* in the *Instructions as to the General Principles,"* he offers us:

"Art. I. Wherever, in a State where there is neither a Grand Consistory nor a Grand Council of Sublime Princes of the Royal Secret, there are any Grand Inspectors General and Princes of the Royal Secret, the Grand Inspector General whose patent and recognition bear the oldest date, or, if there be no Inspector General, then the oldest Prince of the Royal Secret, is invested with the administrative and dogmatic power of High Masonry and takes accordigly the title of Sovereign."[13]

Pike is clearly speaking about the process that was used for John Mitchell to move from the old system to the new one and how he *became* a 33rd. Mitchell was the senior 25th degree Mason in the Charleston area. With the creation of the new 33 degree system, Mitchell moved from the 25th degree (Prince Mason) to the 32nd degree (Prince of the Royal Secret). As the senior 32nd in the area, probably the only one, this provision allowed him to take the title of Sovereign or become a 33rd (and then Sovereign Grand Commander) through his position in the old system and status in the new one.

Mitchell was not *given* the 33rd degree as it is done today, but he *became* a 33rd using the General Principles of the order and the need to create organizations of that order. The Almighty did not kiss His fingers and create John Mitchell as a 33rd. However, a process was defined and used to elevate one to the highest degree when the situation required it. Mitchell did not receive the 33rd in the same manner that we do today, but he received it by means of an administrative process, following the rules that were created *before* he received the degree. Once in possession of the 33rd, he gave it to Dalcho and then set upon the work of creating a supreme council. This would seem to be why Mitchell did not have a 33rd degree patent. But what about Cerneau?

Joseph Cerneau traveled from Cuba to New York, where he created bodies that evolved into a second supreme council of this new 33 degree system in the United States. I have yet to see any records to show how he learned of this new 33 degree system, but there are only so many options. I've also seen nothing to suggest that Cerneau played any role in the planning or the creation of the Charleston Supreme Council. Either Cerneau saw the original Grand Constitutions of 1786 (which I don't believe), or he saw a copy of it, or he met someone who knew of the Charleston Supreme Council and this new system. It only makes sense that Cerneau traveled into the Charleston area for some reason, and he met Masons, maybe members of the Charleston Supreme Council, who told him about the events. It could be at a tavern for dinner or a few drinks. Who knows? But he learned of it, and he liked it. Sadly, there are no records of any such meeting. Such a meeting or meetings are only dictated by logic. He had to learn of this new system somewhere. For all I know, his going to New York may have resulted from his learning of this new system.

I also have no idea if Cerneau went to New York intending to establish a supreme council of this new system or if this new system was, at that time, just something interesting that he filed away in his mind. His going to New York may have had nothing at all to do with Freemasonry. It may have only planned on going to New York to open a jewelry shop there — which he did. We don't have any account *from him* to explain his actions.

But on October 28, 1807, Joseph Cerneau created bodies in New York that would evolve into a second supreme council in the United States. That was the shot that started a true Masonic war, and US Masonry throughout the 1800s was horribly affected by it. We can even today point to current situations that are the direct result of those "wars" — and there is no other word for it.

On one side, Cerneau became a devil and an example of everything wrong with Freemasonry. His very name is today seen in Masonic encyclopedias as a word used to define irregular Masonry.[14] On the other side of the coin, he is an example of how an intolerant, unjust, and power-hungry group is perfectly willing to destroy Masons and Masonic bodies that encroach on what is believed to be "their property." Who was right and who was wrong often depends on who you ask. The basic question boils down to whether Joseph Cerneau had the right to establish the bodies that he established. Let's see if there is a reasonable answer to that question.

There is so much about the early creation of the first supreme council that we simply cannot answer today with clear evidence. So much does not exist. But one of the questions that we *cannot* answer does give us some hope. That question is, will we ever discover new things that were unknown yesterday? Yes, that is very possible. Discoveries are always happening and have happened in the past. For example, it would seem apparent that Albert Pike was unaware of a handwritten copy of the Grand Constitutions that Frederick Dalcho had made. Dalcho was the first Lt. Grand Commander of the Charleston Council and its second Grand Commander. The Dalcho copy of the Grand Constitutions was not discovered until the 20th century. (This copy is fully reproduced in the Harris/Carter *History of the Supreme Council - 1801-1861* on pages 335-346). Pike boldly proclaimed that the French version was a fraud and offered lucid support for his position. Pike seemed to have no idea that what he so soundly proclaimed to be a fraud came directly from the hand of Charleston's second Grand Commander. In fact, the Dalcho handwritten copy makes one point even clearer than Pike's Latin version. Article V in part reads:

> *"There shall be but one council of this Degree in each*
> *Nation or Kingdom in Europe — two in the United States of*
> *America as remote from each other as possible — "*[15]

That's pretty clear. But what I certainly *don't* want to do is try to get into the head of Albert Pike to try and guess at his reason for doing or saying things. Pike *did know* the wording of the Latin version prior to his debate with Drummond but chose not to mention it. It's not impossible that Pike wrote what he did to try to bluff Drummond. Maybe he just wanted him to back down. And that is exactly what Drummond did. He did back down and yielded to Pike's wishes concerning jurisdiction over certain states. But what about the claim that Pike made about Cerneau?

The Grand Constitutions, at least the copies we have, *do* seem to say that the US *shall have* two councils. Charleston was the first, and it seems that Cerneau was the second. Does that automatically make Cerneau valid? Well, in theory, maybe, but the situations were different. We'll get back to this question in a few minutes. But let's look again at the arguments concerning Cerneau with the backdrop of the Grand Constitutions themselves.

Customarily, papers discussing Joseph Cerneau include arguments concerning the Grand Constitutions of 1786 and vice versa. Cerneau is usually accused of acting in violation of these Constitutions. Nineteenth-century defenders of Cerneau typically argued the lack of legitimacy of the Grand Constitutions with the apparent belief that if the Grand Constitutions could be discredited, all charges against Cerneau would likewise be dismissed.

One claim that was often made was that Frederic the Great had been in feeble health at the time the Constitutions were said to be approved and that he was physically unable to have given them consent. Albert Pike went to great lengths to examine the charge that Frederic was not physically able to have executed such a document. Pike meticulously traced the reported events and laid out a detailed report on his position that Frederic could have executed the Grand Constitutions. NMJ Scottish Rite historian Samuel Baynard, however, takes a dim view of *all* versions of the Grand Constitutions of 1786. He writes of Pike's conclusions:

> *Though we admit that our Illustrious Brother did in a masterly manner fully convince us that Frederick on May 1, 1786, was physically able and mentally capable of drafting, signing and promulgating these Grand Constitutions, we have utterly failed to find that he discovered or pointed out to us one scintilla of evidence that Frederick actually did have aught to do with them.*[16]

Pike was obviously aware that his lengthy account did not answer the *actual* question of whether Frederic signed or approved the Grand Constitutions. Pike addressed this point most interestingly. He writes:

> [T]here is not one particle of proof of any sort, circumstantial or historical or by argument from improbability, that they are not genuine and authentic.[17]

As remarkable as it sounds, Pike asks us to prove a negative. That's not how research works! Was Albert Pike, *the Mason*, trying to answer a historical question, or was Albert Pike, *the attorney*, writing a legal brief and maneuvering or leaving out what he felt did not help his case? But we need to stop for a moment and ask again: Which version was Pike defending? Was it the French version that he so soundly proclaimed a fraud? Was it the Latin version? I am not 100% sure. Regardless, Baynard continues:

> *We conclude therefore:*
> *1. That the Grand Constitutions were not promulgated by Frederic the Great;*
> *2. That they were not framed, drawn up or signed in Berlin;*
> *3. That there did not exist in Berlin or even France in 1786, any "Grand Supreme Universal Inspectors, in constituted Supreme Council";*
> *4. That the real date of the Constitutions is subsequent to 1786.*[18]

But if the Grand Constitutions are a forgery, then who forged them? The question did not escape Baynard:

> *It is only natural that the next question should be, Well, then, who did frame them? We do not know. Neither are we unduly disturbed because we do not know. We have our opinion, but it is not substantiated by any evidence that we can call positive or direct, and, therefore, we do not express it as a conclusion.*[19]

OK, to summarize the situation, Pike pronounced the French version of the Grand Constitutions a forgery. He seemed to be debating why the Latin version should be considered legitimate. Baynard rejected *both* versions of the Grand Constitutions, but he does not choose to say who he believes forged them. Regarding the possibility that the Latin version might also be a forgery, Pike tells us:

> *The odious charge has been again and again repeated, that these Latin Constitutions were forged at Charleston. It*

is quite certain that this is not true, because the Supreme Council at Charleston never had them, until it received copies of the editions published by the Grand Commander. If they were forged anywhere, it was not at Charleston: and if anything was forged there, it was the French copy, as it afterwards appeared in the Recueil des Actes.[20]

Pike is saying that whoever created the French version committed forgery. He seems to be saying, without realizing it, that Frederick Dalcho forged them. And elsewhere:

The gentlemen of South Carolina, in that day, did not commit forgery. Whatever the origin of the Grand Constitutions, they came from Europe to Charleston, and were accepted and received by the honorable gentlemen and clergymen who were of the first Supreme Council, in perfect good faith.[21]

If the Grand Constitutions are forged documents, but the original Charleston Council did not forge them, then how did they come into possession of them? Pike theorizes:

This very imperfect French copy, which consists merely of so many Articles, without preface, formality of enactment by any body in Power, or authentication of any sort, contains no list of the degrees, nor even the name of the Rite. It is most probable that de Grasse procured it, in or from Europe, and created the Supreme Council. By Article V of these Constitutions, it requires three persons to constitute a quorum and compose a Supreme Council; and therefore Colonel Mitchell and Dr. Dalcho alone could not have been, by themselves, such a body. Brother de Grasse intended establishing a Supreme Council at Santo Domingo for the French West India Islands; and no other person had any interest to make the Constitutions read so as to allow such a

Council, except his father-in-law, Jean Baptiste Delahogue,
who also resided in Charleston in 1796, 1799 and 1801, and
was also a 33rd, and appointed to be Lieutenant Grand
Commander for the French West Indies. It was for this
reason, evidently, that neither of them was placed on the roll
of members of the body at Charleston.[22]

OK, let's take everything else and put it aside for a moment. Let's look at what is now being offered by Baynard and Pike. Baynard believed that the entire story of the Grand Constitutions was a fabrication. He based his opinion on the total lack of factual evidence supporting the account and the improbability of the reported events. Pike soundly denounced the French version as a fraud (unaware that it seemed to have come from Dalcho) but held to the possibility of the legitimacy of the Latin version (unaware that this version first showed up in France from Cerneau Masons). Pike pointed out his position that the original Charleston Council did not have possession or knowledge of the Latin version and had based their actions on the fraudulent French version. Pike also stated that he believed it was Alexander de Grasse who had brought the forged French version to Charleston and implied that it was de Grasse who might have forged them.

Pike stated that de Grasse was probably the 33rd who, along with Mitchell and Delcho, opened the first supreme council session on May 31, 1801. But the "Birth certificate" of the Charleston council, the "Circular throughout the two Hemispheres," says that deGrasse was a Deputy Inspector General of the 25th degree until February 21, 1802, when he was "appointed" a 33rd by Mitchell and the Supreme Council. Frederick Dalcho also stated in a letter to De La Motta on August 23, 1813, that de Grasse did not receive the 33rd until February 21, 1802. How could De Grasse have helped open the first supreme council in May of 1801 if he was not then a 33rd? We'll return to this "need" of three 33rds in a moment.

There are several logical scenarios that we can explore: The first would be that Mitchell and Dalcho received the Grand Constitutions sincerely believing that they were legitimate. Another would be that Mitchell and Dalcho took part in creating the Grand Constitutions or knew that they were a forgery.

If Mitchell and Dalcho believed that the Grand Constitutions were legitimate, we can look at the series of events with that mindset. Suppose Mitchell and Dalcho believed that they were introducing to the US a European system created some fifteen years before the creation of the Charleston Council. In that case, they could have reasonably assumed that other Supreme Councils of the 33 Degree existed in Europe. Clearly, the Grand Constitutions speak of such a Council in Berlin.

On August 23, 1813, John Mitchell wrote to Emanuel De La Motta concerning De La Motta's report on Joseph Cerneau. Mitchell wrote in part:

> *I am truly surprised and astonished at the conduct of the man you say is called Mr. Joseph Cerneau. No person ever had the degree but the Count de Grasse, and perhaps, but I am not sure, Mr. Delahogue.*[23]

We must stop for a moment to try and understand Mitchell's comment. If Mitchell received a *copy* of the Grand Constitutions and accepted them as legitimate, how could he be so sure that no one else "had the degree"? What about the Supreme Council in Berlin cited in the Grand Constitutions?

The copy of the *Grand Consitutions of 1786* that Mitchell had available to him opens as follows:

> *Made and approved in the Supreme Council of the 33rd duly and lawfully established and Congregated in the Grand East of Berlin on the 1st of May Anno Lucis 5786 and of the Christian Era 1786. At which Council was present in person – His Most August Majesty, Frederic 2nd, King of Prussia, Sovereign Grand Commander.*[24]

Was the "Supreme Council of the 33rd" in Berlin composed of members who did not have the 33rd degree? Why would they not? It makes no sense. Mitchell writes that de Grasse was the *only person* he was certain "had" the degree. What is he talking about? What about the other 33rds in the Charleston Supreme Council after 1801? Mitchell wrote this letter in 1813. Also, by then, SCs of the new 33 degree system had been created in at least the West Indies, Jamaica, France, Italy, and Spain. The comments by Mitchell are extraordinary.

Frederick Dalcho, the Lt. Grand Commander of the Charleston Council, also sent a letter to De La Motta on the same day as Mitchell's letter and also concerning the new Cerneau creation. It should be noted again that the date of Dalcho's letter was *August 23, 1813*. Emanuel De La Motta established the Supreme Council for the Northern Jurisdiction 18 days earlier, on August 5, 1813. Dalcho wrote:

> *It is well known to those who have lawfully received the 33rd degree, that there can be but one Council in a nation or kingdom; and that the Council for the US was lawfully established in this City, May 31st, 1801; consequently any other assuming its prerogatives must be surreptitious.*[25]

What does Dalcho mean by this statement? Well, Article 9 of the Grand Constitutions reads:

"No Deputy Inspector can use his patent, in any country, where a Supreme Council of Inspectors General is established – unless it shall be signed by said Council."[26]

It looks like Dalcho is using a selective combination of Articles Five and Nine in his letter to De La Motta. Let's take a moment and look at the two Articles when read together. Let's say that we are in a country in Europe. The relevant part of Article Five says: *"There shall be but one council of this Degree in each nation or Kingdom of Europe."*[27] Alright, that's pretty clear. One council for each nation or Kingdom in Europe. OK. But now, reread Article Nine to see how it may apply to Europe. Article Nine says that if you go into a country that already has a supreme council, you need to get the original council to approve the creation of another. OK. Got it. So, if Masons of the proper rank establish a supreme council in a country in Europe where no other council exists, that's the one constitutionally approved supreme council. But Article Nine does seem to conditionally remove the one council limit in Article Five by obtaining permission. OK. So, let's say that Masons of proper rank wish to create ten different supreme councils in that European country *and* the original council approves all of them; then all should be fine, right? No other cap can be found as to the number of supreme councils *if* approval is given. But Article Five also says "there shall be two" for the United States. That's different than the one council limit in Europe. What does it mean?

In Albert Pike's debate with Josiah Drummond, Pike argued that the meaning of Article Five was restrictive, that there shall not be *more* than two in the US. Once the second is created, that's it; no more can be created. But how does that restrictive aspect of Article Five apply to Europe? In Europe, would it mean that there shall not be *more* than one council? How does this restrictive interpretation apply to Article Nine? If one is *all* that is allowed, why would you have an article saying that you need to get permission to create another? One is all that is allowed. But maybe the restrictive aspect means that one is all that is allowed *before* you need to get the original council's permission to create others. OK, that brings it back to the original understanding. But then, how does that now apply to the situation in the US? If one is all that is allowed in Europe before permission is necessary for others, then *two* would be the limit in the US before permission is needed. Pike and Dalcho argued that Cerneau was not legitimate because he needed permission from the Charleston Council to exist. Why? The Grand Constitutions provided for one council in Europe and two in the US. It's only if you want an additional number that you would need anyone's permission.

Albert Pike's argument (and Dalcho's argument) only stands up when a selected version of the Constitutions is used along with a single selected Article, ignoring the other Articles. No matter how you cut it, Grand Commander Drummond was right. The Grand Constitutions viewed the northern and Southern areas of the US as if they were two separate nations — one council for each of the two defined areas of the US. And permission is necessary for any more councils in each area. And Drummond was not alone in that position.

So, what of De La Motta's creation? Dalcho's "one council" comment in his letter might well have meant … Charleston and no one else, including De La Motta's creation. Dalcho might *not* have initially approved of the De La Motta Council any more than the Cerneau one. The NJ does seem to have been created without prior approval. But why? Didn't De La Motta know of Dalcho's "one council" rule? If not, why not?

Dalcho said the one council rule was: "well known to those who have lawfully received the 33rd degree." Why would De La Motta, like Cerneau, act in the New York area without prior approval from Charleston? Is Dalcho suggesting that De La Motta did not lawfully receive the 33rd degree? I doubt that. But clearly, De La Motta had a different opinion of the meaning of the Grand Constitutions.

The "birth certificate" of the NMJ, created by De La Motta, tells us: "*there shall be two Grand & Supreme Councils of the 33d Degree for the Jurisdiction of the United States of America, one for the South and the other for the North.*"[28] This would seem to be De La Motta's understanding of the Grand Constitutions. There seems to be great confusion in the Temple.

I am wholly in agreement with Samuel Baynard in his rejection of the legitimacy of all versions of the Grand Constitutions. In the absence of any other reasonable explanation, I believe that John Mitchell and Frederick Dalcho took part in the fabrication of the story of the Grand Constitutions of 1786, either in whole or in part. I believe that Mitchell, Dalcho, and others held reasonable concern regarding the failing and chaotic state of the Order of the Royal Secret. To bring "order" to the "chaos," the new 33 degree system was created. The "cream of the crop" of the degrees and rituals were selected for this new system. It was an inspired creation for which, as we can imagine, a concern developed over whether the whole of Freemasonry would accept it. A royal endorsement would add value to any new Masonic system, and one attached to a set of governing laws might bestow even greater value. I believe the story and situation began to unravel with the discovery of the Cerneau bodies.

Is it possible that De Grasse was the author of the original 33rd degree, as Albert Pike suggested? Sure. I believe that this is very possible. Is it possible that De Grasse came up with the idea of the new 33 degree system to replace the failing 25 degree Order of the Royal Secret? Sure. I also believe that this is possible. Is it possible that De Grasse came up with the story of the Grand Constitutions of 1786? Maybe. Is it possible that the original Charleston Members were innocent victims of a very clever rouse by De Grasse (or someone else) and that they played no part whatsoever in the creation of the 33 degree system or the story of the Grand Constitutions? No. Such a conclusion is not at all supported by the known evidence.

As for Cerneau, well, for a moment, let's take all the many years of published comments about him on both sides and put them aside. Let's take a look at a few things. Both John Mitchell and Joesph Cerneau held the 25th degree from the Order of the Royal Secret. John Mitchell was the founding Grand Commander of the Charleston Supreme Council because he was the senior 25th degree Mason in the unoccupied Charleston area. He announced his authority to create certain bodies by the rights given in the Grand Constitutions of 1786. And yes, I know. Just moments ago, I said I believe them to be a forgery. I do. But for this discussion, it doesn't matter if those Constitutions were real or a forgery or who forged them. Let me explain. Right now, it only matters that the Charleston members accepted them as their rules. They bound themselves to these rules — whoever wrote them. That's what we need to remember. Either they followed their own rules, or they didn't.

Joseph Cerneau did learn of this new creation somewhere. If Cerneau did not take part in the creation of the new system and only learned of it during his travels, then how would he have known for sure if the Grand Constitutions were real or a forgery? Is it possible that Cerneau was told about this new system and initially had no reason to doubt what he was being told? Sure, that's reasonable. Cerneau might have believed the story of the new system coming from Europe and the Charleston council being created by the right of Mitchell's 25th degree. Even if he didn't know much about the system, it seems logical for Cerneau to believe that this happened and that he also had that same right under similar conditions. Once in New York, he decided to create bodies of this new system. And he viewed it as his right due to his rank in the Order of the Royal Secret, just like John Mitchell. It's perfectly logical that he could think this. But were the situations the same? Not really. Let's see if we can look at the *whole* situation.

When we look at the early years of the Cerneau bodies in New York, we can see rather clearly that Cerneau must not have learned much more than just the very basics of this new system. So much of what Cerneau did in the early days dramatically differed from the Charleston creation. While the structure and authority of the Charleston Council did change following its "Birth Announcement" in 1802, the early Cerneau bodies can hardly be recognized as a supreme council of the new 33rd degree system. It resembled more of what he must have known of the old Order of the Royal Secret. But really, that does make some sense.

No records are available to show how Cerneau learned of the new system. Based on Mitchell, Dalcho, and De La Motta's reaction to him, it's doubtful they knew him. It's not unreasonable to think that all he learned of the new system was in casual conversation with someone who knew something about the system. Maybe it was over dinner or drinks in a tavern. We have no idea as there is nothing left by him, no memoirs, a diary, nothing from him to explain his actions.

So, I believe it likely that Cerneau did initially believe the story about the Grand Constitutions. He also must have learned only the very basics of it. Of course, how would the

Masons in New York know if Cerenau was knowledgeable or not about this new system? Also, if De La Motta only visited Cerneau in his shop, how would he know the quality of the work in the Cerneau bodies? So, why would De La Motta, Mitchell, and Dalcho so quickly take such a hostile position about Cerneau? Why didn't they give him any benefit of the doubt? By the time De La Motta arrived, Cerneau and his bodies had been around for a number of years. How did they know that he didn't create his bodies with the same authority, and they just didn't know about it? Could it have been that the Charleston council felt rightfully injured that this Cerneau guy stole what *they knew* that they created, and he didn't even ask? Could the insult and shock of *their* creation being taken without permission have caused them to lose it and go on the attack so quickly? I believe that this is very possible.

And what were the attacks on Cerneau? I have found two main areas of early attack on him. One was that because he did not provide a 33rd degree patent, he could not be a legitimate 33rd. Period. The second was a claim that he was not authorized to create a second supreme council because one already existed in the United States, and he did not receive their permission to create another one. And yes, there was another attack, of sorts, that came later on. It had to do with Cerneau's patent as a Deputy Inspector General of the 25th degree. It limited him to a certain area of Cuba. I see this as more of a distraction or a Hail Mary rather than an attack with any real teeth. Cerneau, even with his minimal knowledge, was clearly trying to establish bodies of the new 33 degree system. If his patent for the old system limited him to only one city block or the whole world, it was still irrelevant.

In this situation, Cerneau's 25th degree patent's only use was as a vehicle to move him from the old system to the new one. It's like saying that a medical doctor in Ohio can't switch professions and become an attorney in California because his medical license limits him to Ohio. But regardless of everything else, he made a lot of mistakes. However, there is one area of criticism of Cerneau that doesn't seem to be mentioned much at all. And does have some teeth. Let's set the stage and look at it.

I have found no convincing records and don't really have an opinion as to why Cerneau traveled to New York. He seems to have arrived there at some time, around late 1806 or early 1807. The records show that Masonry in New York at the time of Cerneau's arrival was complicated. It was divided into two political rival groups. One group was led by a Mason named Daniel D. Tompkins. DeWitt Clinton led the other group. Tompkins and Clinton did not like each other at all.

Tompkins served as Governor of the state of New York from 1807 to 1817. In 1817, Tompkins was elected vice President of the United States. He was an active Mason who would be elected Grand Master of the GL of New York in 1820. Clinton had served as a United States Senator out of New York until 1803, when he was elected as Mayor of New York City. He served as Mayor from 1803 until 1815. Upon Daniel Tompkins' resignation as Governor of New York to accept the Vice

Daniel D. Tompkins

Presidency in 1817, Clinton won a special election to the Governor's office. Tompkins was apparently unhappy that Clinton had won his old Governor's seat and while serving as Vice President, ran against Clinton for the Governor's office in 1820. In a close election, Clinton won reelection. Clinton was also elected Grand Master of the Grand Lodge of New York in

1806. He served as Grand Master from 1806-1819. He was followed as Grand Master by none other than Daniel Tompkins in 1820. Tompkins served only one year as Grand Master.

It seems that the rivalry and then strong dislike between Tompkins and Clinton had existed for a number of years, but it flared up in earnest in 1812 (right before De La Motta arrived) when Clinton ran for the office of United States President against incumbent President James Madison. Clinton lost in a narrow race, and many consider his loss to be Daniel Tompkins throwing his public support behind Madison shortly before the election.

So, upon Cerneau's arrival in New York in 1806 and De La Motta's arrival in 1813, Tompkins was Governor of the State of New York, and Clinton was the Mayor of New York City. Clinton was also Grand Master of New York. Cerneau could well have been pulled into a situation because of what seems to be a desire to be one-up on the other guy. It may have been felt that Cerneau could be of some help. We don't know what was said or exactly what happened.

The reason, or reasons, why De La Motta traveled to New York are equally elusive. Because of De La Motta's actions and the reaction to the situations in New York by Mitchell and Dalcho, I tend to believe that De La Motta was *not* sent to New York by the Charleston Council with clear directions other than, maybe, "report what you find." Maybe there was some talk about something happening in New York, and De La Motta was sent to check it out. I don't know and have not read a clear answer. I do not believe the Charleston Council instructed De La Motta to create a supreme council in New York. Again, like Cerneau, it is possible that De La Motta traveled to New York for reasons other than Freemasonry. But, once in New York, De La Motta made discoveries that he felt required his action. He acted on what seemed to be what he believed was his authority and responsibility as a Sovereign Grand Inspector General.

De La Motta, according to the accounts that exist, somehow learned of Cerneau and visited him at his jewelry shop. They discussed the new 33 degree system. Cerneau apparently informed De La Motta what he had created, and De La Motta asked to see his 33rd degree patent. Cerneau apparently did not have one, which sealed his fate with De La Motta and his place in the history of the US Scottish Rite. I don't know why this was such an open-and-shut case with De La Motta. He knew that this was a new system. Maybe one or both of them had attitudes that rubbed the other badly. Maybe things were said or done that were not recorded. I don't know.

All that is clear is that De La Motta outright rejected Cerneau's legitimacy. But Cerneau was not all that De La Motta discovered. He learned of the bitter division in New York Masonry *and* of a Grand Consistory of the 32nd degree that was *not* under either Charleston *or* Cerneau. It was a body of the new 33 degree system that Charleston apparently knew nothing about. That would seem to be a pretty major surprise. And that is the body upon which I would like to focus for a minute.

On January 21, 1802, John Mitchell "appointed" Alexandre De Grasse to the 33rd Degree and as Grand Commander of the Supreme Council in the West Indies. One of the 33rds created in this 1802 supreme council was a Mason by the name of Antoine Bideaud. Bideaud was a recognized 33rd belonging to a supreme council tracing itself back to the Charleston Council. Bideaud traveled from the West Indies, apparently intending to eventually go to France. He made a stop in New Orleans and then went on to New York, where on August 6, 1806, he created a Grand Consistory of the 32nd degree. He then traveled to France, leaving the new Grand Consistory to fend for itself. Why did he do that?

Looking back today, it may seem odd that Bideaud would create a Grand Consistory and then just take off. But, at that time, this does not seem all that uncommon. It was exactly what de Grasse had done with the supreme council in the West Indies in 1802 and the SC in Jamaica in 1804. It was also a common practice with older rites. Someone with the necessary rank would create bodies, and then they would move on to create bodies elsewhere. It is also exactly what De La Motta did in 1813 in New York. It happened more often than we may realize, but I don't believe it was a good practice. I also believe that it was one of the reasons why the old Order of the Royal Secret developed such organizational problems. But, the point is that this was a Grand Consistory of the 32nd degree that could trace itself directly back to the Charleston supreme council. That's a good thing, right? Well, maybe not. It depends on who you ask. Northern Jurisdiction Grand Commander J.J.J. Gourgas is quoted as saying of the creation of this Grand Consistory.

> *"This act of Bideaud's was completely irregular, unconstitutional. He had no right or power within the United States of America, but was tempted and did succumb at the rate of five times $46 or $230."*[29]

And then is added from Harris and Carter:

> *"Bideaud's patent authorized him to confer degrees and establish bodies "conformable to the Grand Constitutions." He should not have been unaware of the legal prohibitions the Grand Constitutions contained, and the impropriety of ignoring the existence in the United States of the Supreme Council from which his own had dervved."*[30]

These are two extremely interesting statements, and we need to look at them with a curious eye. But first, let's look again at De La Motta. I truly wish that I could have been a fly buzzing around Emanuel De La Motta when he arrived in New York. He found the area was composed of Masons who were divided into two rival groups, both composed of some powerful Masons. And surprise, surprise, both of these groups had bodies of the new 33 degree system of which they were members! How did that happen?

A guy by the name of Joseph Cerneau created one of these bodies (with DeWitt Clinton as the second in charge), and a guy named Antoine Bideaud created the other one (with Daniel Tompkins at the head and Abraham Jacobs amoung the members). Who were Cernau and Bideaud, and under what authority did they act? Cerneau didn't have a 33rd patent, so he *must* be irregular. But who is this Bideaud guy? His patent couldn't be checked because he had already left the area. But, he had claimed to be a 33rd under de Grasse's 1802 supreme council in the West Indies. De La Motta had heard of de Grasse and that supreme council. But, he knew nothing about anyone from any supreme council creating a grand consistory in New York. What's going on?

Think about this situation from how De La Motta may have viewed it. He walked into an area and found not only the Masons divided and hostile towards each other but also that each group had a body of the new 33 degree system that Charleston knew nothing about. Each side pointed to the other side, saying that *they* were the irregular and unauthorized ones. Who, if anyone, was right?

Once again, we don't have any records to explain why Bideaud created his Grand Consistory. If he were only a con-artist seeking money, then you would think that he would have created more of them. He created no such bodies during his stay in New Orleans. It is not impossible, and just as likely as anything else, that he, like Cerneau and De La Motta, walked into the middle of a Masonic dispute in the area. Maybe when he arrived, he just happened to meet the members of one of the groups (the group that included Daniel Tompkins). Maybe they asked him for help. When they learned who he was and this new system of Masonry, they might have felt that this would give them an edge over the other group. They might well have asked him to create the bodies. We don't know. He ended up helping one of the sides over the other, and he created a Grand Consistory.

Bideaud left a register in New Orleans listing established fees for the various degrees. As was normal practice, he charged fees for the degrees. The fees he charged in themselves mean nothing in the way of the charges thrown at him by Gourgas. Fees, as normal, were charged, and those fees went to the one who did the initiations. The fees help pay for the travel and living expenses. The idea that the one giving the initiations would do so free of charge and he would also foot the bill for travel and living expenses is nonsense. This was standard practice. But what is also interesting is that he created a Grand Consistory and not a supreme council. Why didn't he? We have no records to show why he didn't take the next step.

It would seem that Cerneau faced the same situation and took similar actions as Bideaud, only with the other group. The only differences were that Cerneau did not know the new system, and while Bideaud stopped with a Grand Consistory, Cerneau created what he viewed to be (or knew of) a supreme council. The problem, of course, was that Cerneau made quite a few organizational mistakes. Cerneau also may have felt that his "side" was clearly the *correct* side as he had none other than the Grand Master supporting him and serving as his Lt. Grand Commander.

A problem for Cerneau was his unfamiliarity with the new system. Giving him the benefit of the doubt (like was done with the others), Cerneau may have wanted to be of some help. An example of how Cerneau did not know the rules was the fact that he felt that he could create anything at all in the New York area. That area was already occupied. And I don't mean by the Charleston Supreme Council. I mean by Bideaud's Grand Consistory. And I say that regardless of what J.J.J. Gourgas and other SR historians have written. Antoine Bideaud *was* a Sovereign Grand Inspector General of the new 33 degree system.

Yes, if the Bideaud Grand Consistory did not exist, then it seems that Cerneau may have had a valid right (also regardless of what has been said) to follow the same path as John Mitchel to create his bodies in New York. But the Bideaud Grand Consistory did exist when Cerneau arrived in New York. What made Cerneau believe that he could establish anything in the New York area? Well, maybe he didn't know the rules well enough, didn't care about the rules, or he had reason to believe that Bideaud did not have the right to establish what he did. I mean, he had the *Grand Master* on his side, and the *Grand Master* was no friend of the other side. He may well have told him of their perceived "irregularities." Maybe things were not clear-cut, and Cerneau had to decide in an unclear situation.

Now, SR historians have historically badly viewed both Cerneau and Bideaud. Giving either of them the benefit of the doubt does not seem to have been desired. But we need to look at a couple of facts…

1.) The New York Masonic situation was politically and passionately divided

2.) The Grand Master of the Grand Lodge of New York did become Cerneau's Lt. Grand Commander.

It seems that Cerneau, like most Masons, would give serious consideration to a sitting Grand Master.

I have looked at the Cerneau, Bideaud, and Charleston situations and actions for many years. SR historians have vilified Bideaud and Cerneau from the beginning. Cerneau, of course, is vilified every time his name is mentioned. But when all the accusations and published accounts are examined, I find confusion, bad or self-serving logic, and excuses on all sides. I find that no one was entirely right or wrong. Everyone made errors. And everyone wanted you to look at what "the other guy" did but not at anything they did themselves.

Bideaud involved himself in a local Masonic squabble. He took sides. He created bodies in an area that the rules said was unoccupied. He charged a fee for the degrees. The idea that, because of that, he was a petty con artist trying to make money off his rank in the Scottish Rite is very unfair and wholly unsupported. That was standard practice at that time, before and after that time, and we know it.

So why did De La Motta, of equal rank to Bideaud, feel the need to "heal" what Bideaud had done and then turn around and create a Supreme Council out of his Grand Consistory? There is nothing that I have seen that shows that Bideaud acted outside of his authority. According to the *Grand Constitutions*, that area was considered unoccupied. It was as if it were a separate nation regardless of what has been claimed by selective readings of it.

But playing armchair quarterback, yes, Bideaud may have saved himself a lot of bad press by saying, "Geeze, I'm so sorry that this situation exists in your area. I wish all of you the very best of luck, but I have to leave." And then he should have gone on to France. It was the same with Cerneau. But the difference in his case was that the *Grand Master* became involved in what Cerneau was doing. We don't know exactly what happened, but the Grand Master did become his Lt. Grand Commander. I'd say that the Grand Master liked and approved of what Cerneau was doing. But, again, playing armchair quarterback, Cerneau might have said about the same thing that Bideaud should have said. He should have told the Grand Master that he did not know what was happening in the area and did not fully know or understand this new system. All he could do was wish all the parties well. But we have to understand that Cerneau does not seem to have been just passing through the area like Bideaud. He did open up a jewelry shop and remained in the area for some years. If you are brand new to an area and pulled into a situation in which the Grand Master might be seeking your aid, you may well have taken the same path as Cerneau. We just don't know all of the details. Should he have done it? Well, he was a Deputy Inspector General. Regardless of what he should have done or might have done, he did create those bodies. And he has paid a high price ever since.

And what of De La Motta? I've seen nothing that he was under specific orders from Charleston to act in a certain manner, depending on what he found. In fact, from what I have read, it seems that Charleston knew nothing, or very little, about the situation in New York. It seems that De La Motta walked into a wholly unexpected situation. And it was not as if De La Motta could pick up a telephone and call the members at Charleston. Yes, again, playing armchair quarterback, it may have gone better if De La Motta had just sat back and waited for instructions from Charleston. But he didn't. He also made a decision. He felt that Cerneau was irregular. He felt that problems existed with the Bideaud Grand Consistory, so he healed it. He then advanced the Bideaud Grand Consistory to a supreme council by what he saw as his right as a Sovereign Grand Inspector General in what he viewed as an unoccupied area. It became the Northern Masonic Jurisdiction. He made decisions and acted on them. Then, he received letters from the Charleston Council.

On August 5, 1813, Emanual De La Motta created the Northern Council with Daniel D. Tompkins as Sovereign Grand Commander. On August 23, 1813, letters were written to De La Motta by both John Mitchell and Frederick Dalcho. The letters must have given De La Motta some concern. Mitchell told him that no one except maybe de Grasse and Delahogue ever "had" the 33rd degree. I have no idea how De La Motta understood that, but I imagine it caused a bit of confusion with him. Then Dalcho told him that the Grand Constitutions provided for only *one* supreme council in the United States, and that was at Charleston. That was clearly *not* what Bideaud, Cerneau, De La Motta, Drummond, Baynard, and quite a number of others believed. It was also *not* written in the copy of the Grand Constitutions in Dalcho's hand. But it is what Dalcho wrote to De La Motta.

I do not accept that the Grand Constitutions of 1786 were legitimate. But I have found no evidence that the original Charleston Supreme Council was created for any ill purpose. I believe that its creation was an effort to help. I believe a very workable and meaningful system was created with a story born out of insecurity and doubt that the new system would be accepted without such a story. I've seen nothing that has given me reason to believe that the Charleston Supreme Council was created only to be of benefit to its creators.

In hindsight, I believe that they should have been open about how the new system was created, and they should *not* have reacted so quickly and harshly to Cerneau. At the very least, it was display in very poor tactics. I mean, think about it. By the time De La Motta arrived in New York, both the Cerneau and Bideaud bodies had existed enough years to have established themselves. On one side, you had the Governor of New York and, on the other, the Mayor of New York City, who also happened to be the Grand Master. They didn't like each other. They were skilled and powerful rivals. These were not at all stupid men who were unable to get things done. They were seasoned leaders — inside and outside of Freemasonry. They were also not at all afraid of battle.

But then De La Motta gets in the middle of them and says, "OK, I will make you guys here legitimate, but you other guys are done. You are simply irregular." *Really?* Forget about Cerneau. Forget about everything that you have been taught about this whole situation. Stop for a minute and try to put yourself back to *that* time and look at it through their eyes, with *those* players.

De La Motta is not only telling the sitting Grand Master that he's irregular, but he is telling that to the guy who just months prior came within inches of being elected President of the United States! And then, after saying *that* to *that* guy, De La Motta creates the same thing that Cerneau created. I can't see how, in any way, De La Motta thought that this was a good idea. And all because De La Motta didn't believe that Cerneau was a 33rd?

Not quite 30 years after the creation of the Charleston Council and just over 15 years after this event with Cerneau, Moses Holbrook was the Grand Commander of the Southern Jurisdiction. Holbrook *didn't know* how *Mitchell* became 33rd, and he questioned Frederick Dalcho about it. Dalcho said that he didn't … recollect. Maybe he signed some obligation from some Prussian for it. *Really?* How in the *world* could the Charleston Council, at that time, not possess and well know the proof of how Mitchell received the 33rd? How could that not be front and center in the archives of the Charleston Council? Cerneau and Cerneau Masons were attacked in every way possible because they could not provide documentation as to how Cerneau received the 33rd degree. Now we see that the Charleston Council *itself* and its leaders, at the very time that they were so harshly attacking Cerneau, didn't even know how their first Grand commander received his 33rd. It's astonishing. It's very disturbing.

I see no reasonable debate on this issue. The members of the Charleston Council *had* to know that they were living in a glass house. I believe De La Motta, Mitchell, and Dalcho should have stopped dead in their tracks once they learned of the situation in New York and who they were dealing with. Mitchell and Dalcho should have gotten themselves up to New York as quickly as they could. De La Motta should have gone to his hotel room and stayed there till Mitchell and Dalcho arrived. Mitchell and Dalcho should have sat down with all interested parties and said, "OK, let's talk." I don't care who created what or who had what authority. They had a great opportunity and were also facing a very serious situation. They should have put aside all this "You can't exist unless *I say* it's OK" ego nonsense. Regularity is subjective. They should have stayed locked in that room until they could find a way to all work together for the unified benefit of this new, enlightened system. But they didn't. They went on the attack. Powerful New York Masons, who had abundant ego and skill at battle, were attacked. And they fought back — hard.

Freemasonry throughout the United States had no idea what in the world was going on, but they paid the price. It was foolish, unnecessary, and against everything the Scottish Rite teaches. And everyone was to blame.

It has been more than 200 years since the creation of the Charleston Council. The creators of the Scottish Rite, as well as all parties involved, were human, and humans sometimes make mistakes in judgment. I believe it is time to be more lenient in our judgments. Did Cerneau make mistakes? You bet. Did Charleston make mistakes? You bet. But it's time to let all this go.

We do not know the why of Cerneau's actions. We do know that many good Masons supported and followed his Masonry. A good number of Grand Lodges embraced the so-called "Cerneau Masonry." Others denounce it to this day and probably don't remember why. And, yet, we can find many valuable contributions to the Scottish Rite by Cerneau Masons.

When we look back to the early Charleston Supreme Council and the years right before its creation, we see a great mess in the old 25 degree system. No matter what mistakes the Charleston Council made or how they acted, they did give us something extraordinarily worthy. We must stop fighting a 200 year old unnecessary and self-damaging war.

We are in a new day and a new age. Things are changing around us at near break-neck speed. The young members of the Scottish Rite want its teachings and philosophy of honor, integrity, and ethics. They want their lodges and bodies to be more than a reading of the minutes and a hot meal. They don't give a blue flip about some 200-year-old pointless argument about who was right and who was wrong. We must move on. We need to close that chapter completely. We must do the work that needs to be done. Our craft lodges and all other bodies need help. If Freemasonry wants to survive, it must change with the world. But I don't mean turning into something that we have never professed. I mean making sure that we *are* what we have *always* professed. We must realize that the Scottish Rite has a cloudy history. We must realize that much of our history is opinion rather than provable fact. We must stop insisting that our members believe anything to keep "our guys" in a positive light. It's OK to mess up. We are all human. But we must not have one standard of judgment for us and another for them. That's not what we teach.

Notes:

1. Today, the official name is "*The Supreme Council [Mother Council of the World] of the Inspectors General Knights Commander of the House of the Temple of Solomon of the Thirty-third degree of the Ancient and Accepted Scottish Rite of Freemasonry of the Southern Jurisdiction of the United States of America*" — but more commonly known simply as the "*Southern Jurisdiction.*"
2. R. Baker Harris and James D. Carter, *History of the Supreme Council, 33° (1801-1861)*, (Washington, D.C.: The Supreme Council, 33° Southern Jurisdiction, USA, 1964), 337.
3. Albert Pike, *The Grand Constitutions of Freemasonry* (New York: The Supreme Council, 33° Southern Jurisdiction, USA, 1872), 282-283.
4. Henry C. Clausen, *Authentics of Fundamental Law for Scottish Rite Freemasonry* (San Diego: The Supreme Council, 33° Southern Jurisdiction, USA, 1979), 9-10.
5. *Transactions of the Supreme Council of the 33D for the Southern Jurisdiction of the United States* (New York: Masonic Publishing Company, 1869), 19.
6. Ibid., 22-23.
7. Pike, *The Grand Constitutions of Freemasonry*, 289. Pike altered the English translation of the French version of Article five to: "...but two in the United States of America..." to emphasize his point concerning his interpretation of the meaning of this phrase.
8. Ibid., 283.
9. Albert Pike, *The True Secret Institutes and Fundamental Bases of the Order of Ancient Free and Associated Masons* and the *Grand Constitutions of the Ancient Accepted Scottish Rite of the Year 1786.* (New Orleans: The Supreme Council,

33° Southern Jurisdiction, USA 1859), 163-165. In Pike's 1872 (A.M. 5632) *The Grand Constitutions of Freemasonry*, he altered the original translation of the Latin version to read as follows: "*In each great nation of Europe, and in each Kingdom or Empire, there shall be a single Council of the said degree. In the States and Provinces, as well on the Continent as in the Islands, whereof North America consists, there will be two Councils, one at as great a distance from the other as may be possible.*" Pike, the master linguist, replaced the word "shall" with "will" in his 1872 edition, which, while having the same basic meaning, was not such an obvious problem to inattentive readers. The edited edition carries the note, "Re-translated from the Latin by Albert Pike, 33°, Sov. Gr. Commander. A.M., 5632" p. 213. Pike maintained the accuracy of his 1859 translation, at least, until 1868, as the questioned portion of Article Five is reproduced in the 1868 *Transactions* of the SC SJ exactly as they appeared in the 1859 translation on page 28.

10. Samuel Harrison Baynard, Jr., *History of the Supreme Council, 33° Ancient and Accepted Scottish Rite Northern Masonic Jurisdiction of the United States of America and its Antecedents* (Boston: The Supreme Council, 33° Northern Masonic Jurisdiction, USA, 1938), Vol. I, 175-179. This quotation is taken from the facsimile reproduction of the 1813 "birth certificate" for the Northern Jurisdiction (reproduced on page 176). In addition to the facsimile is a printed transcript of the "birth certificate " provided to us by Ill. Brother Baynard. Interestingly, the printed transcription omits a number of words and phrases that appear in the facsimile. The phrase, for example, "one for the South and one for the North" (line 26 of the facsimile), does not appear in the printed transcription.

11. Harris and Carter, *History of the Supreme Council, 33° (1801-1861)* , 95.

12. Henry Wilson Coil, *Coil's Masonic Encyclopedia* (New York: Macoy Pub. & Masonic Supply Co., 1961), p. 125.

13. Pike, *The Grand Constitutions of Freemasonry*, 117.

14. See: "Cerneauism" in *Coil's Masonic Encyclopedia*, 125-125. This term is used in many Masonic publications for any Masonic body in support of Cerneau or under the jurisdiction of a "Cerneau Masonic body." A number of bodies including Grand Lodges became "Cerneau" in the early to mid 1800's.

15. Harris and Carter, *History of the Supreme Council, 33° (1801-1861)*, 340.

16. Baynard, *History of the Supreme Council, 33°*, 101.

17. Pike, *The Grand Constitutions of Freemasonry*, 170.

18. Baynard, *History of the Supreme Council, 33°*, 115.

19. Ibid., 116.

20. Pike, *The Grand Constitutions of Freemasonry* 126.

21. Ibid., 195.

22. Ibid., 134.

23. Harris/Carter, *History of the Supreme Council, 33° (1801-1861)*, 117.

24. Ibid., 337.

25. Ibid., 118.

26. Ibid., 342.

27. Ibid., 340.

28. Baynard, *History of the Supreme Council, 33°*, 176. See note 10 for more information.

29. Harris/Carter, *History of the Supreme Council, 33° (1801-1861)*, 109

30. Ibid., 109.

The Elimination of the French Influence in Louisiana Masonry

Unlike other areas of the United States, Masonry did not begin in Louisiana with the introduction of British-style Masonry. Louisiana was originally established as a French territory. The French culture remained in Louisiana throughout the Spanish reign and after the area became part of the United States. As a result, the Masons of Louisiana logically favored French-styled Masonry. However, with the growing influx of "Americans" and the American culture, British-style Masonry began to grow in significance in the state. These two influences created a unique situation in Louisiana. While Perfect Union Lodge (long believed to be Louisiana's first Masonic lodge[1]) obtained its charter as a York Rite (American-Webb) Lodge from the Grand Lodge of Ancient York Masons of South Carolina in 1793, the lodge worked in the French language (as did the Grand Lodge from its birth in 1812 until 1850) and was French in nature. Just before the Grand Lodge of Louisiana formed, the only two English-speaking lodges in New Orleans (Louisiana and Harmony) withdrew from the Masonic convention created to form the Grand Lodge. This resulted in the Grand Lodge being formed by five French-speaking Lodges.[2]

As the steady stream of English-speaking "Americans" came into New Orleans, the impact was felt on the New Orleans culture and New Orleans Masonry. By a vast majority, the English-speaking Masons who came to New Orleans were of the York Rite (American Preston/Webb ritual) and found little interest in the French-speaking New Orleans Masonic lodges. The developing conflict between the various Masonic rites in New Orleans (French, Scottish, and York) can be viewed as a conflict between the co-existing New Orleans cultures. The established French-speaking population wanted to maintain its dominance over the culture and Masonry in New Orleans. The English-speaking citizens of New Orleans felt that their needs were not being accommodated by the French establishment. A revolt was inevitable.

The Grand Lodge and the Grand Consistory

In January 1833, a concordat was entered into between the Grand Consistory of Louisiana and the Grand Lodge of Louisiana.[3] This event can be seen as the catalyst for the schism in Louisiana Masonry that was soon to take place. In order to attempt to understand the significance of this concordat and the reasons behind it, a brief history of the Grand Consistory of Louisiana is necessary.

The Grand Consistory of Louisiana was organized and chartered in 1811 by the Supreme Council at Kingston, Jamaica.[4] Upon Louisiana achieving statehood in 1812, the *Grand Consistory* would seem to be no longer in a territory that could be considered "open" and could no longer remain under the jurisdiction of a foreign supreme council. Since fraternal relations between the Supreme Councils at Charleston and Kingston existed,[5] it would be logical to assume that the Grand Consistory would pass under the jurisdiction of the Charleston Council. However, this did not completely happen. The Grand Consistory (or, at least, part of it) passed under the jurisdiction of the Cerneau Bodies in New York in 1813 (considered irregular by the Charleston Council). At this point, the Grand Consistory of Louisiana reorganized into the Grand Council of Louisiana of Princes of the Royal Secret, 32°.[6] It was still a Scottish Rite body of the 32nd degree, but under a different system of Masonry — the Cerneau system.

DeWitt Clinton

Why would the Grand Consistory make this seemingly unusual move and place itself under a supreme council that was considered irregular? The answer may come from the fact that the Cerneau Council was composed of members of the regular Grand Lodge of New York. DeWitt Clinton was a long-time Grand Master of the Grand Lodge of New York, held in very high regard, *and* was the Deputy Grand Commander of the Cerneau Council. The Charleston Council was composed of members of what was then the irregular Grand Lodge of South Carolina.[7] The only logical answer for the Grand Consistory's action was that it considered Charleston to be (or had become) the irregular supreme council. The Grand Consistory of Louisiana was not the only body to begin favoring the Cerneau bodies over the Charleston Council. The Grand Commander of the Supreme Council of Kingston, Jamaica, J.J. Itter, is listed as an Honorary member of the Cerneau Sovereign Grand Consistory (the name of their supreme council) in the 1818 register of members.[8] This register is reprinted in Folger's *Ancient and Accepted Scottish Rite in Thirty-three Degrees* and carries the note:

> *This Pamphlet is annexed because it is a much more perfect one, than those published in 1813, 1814, 1815, and 1816. The others are not as full, and this is precisely like the preceding ones in every respect, the Author has preferred the one of this date.*[9]

While it is dangerous to draw the conclusion that Itter was an Honorary Member of the Cerneau Sovereign Grand Consistory from its creation based on Folger's unverified statement, J.J.J. Gourgas wrote to Emanuel De La Motta on 3 July 1815:

> ... *we have one [communication] which says that I.I.[sic, read J.J.] Itter, the Sn. Gr. Cr. there, loves money much, is a second Joseph Cerneau there and entirely devoted to him, that it is needful to take precautions for the correspondence with the Supe. Gd. Council, and even that the said Itter is the grand director and manager of everything; it is recommended, however, as a precaution, to correspond and direct to Ill. Br. Morales, formerly the Sn. Gd. Comr., &c., &c., &c ...* [10]

It does seem that the Supreme Council in Jamaica (or, at least, part of it) had switched to the Cerneau camp.

The battles between the Cerneau Council and the Councils in the Southern and Northern Jurisdictions (and additionally the problems resulting from the anti-masonic movements across the U.S.) would soon take its toll on all of the U.S. supreme councils. By the late 1820s, the Cerneau Council fell apart and ceased being active. John Holland, who was long-time Grand Master of the Grand Lodge of Louisiana and Commander in Chief of the Grand Council of Louisiana of Princes of the Royal Secret, 32°, sought in vain to contact the Cerneau Council. When it became clear that the Cerneau Council was no longer active (and after having received communications from the Council in the Northern Jurisdiction), the Grand Council of Louisiana decided to pass under the jurisdiction of the Charleston Supreme Council in 1831.[11] While under the jurisdiction of the Charleston Council, the renamed Grand Consistory of Louisiana chartered two

Scottish Rite Symbolic Lodges (Les Trinosophes & La Liberale) most likely using Emanuel De La Motta's 1814 *Rejoinder* as their justification.[12] With the growing friction between the two New Orleans cultures, the French-controlled Grand Consistory might also have taken this action to carve out a stronghold not only for the French-speaking concerns but also for the Scottish Rite. It should be noted that while relations between the French and English-speaking Masons of New Orleans were of a volatile nature, the relations between the French-speaking French Rite and French-speaking Scottish Rite Masons were also in a deteriorating state. The Grand Lodge, at that time, was strongly influenced by the French Rite [13] and clearly did not want to see control of symbolic lodges lost to the Grand Consistory. In 1833, a concordat was entered into between the Grand Consistory and the Grand Lodge whereby the Grand Lodge would issue symbolic charters for the York Rite, French Rite, and Scottish Rite and provide Symbolic Chambers for the management/education of the various lodges in the Grand Lodge. In exchange, the Grand Consistory relinquished its right to charter symbolic lodges. This might have settled some of the problems existing between the French and Scottish Rites, but it created more problems between the French and English-speaking Masons.

The Grand Council Becomes Again the Grand Consistory

By the early 1830s, the Charleston Council appeared to have met the same fate as the Cerneau Council.[14] On 1 September 1832, the Marquis de St. Angelo (Santangelo) visited the Grand Consistory and explained the state of affairs of High Degree Scottish Rite Masonry in the U.S. He announced that the United Supreme Council of the Western Hemisphere had been organized and informed them of the obvious benefits of passing under its jurisdiction.[15] Realizing that this Council was a reorganization of the Cerneau Council and that the Charleston Council in the Southern Jurisdiction and the De La Motta Council in the Northern Jurisdiction were no longer active, the Grand Consistory resolved to pass under St. Angelo's Council on the same day of his visit. Once again, it must be realized that Cerneau Masonry was not universally deemed irregular at this time. Lafayette had been well received by the Grand Lodge of Louisiana on 14 April 1825. Just eight months earlier, on 15 August 1824, the Cerneau Council conferred the 33° on Lafayette and, despite contradictory statements by the Charleston Council,[16] he considered *himself* a Cerneau Mason until his death in May of 1834.[17] Unfortunately, the United Supreme Council of the Western Hemisphere (even with entering into a treaty with the Supreme Council of France in 1834)[18] was not to be a long-lived supreme council. In 1839, the Marquis St. Angelo (Santangelo) returned to New Orleans as the Lt. Grand Commander of the United Supreme Council of the Western Hemisphere and, due to the near death of that Council, organized the Supreme Council for the United States of America sitting in New Orleans on 27 October of that year.[19] The Supreme Council of Louisiana (as it became known) was received by both the Grand Lodge and Grand Consistory of Louisiana, and fraternal relations were established between all bodies.[20] The United Supreme Council of the Western Hemisphere lingered on until the early 1840s and then died. On 9 October 1846, the Grand Consistory of Louisiana passed under the Jurisdiction of the Supreme Council of Louisiana.[21]

The English-speaking Masons found no comfort in the Concordat of 1833 nor the fact that a Symbolic Chamber would be created for the management of the three Rites in Louisiana Masonry. The English-speaking Masons felt that the York Rite should be the sole rite in the Grand Lodge. The various activities of the New Orleans Scottish Rite Masons could have been viewed as further evidence of instability in the "French"

Masonry. The unrest reached the boiling point in 1844 with a new Constitution for the Grand Lodge of Louisiana. The three Rites were officially recognized by the Constitution, and this seemed to be the breaking point for the York Rite Masons. 1844 would also be a turning point in Louisiana Masonry for both the Grand Lodge *and* the Scottish Rite bodies.

Ray Baker Harris states:

> *Oddly enough, as a revival of the Southern Supreme Council began in Charleston in 1844, in the same year, and completely unrelated, and independently, Gourgas and Yates were resuming discussion of the possible revival in the Northern Jurisdiction.*[22]

The revived Charleston Council was, undoubtedly, aware of the Supreme Council in New Orleans as the Council's "birth announcement "survives in the Holbrook papers in the Archives of the Southern Jurisdiction.[23] The Charleston Council neither protested nor took action against the Supreme Council of Louisiana—at that time. In 1845, a powerful Past Grand Master of the Grand Lodge of Louisiana became the Grand Commander of the Supreme Council of Louisiana. New Orleans Criminal Court Judge Jean-Francois Canonge served the Grand Lodge of Louisiana as Grand Master in 1822-24 and 1829 and also served as Commander in Chief of the Grand Consistory of Louisiana from 1843-46. Canonge had served as the Grand Senior Warden of the Cerneau Grand Council of Princes of the Royal Secret, 32° in Philadelphia in 1818[24] and was a founding member of the Supreme Council of Louisiana in 1839. It was during his administration that the Grand Consistory passed under the jurisdiction of the Supreme Council of Louisiana. With the influential Canonge as Grand Commander and numerous Past Grand Masters and Grand Lodge Officers serving as members and officers of both the

Grand Consistory and Supreme Council of Louisiana, it is likely that the newly revived and unstable Charleston Council did not wish (remembering the battles with the New York Cerneau Council) to directly confront the New Orleans Scottish Rite Bodies.

Enter the Grand Lodge of Mississippi

The New Orleans English-speaking York Rite Masons felt that the 1844 Constitution of the Grand Lodge of Louisiana altered the Grand Lodge into a body that was no longer an Ancient York Rite Grand Lodge. The decision was made to sever their association with the Grand Lodge and organize themselves into what they felt was proper York Rite Masonry. A committee was formed, and a letter of grievance was brought before the Grand Lodge of Mississippi on January

John A. Quitman

23, 1845.[25] The Grand Master of the Grand Lodge of Mississippi was Mexican War hero and former governor of Mississippi, John A. Quitman. The Grand Lodge of Mississippi appointed a committee to go to New Orleans in order to examine the situation. One year later, on January 21, 1846, the committee presented two reports before the Grand Lodge of Mississippi concerning the events in New Orleans. The first report was presented on behalf of the "majority" of the committee:

> *The committee to whom was referred the controversy between the Ancient York Masons of the State of Louisiana, on one side, and the Scotch and French Masons of said State, on the other, have duly considered the subject, and beg leave to report the following resolutions:*

1. Resolved, That no Grand Lodge of Scotch and French, or Modern Masonry can assume jurisdiction over any Ancient York Mason, or body of such.

2. Resolved, That it is not consistent with Ancient York Masonry, to unite with Scotch and Modern Masonry, or either of them, in the formation of a Lodge, Grand or Subordinate.

3. Resolved, That there is no Grand Lodge of Ancient York Masons within the limits of the State of Louisiana.

4. Resolved, That this Grand Lodge has the power, and it is its duty on proper application, to issue Dispensations and Charters to bodies of Ancient York Masons within the limits of the State of Louisiana, until the constitution of a Grand Lodge within that State.

5. Resolved, That we entertain the highest opinion of the distinguished body known as the Grand Lodge of Louisiana, and are willing to contribute as much as possible, consistent with our obligations, to aid and protect Ancient York Masons, wheresoever dispersed, and to maintain our Order pure and unmingled, to preserve friendly relations with that honorable body.

6. Resolved, That under no possible circumstances would this Grand Lodge assume jurisdiction over a Scotch or Modern Mason, or body of such, such assumption being alike inconsistent with their rights and our principles.

DUDLEY S. JENNINGS, R. N. DOWNING, J. J. DOTY, Committee [26]

The undersigned, a member of the committee to whom was referred so much of the Address of the M. W Grand Master, as relates to the M. W Grand Lodge of Louisiana, and also the verbal report of the committee appointed to visit that M. W. Body, begs leave to state by way of minority report, That the M. W. Grand Lodge of the State of Louisiana was organized exclusively after the

Ancient York Rite, and so remained for a number of years, until it accumulated the Scotch and French Rites. Said Grand Lodge is constituted by free and voluntary meetings of the Subordinate Lodges of the State, represented for life by the Master of each Lodge, who has presided over his Lodge for one year, and temporally by the Senior and Junior Wardens. According to the information now before the undersigned, there are now in active operation fourteen Lodges working in the Ancient York Rite; four in the Scotch Rite, accumulating the York and Modern Rite, and two in the Modern Rite, accumulating the Scotch and York Rite.

The undersigned would further respectfully submit, that no one of the fourteen Lodges above named, (as the undersigned believes,) has made any official complaint to this body of any improper or unmasonic conduct on the part of the M. W. Grand Lodge of Louisiana.

The undersigned is aware of the fact that St. Albans Lodge, No. 28, Louisiana, did, on the 9th July last issue a circular, addressed to the York Lodges in that State, requesting them to meet in convention and form a Grand Lodge of York Masons. The undersigned has yet to learn that more than one other Lodge of the State of Louisiana accepted or acted on the proposition of the said St. Albans Lodge. The undersigned would further represent that the M. W. Grand Lodge of Louisiana was constituted exclusively in the York Rite, that it is still a York Rite Grand Lodge, accumulating the Scotch and Modern Rite; that it grants charters authorizing Masonic work and labor in the York Rite exclusively, and that it also grants charters authorizing work in either the Scotch or French Rite, but invariably requires, in the later cases, that the York Rite shall always be communicated upon the candidate for the degrees in the latter Lodges. All the Masons of Louisiana are thus strictly Ancient York, though many of them possess also the French and Scotch Rite. These Rites obtain generally throughout the world, and any reflection upon the organization of the M. W.

Grand Lodge of Louisiana would equally reflect upon the conduct and proceedings of the Supreme Bodies of Masonry in France, Scotland and other nations, where these Rites are peculiarly esteemed. The undersigned would respectfully submit that this Grand Lodge do respectfully and fraternally remonstrate with the M.W. Grand Lodge of Louisiana upon its tolerance or the use by its Subordinate Lodges of ***** or their peculiar charts. The following resolutions are submitted:

1. Resolved, That this Grand Lodge finds nothing in the proceedings of the M. W. Grand Lodge of Louisiana, which demands a termination of the Masonic relations hereto fore existing between them.

2. Resolved, That this Grand Lodge would not, (at least under present circumstances,) feel itself justified in granting Dispensations or Charters to any body of Masons in the State of Louisiana.

All of which is respectfully submitted,

H.W. Walter [27]

A second "counter" report was made, but the outcome of the events of 21 January (despite the efforts of the two "counter" reports) was the chartering of George Washington Lodge in New Orleans and Lafayette Lodge in Lafayette[28] by the Grand Lodge of Mississippi on 22 February. Relations were severed between the Grand Lodges of Louisiana and Mississippi, and the Louisiana Lodges chartered by the Grand Lodge of Mississippi were declared clandestine by the Grand Lodge of Louisiana. In total, the Grand Lodge of Mississippi would charter seven Lodges in New Orleans by 1848.[29] These seven Lodges would unite to form the Louisiana Grand Lodge of Ancient York Masons on March 8th, 1848. The Grand Lodge of Mississippi received admonishes from most U.S. Grand Lodges, and the majority openly condemned its action.[30] While the future for this splinter group of the Grand Lodge of

Louisiana may have looked bleak, several events would take place to not only strengthen the position of the English-speaking New Orleans Masons but assure them of total victory and the loss of French control over *all* forms of Louisiana Masonry.

19 January 1848 would bring the death of Jean-Francois Canonge, the Grand Commander of the Supreme Council of Louisiana. In his place would be elected James Foulhouze as Grand Commander. Foulhouze had been appointed Grand Secretary of the Supreme Council in 1847 [31] and had received his 33° only two years earlier from the Supreme Council of the Grand Orient of France.[32] The election of Foulhouze as Grand Commander bypassed a number of senior members of the Council and clearly, established the popularity of Foulhouze with the Council. Foulhouze had brought with him various rituals from France[33], which he rewrote for the New Orleans Council.[34] Foulhouze was a brilliant man who would soon be elected as a District Court Judge. The former Roman Catholic priest turned lawyer, and Mason was obviously recognized as possessing great ability with Masonic philosophy and high organization and leadership ability (as his later battles with the Charleston Council would prove). Foulhouze was not, however, a Past Grand Master, and his influence in the Grand Lodge was limited. During the same month as the death of Canonge, the Charleston Council was taking an action that would greatly strengthen its own position and further weaken the hold of the French-speaking New Orleans Masons. Albert Mackey (the Grand Secretary of the Charleston Council) sent a notice to the *Freemason's Monthly Magazine*[35] (Boston), which read:

> *At a special session of the Supreme Council ... for the*
> *Southern Jurisdiction of the United States of America, our*
> *Illustrious Brother John A. Quitman ... Major General in the*

Army of the United States, was elected to fill a vacancy in this Supreme Council, and was duly and formally inaugurated a Sovereign Grand Inspector General of the 33d. All Consistories, Councils, Chapters and Lodges under this jurisdiction are hereby ordered to obey and respect him accordingly.[36]

It is interesting to note that at the same special session of the Charleston Council (or very soon after), Achille Le Prince was elected as an SGIG[37] yet no notice in a national Masonic magazine was apparently published. It is also interesting to examine the selection of Quitman as a member of the Charleston Council. Obviously, Quitman was a powerful and well-known individual who would be an asset to the Charleston Council, but would his actions against the Grand Lodge of Louisiana be a source of embarrassment to the Charleston Council? In December of 1848, the Grand Lodge of South Carolina issued a statement and a resolution concerning the actions of the Grand Lodge of Mississippi. The South Carolina Committee considered all points of the arguments of the Grand Lodges of Louisiana and Mississippi. While it did not condone the cumulating of rites by the Grand Lodge of Louisiana and hoped that *"the anomaly of mixed rites will be abolished by the Grand Lodge of Louisiana, "*[38] it also found no cause for the Grand Lodge of Mississippi to "invade" the jurisdiction of the Grand Lodge of Louisiana. In addition, the report states:

Your committee sincerely regret that by the formation of another Grand Lodge in the City of New Orleans, there has been another flagrant violation of the rights of the Grand Lodge of Louisiana. This new body is under the title of Louisiana Grand Lodge of Ancient York Masons. [39]

Resolved that the Grand Lodge of Louisiana did not forfeit their right of jurisdiction in Louisiana by the course they adopted in cumulating the degrees, altho this Grand Lodge disapproves of such improper acts and mal practices, and is desirous to learn that they have been abolished; and the ancient landmarks restored.

Resolved that the Grand Lodge of Mississippi, in granting warrants to establish new Grand Lodges within the State of Louisiana, made a premature and unlawful entry into a foreign jurisdiction which was not warranted by the occasion, and, to say the least, was a violation of that courtesy, which ought to exist between Grand Lodges.

Resolved that without speedy conclusion to the differences between two Grand Lodges now erected in Louisiana, the Grand Lodges throughout the United States ought to adopt some stringent method of depriving one, or the other, of the right of assuming authority which certainly only one is entitled to.

A E. Miller, J.H. Honour,
Z.B. Oakes, J.G. Norris, J.C. Barber. [40]

While the resolution of the Grand Lodge of South Carolina was not harshly critical of the Grand Lodge of Mississippi and did place some of the blame on Louisiana, it is most significant that any criticism, at all, of Mississippi by the Grand Lodge of South Carolina occurred. Two of the five members of the Grand Lodge of South Carolina committee were also Active Members of the Charleston Supreme Council. J.C. Norris was the Grand Treasurer, and J.H. Honour was Grand Commander! When the officers of the Charleston Supreme Council and the officers of the Grand Lodge of South Carolina for 1848 are compared, an interesting picture is painted.

John H. Honour—Grand Commander of Charleston Council & Grand Treasurer of Grand Lodge; Charles M.

Furman—Lt. Grand Commander of Charleston Council & Grand Master of Grand Lodge (1838-40, 1847-48); James Norris—Grand Treasurer of Charleston Council & Past Grand Master of Grand Lodge (1846); Albert G. Mackey—Grand Secretary of Charleston Council & Grand Secretary of Grand Lodge; James Burges—S. G. I. G. in Charleston Council & Grand Senior Warden of Grand Lodge; Achille Le Prince—S. G. I. G. in Charleston Council & no elected office in Grand Lodge; William S. Rockwell—SGIG from Georgia; John R. McDaniel—SGIG from Virginia; John A. Quitman—SGIG from Mississippi.

Out of the six members of the Charleston Council that lived in South Carolina, only one was not a high-ranking Grand Lodge Officer. The Grand Master, Charles M. Furman, was the Lt. Grand Commander of the Charleston Council.

Stating that the Grand Lodge of Mississippi had acted improperly was admitting that a newly elected Sovereign Grand Inspector General of the Charleston Council had acted improperly *prior* to his election. Why then was Quitman elected to this office? In fairness to the Charleston Council, it must be noted that a man should not be condemned before all the evidence is examined. Quitman was made an Active Member of the Charleston Council nearly a year before the Grand Lodge made its rulings on Quitman's Grand Lodge. It must also be noted that the Charleston Council was not obligated to act in harmony with the Grand Lodge of South Carolina nor have the same agenda. The Grand Lodge of South Carolina was, in no way, threatened by the existence of any Masonic body in New Orleans. The Charleston Council, however, was *very much* threatened by the well-organized New Orleans Scottish Rite bodies — the *only* Scottish Rite Bodies in the U.S. to remain active during the "dormant" period of the Supreme Councils of the Northern and Southern jurisdictions.[41] While wearing the "Supreme Council" hat, Grand Commander John Honour, as well as the other Charleston Council members, were obligated to do all in their power to assure that the Charleston Council would survive. This included recruiting the powerful and very influential John Quitman. While wearing the "Grand Lodge" hat, John Honour and the rest of the Grand Lodge were obligated to chastise Quitman (although not mentioning his name) through the unwarranted actions of the Grand Lodge of Mississippi (actions which, however, would ultimately prove helpful to the Charleston Council).

The Takeover of the Grand Lodge

The Louisiana Grand Lodge of Ancient York Masons was organized on March 8, 1848, and was recognized by only one other Grand Lodge — The Grand Lodge of Mississippi. In 1849, John Gedge was elected Grand Master of the Louisiana Grand Lodge of Ancient York Masons. Despite the regularity question of the Louisiana Grand Lodge and the lack of support for this new Grand Lodge around the world, the Grand Lodge of Louisiana merged with this body in 1850. The Grand Lodge of Louisiana was left with little choice in this matter. The fact that the Grand Lodge of Louisiana was overwhelmingly considered the "regular" Grand Lodge was not sufficient to overcome the internal problems stemming from the cultural divisions in New Orleans. By mid-1849, it was realized that the English-speaking lodges that had remained loyal to the Grand Lodge were showing signs that continued loyalty would, most likely, not happen. The division between the French-speaking Scottish and French Rite New Orleans Masons only contributed to the dilemma. Obviously, realizing that the total collapse of the Grand Lodge of Louisiana was a very real possibility, the Grand Lodge of Louisiana and the Louisiana Grand Lodge entered into talks designed to merge the two bodies.[42] That merger took place in June of 1850 with the approval of a new

Constitution of the Grand Lodge of Louisiana of Free and Accepted Masons. Under the terms of the agreement of the merger, the Louisiana Grand Lodge members declared irregular would be declared "regular" by the Grand Lodge of Louisiana. All Lodges chartered by the Louisiana Grand Lodge (or by the Grand Lodge of Mississippi in Louisiana) would also pass under the jurisdiction of the new Grand Lodge of Louisiana. The one phrase that was agreed upon that would result in *great* unrest with the French-speaking New Orleans Masons was Article II Section 2, which read:

> *It* [the *Grand Lodge of Louisiana*] *is constituted as a Grand Lodge of Free and Accepted Masons, and in that capacity recognizes nothing but pure Ancient Free Masonry, consisting of the three symbolic degrees of Apprentice, Fellow Craft and Master Mason, and is forbidden to tolerate any distinctions derogatory to the character in which it is constituted.*[43]

Believing that this phrase would result in the Grand Lodge of Louisiana maintaining its former position concerning the several rites in New Orleans, the French-speaking New Orleans Masons agreed to the new Constitutions. After the Constitution was passed, the "new" Grand Lodge of Louisiana (then controlled by the English-speaking Masons) announced that "pure Ancient Free Masonry" was the equivalent of "Ancient York Rite Masonry." All non-York Rite Lodges were instructed to turn in their charters in order to receive York Rite charters.[44] The French-speaking New Orleans Masons flew into a rage. Charges of trickery abounded. Two French-speaking lodges (Polar Star and Disciples of the Masonic Senate) and a Spanish-speaking lodge (Los Amigos Del Orden) applied to the Supreme Council of Louisiana for relief. The Supreme Council of Louisiana announced that since the Concordat of 1833 between the Grand Lodge of Louisiana and the Grand

Consistory of Louisiana (at that time the highest-ranking body of Scottish Rite Masons in the State) had been violated by the new Grand Lodge, the Supreme Council would have no choice but to grant the relief sought by the lodges and issue Scottish Rite charters to the subordinate Scottish Rite Symbolic Lodges.[45]

If the goal of the new 1850 Grand Lodge Constitution and the merger with the Louisiana Grand Lodge was to bring peace to *all* the Louisiana Masons, it was a total failure. If the goal was to remove the power base in the Grand Lodge from the French-speaking New Orleans Masons, it was, indeed, a success. The French-speaking New Orleans Masons became split after 1850. One faction, outraged at the turn of events, wished nothing more to do with the Grand Lodge and saw the Supreme Council as the only hope of maintaining the French interests. The other French faction, most likely simply tired of the squabbles, remained with the Grand Lodge in the hopes of possibly still bringing unity to the troubled Grand Lodge.

In 1851, John Gedge, who two years earlier was the Grand Master of the irregular Louisiana Grand Lodge, was elected Grand Master of the Grand Lodge of Louisiana. Any thought that the "new" Grand Lodge of Louisiana was *not* under the control of the English-speaking Masons was clearly eliminated. The Grand Lodge and Supreme Council, once closely related bodies, were now opposing forces. With Louisiana Masonry in a state of turmoil and the once powerful Supreme Council of Louisiana fighting for order and realizing that it was no longer a stable authority, the time for the Charleston Council to act was at hand.

A New Scottish Rite in New Orleans

At the invitation of John Gedge, Albert Mackey came to New Orleans in 1852 and established, for the Charleston Supreme Council, a Consistory of the 32° (not a Grand Consistory as is sometimes reported). Obviously, the New Orleans Scottish Rite bodies charged that this was an outrageous invasion of territory. Not only was the fact that the Consistory was organized in New Orleans, but the manner in which it was created was the subject of severe criticism. James Foulhouze would comment in his *Historical Inquiry:*

Albert Mackey

> *Gedge knew where the deception lay, and that it was no accident but the result of artful design. He hated the Scotch Rite, and had attempted all in his power to destroy it. The question therefore for him was to find out how he could carry out his purpose, and he was unscrupulous about the means to employ, he conceived the idea of becoming a Scotch Mason himself if it was possible. He succeeded in finding at Charleston a man as unscrupulous as himself, a man of whom one who is now a chief supporter of the Charleston Consistory in Louisiana said in 1853 that an eternal shame should weigh upon him for what he (Mackey) then did. That man was A.G. Mackey. He came at Gedge's request to establish a Consistory for the government of the supreme power at Charleston, appointing Gedge as the Commander, and therein conferring the High Degrees of what they are pleased to call the Scotch Rite in a manner as to create disgust even to those who now exalt him as their most potent monarch, if we may believe the same authority.* [46]

James Foulhouze is usually judged unkindly by most Masonic historians (either fairly or unfairly). Foulhouze clearly had little use for the Charleston Supreme Council, and his anger at the Charleston Council is evident. These facts aside, this statement by Foulhouze should be examined for accuracy. Foulhouze claimed that an unnamed Charleston supporter charged that the manner in which the "Mackey" Consistory was created was an "eternal shame" on those conferring the degrees. That unnamed Mason was Charles Laffon de Ladébat, 33°. After the Concordat of 1855 merged the New Orleans and Charleston Councils, Ladébat became an Active Member and Officer in the Charleston Council. In 1853, Ladébat wrote about the Grand Lodge events of 1850 and the new Consistory as follows:

Charles Laffon de Ladébat

In presence of such despotic, anti-masonic conduct, the Scotch BB.: resisted as men, as Masons, and formed an independent corporation under the only M.: authority existing in Louisiana "de jure et de facto." The balance remained with the new Grand Lodge, swore obedience to her, through indifference rather than from conviction. Soon after this, the very same Sectarian [John Gedge], in his restlessness, caused Br.: Albert G. Mackey to come from Charleston, in order to establish a Grand Consistory, exactly as if there never had existed a Supreme Council of the Scotch Rite in Louisiana. Our sectarian, after abolishing the Scotch Rite, wished to re-establish it in order to be at the head of it. This Consistory has been inaugurated, you know it M.: W:, for you were admitted into it for proper causes. The manner in which the degrees were conferred in this spurious

Consistory is and will be an eternal shame to the Br.: who has conferred them.[47]

The same anger and emotion that is contained in the Foulhouze quotation is also present in this statement by Ladébat. It was, clearly, a time of high emotion and divided passions. From these two quotations, it is not only apparent that the New Orleans Scottish Rite Masons disapproved of the creation of this Charleston Consistory in New Orleans, but they also found something very disturbing in the manner in which the Scottish Rite degrees were conferred on the members of this new Consistory. To try and understand Ladébat's "eternal shame" statement, we must attempt to trace the source of the problem. The following circumstances should be noted: The *Charleston Council*, at the time of its creation, worked a different form of the present 33-degree system. The *1802 Charleston Manifesto lists* the 29° as Knight Kadosh and the 30°, 31°, and 32° all as Prince of the Royal Secret.[48]

The Supreme Council of Louisiana (as did the Grand Consistory of Louisiana) worked in the 33-degree system with the degrees as they exist today (29° — *Knight of St. Andrew*, 30° — *Knight Kadosh*; 31° — *Grand Inspector Inquisitor Commander*, 32° — *Prince of the Royal Secret*).[49]

In the 1845 *Charleston Manifesto*, the Charleston Council lists the names of the Council's degrees nearly as they appeared in the *1802 Manifesto*. The 1845 *Manifesto* suggests that the revived Charleston Council had possibly not revised its rituals or did not have possession of its revised rituals.[50]

The Charter for the *1852 "Mackey" Consistory* in New Orleans lists the bulk of the degrees exactly as listed in the 1845 & 1802 Manifestos, including the 29° as the K-H degree. The 30°, however, is listed as Knight of St. Andrew, 31° — Grand

Inquiring Commander, and the 32°— Sublime Prince of the Royal Secret.[51]

On March 20, 1853, Albert Mackey *communicated* the degrees from the 4th to the 32nd to Albert Pike at Charleston.[52]

Since Albert Mackey, alone, came to New Orleans and conferred the Scottish Rite degrees from the 4th to the 32nd on the Masons who formed the 1852 New Orleans/Charleston Consistory, it is reasonable to assume that Mackey (like he did with Pike) *communicated* and did not *confer* the degrees (as there was no degree team). If, in addition to this and the general dissatisfaction of creating a Consistory in an area viewed as "occupied," Mackey used the degree names as listed on the 1852 "Mackey" Consistory or drastic variations of the known rituals, this could have been viewed by the New Orleans Scottish Rite Masons as an *incredible* deviation from the accepted Scottish Rite manner of initiation and rituals known in New Orleans. The combination of these events could have prompted Ladébat's *"eternal shame"* statement. It is quite clear that the 1852 Consistory flamed the fires and resulted in a "quick burn" of tempers in the French-speaking New Orleans Masons.

The Concordat of 1855

The speed and total loss of the Grand Lodge of Louisiana by the French-speaking Masons caused obvious confusion and uncertainty as to the future. Without a powerful leading force, they began to split into factions. James Foulhouze, as Grand Commander, sought to unite all the French-speaking Masons under his banner. Whether it was because of the rapid advancement of Foulhouze (resulting in uncertainty as to his ability) or simply personality conflicts, Foulhouze was not able to unite all the French Masons. The conflict of opinions within the Supreme Council of Louisiana as to the direction to proceed can reasonably be seen as a contributing factor to the resignation of Foulhouze[53] and nearly all of the officers of the Supreme Council of Louisiana by December of 1853.[54] On 7 January 1854, Charles Claiborne was elected Grand Commander of the Supreme Council of Louisiana. Claude Pierre Samory was elected Lt. Grand Commander, and Charles Laffon de Ladébat was appointed Grand Secretary. Samory and Ladébat were part of the French-speaking faction that split from Foulhouze during the 1850-53 turmoil. 1854 was devoted to negotiations with the Charleston Supreme Council. 16 February 1855, the concordat merging the New Orleans and Charleston Supreme Councils was signed in New Orleans. John Gedge, who had spearheaded the movement of the Louisiana Grand Lodge and the 1852 Consistory, would not live to see the concordat between the New Orleans and Charleston Councils — he would die on 13 April 1854.

Claude Pierre Samory would be the first former member of the Supreme Council of Louisiana to be elected an Active member of the Charleston Council.[55] Following Samory would be Ladébat in 1859.[56] The Grand Consistory of Louisiana would absorb the 1852 Consistory during the Concordat of 1855, and on 17 December 1856, Albert Pike would be unanimously elected Commander in Chief of the Grand Consistory of Louisiana — an office that he would hold until his 1859 election as Grand Commander of the Charleston Council.

Ultimately, the French Rite would seemingly disappear from Louisiana Masonry.[57] The French domination of the Grand Lodge and the Scottish Rite Bodies would end.[58] Samory and Ladébat would both move to France in the mid-1860s.[59] The elimination of the French control of Louisiana Masonry was complete. In citing his reasons for his upcoming resignation from the Charleston Council, Charles Laffon de Ladébat summed up the Louisiana situation to Albert Pike in an 1860 letter:

> *My resolution of retiring from active practice is 5 years old & more. Hear what I wrote to Mackey January 31, "When the work will be accomplished, when everything will be in proper order & well understood, I will retire willingly & leave the management of all to more competent but not to more devoted hands." We know that the foreign influence will & must be superseded by the American element. Now that time has come & as I believe that, even in Masonry, Americans must rule in America. I, a frenchman, must retire — in due time.*
>
> *I believe readily that you did not want the office, but the office wanted you & it will be a great pleasure for me to remember ... that I was not the last to devise the means of placing you at the head of the order, 1st by making you a 33rd against the will of Messrs. Furman & Honour: 2nd by vacating my office of Deputy in your favor, & twice you got in the S. C. & especially twice you were unanimously elected to the Presidency, I consider myself as having done my duty, all my duty, all I could do. The lifeless council of Charleston was revived; it lives now! Only now tho!* [60]

Notes:

1. The first known craft lodge in Louisiana was the ecossais lodge *Perfect Harmony* chartered on 16 July 1752 in New Orleans by *Perfect Union Lodge* in Martinique. *Sharp Document #40* is located in the Archives of the Supreme Council Northern Masonic Jurisdiction USA in Lexington, Massachusetts. See also: *The Sharp Documents, Volume IV* (Rennes, France: The Latomia Foundation, 1993) 1.
2. Perfect Union, Charity, Concorde, Perseverance & Polar Star. All except Charity and Concorde are still active.

3. *Proceedings of the Grand Lodge of the State of Louisiana* (New Orleans: 1848) 16.

4. R.F. Gould, W.J. Hughan, A.F.A. Woodward, D.M. Lyon, J.H. Drummond, E.T. Carson, T.S. Parvin — Editors, *A Library of Freemasonry*, Vol. V (Philadelphia: The John C. Yorston Publishing Co., 1923) 299.

5. Ibid., 298-299.

6. *Minutes Book of the Grand Consistory of Louisiana* (1822-1846). Located in the *New Orleans Scottish Rite Bodies*. New Orleans, Louisiana. In the Cerneau Scottish Rite, a body of the 32nd degree was called a "Grand Council" and not a "Grand Consistory" as in the Charleston Scottish Rite system.

7. Alain Bernheim, Introduction, *Outline to the Rise and Progress of Freemasonry in Louisiana,* by James B. Scot (New Orleans, LA: Cornerstone Book Publishers, 2008 reprint of 1873 edition) XIV.

8. Robert B. Folger, *The Ancient and Accepted Scottish Rite in Thirty-three Degrees* (New Orleans, Cornerstone Book Publishers, 2011 reprint of 1862 edition) 186.

9. Ibid., 181.

10. *Transactions of the Supreme Council of the 33d Degree for the Southern Jurisdiction USA* (SC SJ USA: Washington, D.C. reprint 1878) 14-16; Alain Bernheim, *Further Light on the Masonic World of Joseph Glock* (London: Ars Quatuor Coronatorum Vol. 100, 1987) 46.

11. *Minutes/Grand* Consistory, 21 February 1831 & Bernheim, Introduction, *Outline*, XVI.

12. De La Motta stated: *"I have nothing further to say, except, that although Sublime Masons have not in this country initiated into the Blue or Symbolic Degrees, yet their Councils possess the indefeasible right of granting warrants for that purpose. It is common on the continent of Europe, and may be the case here, should circumstances render the exercise of this power necessary. [...] E. De La Motta, Esq."* Joseph McCosh, *Documents Upon Sublime Freemasonry* (New Orleans, LA: Cornerstone Book Publishers, 2018 reprint of 1823 edition) 62. De La Motta took this statement from Frederick Dalcho's (the Charleston Council's then Lt. Grand Commander) 1803 *Oration*. Bernheim, Introduction, *Outline*, XXIII.

13. Ray Baker Harris, James D. Carter *History of the Supreme Council, 33° Southern Jurisdiction, USA (1801-1861)* Washington, D.C.: The Supreme Council, 33° 1964), 30, 35.

14. The exact date that the Charleston Council went dormant cannot be determined.

15. *Minutes Grand Consistory* & Bernheim, Introduction, *Outline, XXV-XXVII.*

16. Harris/Carter, *History,* 158.

17. On 10 May 1834 (ten days before his death), Lafayette wrote in the Golden Book of the *United Supreme Council of the Western Hemisphere* (held by Comte de St. Laurent): *I owe today the great favors which the Grand Council of the Western Hemisphere has designed to bestow upon me. I accept them with deep gratitude and will try to merit them through* my *zeal.* The Lafayette document is in the Archives of the *Supreme Council of France.* Photocopy in possession of this author. Reprints of this statement are in Julius F. Sachse's *The History of Brother General Lafayette's Fraternal Connections with the R. W. Grand Lodge, F.& A.M., of Pennsylvania* (Philadelphia: The Committee on Library by Resolution of the *R.W. Grand Lodge, F.& A.M., of Pennsylvania,* 1916) 21·23 and Robert Folger's 1862 *Ancient & Accepted Scottish Rite in Thirty-three Degrees* (p. 220). Many thanks to Claude Gagne, 33°, Grand Archivist of the *Supreme Council of France,* for his assistance.

18. Harris/Carter, *History,* 216.

19. "Birth Announcement" of the *Supreme Council of the United States of America Sitting in New Orleans,* located in the Archives of the *Supreme Council Southern Jurisdiction, USA* in Washington, D.C. Photocopy in possession of this author. Scot, *Outline,* 53, 54

20. Ibid 54;

21. *Minutes Grand Consistory,* 9 October, 1846 & Bernheim, Introduction, *Outline,* 29.

22. Scot, *Outline,* 224.

23. Ibid., 220.

24. Folger, *Ancient And Accepted Scottish Rite,* 286.

25. *Proceedings of the Grand Lodge of Mississippi A.F.&A.M. 1818-1852* (Jackson, Miss: Clarion Steam Printing Establishment, 1882) 309.

26. Ibid., 320-321.

27. Ibid., 321-322.

28. The town of Lafayette was a suburb of New Orleans in the 1800s, located in what is now considered the "uptown" area of New Orleans.

29. George Washington, Lafayette, Warren, Marion, Crescent City, Hiram & Eureka.

30. *Grand Lodge of the State of Louisiana Report and Exposition* (New Orleans: J.L Sollee, 1849) 5-34.

31. James Foulhouze, *Historical Inquiry* (New Orleans: Cornerstone Book Publishers, 2011 reprint of 1859 edition) 62.

32. Ibid., 60.

33. Charles Laffon de Ladébat, *Ancient and Accepted Rite. Thirtieth Degree* (New Orleans: 1857) xxvii.

34. Charles Laffon-Ladébat states in a footnote of his published 18° ritual: *The philosophical explanation of this and of all the other Degrees from the First up to the Thirtieth inclusive, is taken from the work of Ill.: Bro.: J. Foulhouze, 33d, with*

some slight alterations, of which, the author willingly assumes the responsibility. Ladébat, *Ancient and Accepted Scotch Rite. Eighteenth Degree* (New Orleans: 1856) 123. Foulhouze had also rewritten the 33° for the *Supreme Council of Louisiana.* See: James D. Carter, *History of the Supreme Council, 33° SJ USA* (1861-1891) (Washington, D.C.: The Supreme Council 33°, 1967) 37-38.

35. The title of this magazine is sometimes given as *Freemasons' Magazine.* Many thanks to Alain Bernheim for this discovery.

36. Charles S. Lobingier, *The Supreme Council, 33°* (Louisville, KY: The Standard Printing Co., Inc., 1931) 172; Harris/Carter, *History, 236.*

37. Ibid., 236-237.

38. It was the apparent early policy of the Grand Lodge of Louisiana to take a position of non-involvement in areas concerning the rituals of the Lodges under its jurisdiction. In 1844, Germania Lodge #46 was issued a charter as a York Rite German-speaking Lodge. Its original German ritual, however, was a mixture of the York, French and Scottish Rites. Arturo de Hoyos, Introduction, *The Liturgy of Germania Lodge No. 46 F.&.A.M.* Translated & edited by Arturo de Hoyos (New Orleans: Michael R. Poll, 1993) v.

39. *Grand Lodge of Louisiana Grand Annual Communication. First Quarterly Session* (New Orleans: J.L. Sollee, 1849) 28-29.

40. Ibid., 28-29.

41. The Cerneau Bodies in New York, the Charleston Supreme Council (SJ), and the De La Motta Supreme Council (NMJ) in New York all ceased being active bodies from a period roughly between the 1820s to the mid-1840s. The Grand Consistory of Louisiana remained active during this period of time.

42. Scot, *Outline, 78-80.*

43. *Constitution of the Grand Lodge of the State of Louisiana of Free and Accepted Masons* (New Orleans: The Crescent Office, 1850) 3.

44. Charles Laffon de Ladébat, *The Schism between the Scotch & York Rites* (New Orleans: Cornerstone Book Publishers, 2008 reprint of 1853 ed.) 7-8.

45. Scot, *Outline, 86-87.*

46. Foulhouze, *Inquiry, 62-63.*

47. Ladébat, *Letter to Hill, 9.*

48. Harris/Carter, *History, 319-325.*

49. *1846 General Regulation of the Supreme Council of the USA Sitting in New Orleans. Minutes/Grand* Consistory.

50. Harris/Carter, *History,* 229-231. Note: The Scottish Rite Rituals, as transcribed by Albert Pike in 1854 & 55, show the degree structure closer to today's structure, with, for example, the 30° being the K-H degree rather than the 29°. It is possible that Albert Mackey, realizing the problems with the degree structure and reasonably embarrassed by the legitimate uproar of the New Orleans Scottish Rite Masons, restructured the degrees or located

them at some point between 1852 and 1854. Thanks to Arturo de Hoyos for the information concerning the Pike Manuscript Rituals.

51. A photographic reproduction of the 1852 "Mackey" Consistory is located in the George Longe Papers, Amistad Research Center, Tulane University, New Orleans, LA. A framed copy of this document is also located in the New Orleans Scottish Rite Bodies. New Orleans, Louisiana.

52. Ibid., 244.

53. In his 1858 work, Joseph Lamarre states: *In 1853, Ill. Bro. James Foulhouze resigned his membership in the ex-S.C., because III. Bro. Charles Claiborne, 33d had ridiculed his costumes, his masonic frocks.* Lamarre. *A Masonic Trial In New Orleans - May 22, 1858* (New Orleans: J. Lamarre, 1858) 24. It seems unthinkable that this could have been the sole reason for Foulhouze resigning his office in the Supreme Council of Louisiana, but it is an interesting look at the volatile atmosphere.

54 Folger, *Ancient And Accepted Scottish Rite, 312-314.*

55. 18 November 1856. Harris/Carter, *History,* 252.

56. Albert Mackey wrote to Ladébat on 27 February 1859, informing him of his election. Ladébat wrote back to Mackey on 19 March, accepting the office and, interestingly, expressed a desire for a supreme council to be established in each state. Ibid., 266.

57. Following the 1850 *Constitution of the Grand Lodge of Louisiana,* the French Rite was not accommodated by the Grand Lodge. With no superior body for the government of the French Rite Lodges, they eventually lost their identity and their unique nature. An attempt was made in the late 1800s to revive the French Rite in New Orleans through the short-lived *Grand Orient of Louisiana* (French or Modern Rite). This body was created in 1879 but, possibly due to little support, did not last longer than ten years. See: *The Grand Orient of Louisiana: A Short History and Catechism of a Lost French Rite Masonic Body,* Introduction by Michael R. Poll (New Orleans: Cornerstone Book Publishers, 2008 reprint of 1886 edition).

58. On 7 October 1856, James Foulhouze and the other former officers of the Supreme Council of Louisiana who resigned in 1853 announced that the body had never ceased to exist. The Supreme Council of Louisiana (under Foulhouze) and the Charleston Council (under Pike) engaged in bitter attacks. For presently unknown reasons, Foulhouze would seem to have abandoned the Supreme Council of Louisiana in the mid-1860s.

59. Samory would return to New Orleans and die there on 30 July 1889, and Ladébat would remain in France and die there on 22 December 1882.

60. Charles Laffon de Ladébat to Albert Pike June 24, 1860. Original in the Archives of the Supreme Council Southern Jurisdiction, *USA.* Photocopy in possession of this author.

Creole Freemasons of New Orleans

The mid-1800s were a terrible time for Louisiana Freemasonry. Masonry in the state became split into two unyielding factions — the English-speaking Masons and the French-speaking Masons. To better understand the situation, we must go back to the early days of Freemasonry in Louisiana.

The French established the territory of Louisiana. Louisiana was French in culture as well as language. The earliest record we presently have of Freemasonry in Louisiana is contained in the *Sharp-Bordeaux Documents*. These documents tell us of a lodge established in New Orleans in 1752.[1]

Old New Orleans

New Orleans was an important U.S. shipping port. Merchants found it cheaper, simpler, and safer to transport goods down the Mississippi to New Orleans and out by ship through the Gulf of Mexico to wherever they were going. With the ships that would bring goods and tourists to New Orleans came Masons visiting the city. These visitors, including travelling Masons, were mostly English-speaking.

Freemasonry in New Orleans reflected the culture of the city. The Grand Lodge of Louisiana was created in 1812 by five French-speaking lodges. The Grand Lodge itself was French-speaking. This meant that New Orleans Freemasonry, in those early days, was French not only in language but by culture.

The English-speaking Masons who visited New Orleans did not understand or seem to like the Freemasonry they found in the city. By the 1820s, 30s, and later, Masonic visitors to New Orleans found lodges working in at least three different rituals and up to five different languages.

Freemasonry in the United States outside New Orleans was, by far, English-speaking and York Rite (or American Webb) ritual. The English-speaking Masons in New Orleans grew frustrated at what seemed to be an un-Masonic deviation from what they viewed as proper Freemasonry. The Grand Lodge grew frustrated as their position was that they were trying to accommodate as many different Masons as possible.

If a group of regular Freemasons speaking a particular language and working in an approved ritual sought to create a lodge, then the Grand Lodge saw no problem issuing them a charter to work in the language and ritual of their choice. The English-speaking Masons felt that this was unacceptable. In their view, the Grand Lodge should only accommodate English-speaking Masons working in the York Rite/American Webb ritual. The Grand Lodge viewed this as self-serving and unreasonable.

The two sides held firm to their positions, and this was the general heart of the conflicts in Louisiana Freemasonry.

The problem for the English-speaking Masons was that they were in the minority. While the English-speaking Masons were growing in number, it was still about a 60/40 split (and that's a rough estimate) between the two sides. Regardless of the minority status of the English-speaking Masons, they were successful in taking over the Grand Lodge of Louisiana in 1850.

The Vieux Carre, New Orleans

From all records and accounts I have seen over the last 35 to 40 years, the French-speaking Masons seemed split regarding how they should deal with the English-speaking Masons. Because the French-speaking Masons were divided, the English-speaking Masons were able to drive a wedge between them and create three groups instead of two. While the English-speaking Masons were the minority, they became the majority against the two smaller French-speaking factions. It seems that the divide and conquer tactic worked.

I have always had a problem trying to understand why the French-speaking Freemasons allowed themselves to be split into two in such a manner. I couldn't understand why they couldn't remain unified. Had they remained unified, the English-speaking Masons could not have taken over the Grand Lodge, and the trouble that followed might have been avoided.

So why did they do it? Why could they not come together and work together for their own best interest? That's what I would like to explore now.

When we study history, it's important to understand not only what happened but to try and understand *why* something happened. If we don't understand why something happened, our understanding of the whole situation may be skewed or incomplete.

We know that Freemasonry in Louisiana was divided. We understand that the French-speaking faction lost the battle even though they were in the majority. It seems that to understand why the French-speaking Masons acted as they did, we need to step outside of Freemasonry. We need to look at the city of New Orleans, its citizens, and its culture.

In New Orleans, there is a group of people who call themselves Creoles. But quite a bit of misunderstanding exists concerning exactly who is a Creole.

From my study, there are three main areas of misunderstanding about Creoles. One is that being a Creole has something to do with race. That's false.

The second is that a Creole is a Creole is a Creole. In other words, the belief is that there is no difference between a Creole from New Orleans and a Creole from, say, the West Indies. That is also false.

And the third misconception is that there is no cultural difference between a Creole and a Cajun from Southwest Louisiana. It is often felt that they are simply two names for the same thing. Again, that's false.

In the early days of Louisiana, the term Creole simply meant someone born somewhere in Louisiana. It was used to identify native born citizens of Louisiana. But, around the 1820s, a unique and complex social structure began to develop around the Creoles. Three factors had to be present to be defined as a Creole and accepted into their social structure.

First, it was felt that Louisiana was too large an area, and many outside of the New Orleans area did not embrace the French or Creole culture. It was felt that to be a Creole, they needed to be born in New Orleans or an area up the River Road to about the town of Vacherie.

The second element was that they needed some French blood in them. It didn't matter how much; it was just required that they be part French.

The third element that was needed was to have some Spanish blood. Again, it didn't matter how much Spanish blood or what else might be in the individual's heritage.

All that mattered for one to be defined a Creole was to be born in New Orleans (or the selected area), to have some French blood, and to have some Spanish blood. If all three of these elements were not present, then the individual was not considered a Creole. With that, the Creoles established a complex society with many unique customs.

While these customs and social structures were felt to be agreeable and even necessary to the Creoles, they were often considered unacceptable to many non-Creoles. The Creoles were often viewed to be morally problematic not only because of their customs and society policies but in how they defined themselves.

Many English-speaking visitors and citizens of New Orleans found that the Creoles were too accepting, for example, of those who were not white. In fact, many were shocked when individuals were introduced as Creoles who were clearly not white.

The problems with the Creoles were not limited only to the English-speaking citizens of New Orleans. Many of the French-speaking citizens were not considered Creoles and sometimes disagreed greatly with Creoles on many different things — although their attitude regarding race was not one of them. In fact, if we look at a breakdown of the leading New

Orleans French-speaking Freemasons of the mid-1800s, we will see an interesting situation.

The French-speaking New Orleans Masons were split into two ritualistic groups. One group were members of the French or Modern Rite, and the other group members of the Scottish Rite. But I had a problem with the logic of this theory. I couldn't understand how simply belonging to a different rite would explain the split or division between the two groups.

Both the French and Scottish Rites in New Orleans were French-speaking and somewhat similar in ritual. There was nothing in the ritual of either rite that would explain any sort of natural division. I then began looking at those who composed the different rites. A pattern began to develop.

For the most part, the Creoles were members of the French Rite, and the non-Creole French-speaking Masons were members of the Scottish Rite. But still, there were exceptions and some overlapping. For example, let's look at the New Orleans Scottish Rite of that time and a few of its leaders.

James Foulhouze, Pierré Soulé, Claude Samory, and Charles Laffon de Ladébat were leading New Orleans Scottish Rite Masons of the mid-1800s who were all French-speaking. But none of them were Creoles. Foulhouze and Soulé were born in France. Samory was born in Charleston, SC, and Ladébat in Jamaica. But this does not mean that all the members of the New Orleans Scottish Rite were not Creoles.

The Lt. Grand Commander of the Supreme Council of Louisiana, Thomas Wharton Collens, was from a Creole family, and there were others. But the general trend in the mid-1800s was that the Creoles seemed to favor the French Rite and the non-Creole French-speaking Masons leaned to the Scottish Rite.

There are even unconfirmed reports that if one gave any thought of becoming Grand Master of the Grand Lodge of Louisiana, then it was necessary to belong (at least as a plural member) to one of the French Rite lodges. At the same time, exceptions were not uncommon. What did become clear was that it was not the rite that one belonged to that can be seen as the source of the split between the French-speaking Masons in New Orleans. It was the cultural differences between the Creoles and non-Creoles. The Creoles simply thought and acted differently than non-Creoles, regardless of the language spoken.

These differences were at the heart of why the French-speaking New Orleans Masons could not agree on a plan to defend the Grand Lodge.

But, if we look closer at the situation, it seems far more complicated and difficult for the French-speaking New Orleans Masons. The disagreements as to the best course of action were not limited to the Creoles and non-Creoles.

For example, of the non-Creoles, James Foulhouze and Pierré Soulé felt that the best course of action in the Scottish Rite struggle was to support the Supreme Council of Louisiana. While Claude Samory and Charles Laffon de Ladébat chose to support the Charleston Supreme Council.

New discoveries also suggest a strong split between the Creoles regarding how they felt they should respond to the English-speaking takeover of the Grand Lodge. With these additional fractures within the French-speaking Masons, it becomes clear that their disorganization and failure to unite as a solid group resulted in their failure to properly defend the Grand Lodge (or the Scottish Rite) from takeover.

The philosophy of divide and conquer can be seen as a main source of success for the English-speaking Masons. Of course, it is far less clear if the English-speaking Masons actually orchestrated these events or only benefited from the French being unable to agree and unify.

New research and discoveries are shedding light on the activities and divisions of the Creoles in Louisiana Masonry. While the French Rite seems to have been the rite of choice for many of the Creole Masons, it should not be assumed that they were all in lockstep with each other regarding attitudes or opinions.

Most Masons in New Orleans (both Creole and non-Creole) were Roman Catholic by religion. In fact, the first Grand Master of the Grand Lodge of Louisiana was the blood brother of the Bishop of New Orleans. Many of the Roman Catholic Masons were Church Wardens for the St. Louis Cathedral well into the mid-1800s and played a part in the selection of the parish priest. Their devotion to the Roman Catholic Church and how that might be applied to Freemasonry varied from Creole Mason to Creole Mason.

We should understand, however, that the position of the Roman Catholic Church towards Freemasonry has historically been negative. Many Roman Catholic Freemasons have been ex-communicated from the Church solely for their Masonic membership. In New Orleans, while Freemasonry was often viewed as unacceptable for non-Masonic Creoles, it was not only acceptable but often desirable within the Creole Masonic community.

In 1850, with the takeover of the English-speaking Masons, the new Grand Lodge informed all lodges to turn in their charters to receive York Rite charters. The new Grand

Lodge was intent on making its desire of an English-speaking and York Rite only Grand Lodge a reality.

Three lodges petitioned the Supreme Council of Louisiana for relief. The Supreme Council of Louisiana granted their request and, for the first time in its history, worked a complete 33-degree system. The action of the Supreme Council of Louisiana was based on the Grand Lodge's violating an 1830s agreement where the Grand Lodge agreed to provide for non-York Rite Lodges under its jurisdiction.

The result of that agreement was the Grand Lodge officially recognizing the York Rite, Scottish Rite, and French or Modern Rite. The Grand Lodge began granting charters to lodges in whichever rite the lodge chose to work. This was also the time of the creation of the Chamber of Rites where the Grand Lodge officially supervised the ritual of each of the three rites.

The three lodges that petitioned the Supreme Council of Louisiana were Etoile Polaire #1 (Polar Star), Los Amigos Del Orden #5 (which is today Cervantes #5), and Disciples of the Masonic Senate #5. You might notice that two of the three lodges carried the number 5. But Etoile Polaire also carried the number 5 at the time of the creation of the Grand Lodge.

With the change in the Grand Lodge's constitution of 1833, Etoile Polaire requested and received two additional charters. It received the first Scottish Rite charter, the first French or Modern Rite charter, and it maintained its York Rite charter. Yes, that one lodge had three charters and three sets of officers — one set for each rite. The 1833 Grand Lodge *Proceedings* show the lodge meeting on three different nights each week — one for each of its rites worked. The Grand Lodge is missing all its *Proceedings* from that date until the early 1840s.

We have no idea what happened during those "lost years," but the next we see of Etoile Polaire was that they possessed one charter — a Scottish Rite charter, and they were meeting as a Scottish Rite lodge. I have no idea what happened to cause them to turn in their York and French Rite charters.

Los Amigos Del Order carried the number 5 as it was the fifth lodge to receive a Scottish Rite charter. Disciples of the Masonic Senate carried the number 5 as it was the fifth lodge to receive a French or Modern Rite charter. This means that the Supreme Council of Louisiana took in two Scottish Rite lodges and a French Rite lodge.

The English-speaking Masons were not satisfied with taking over the Grand Lodge in 1850. They sought to remove the French influence from all aspects of Louisiana Masonry. The Scottish Rite was their next target.

In 1852, a consistory of the 32nd degree was created by the English-speaking Masons in New Orleans under the jurisdiction of the newly revived Charleston Supreme Council. This action caused great upset with the French Masons in New Orleans. But their upset could not overcome their divisions and differences of opinions as to the best course of action.

The Supreme Council of Louisiana became split and divided on how best to secure the future of Freemasonry in Louisiana. This division resulted in half of the supreme council agreeing to a merger with the Charleston Council and the other half refusing to take part in such an action.

In 1855, half of the Active Members of the Supreme Council of Louisiana signed a Concordat (or agreement) with the Charleston Supreme Council — known today as the Southern Jurisdiction — and half refused to participate and walked away. As a side note, most of the ones who signed this

1855 Concordat on the New Orleans side were merchants by profession. The ones who walked away refusing to sign were mostly lawyers and judges. What that means may be a matter for a later debate, but I have always found it interesting.

Following the signing of the 1855 Concordat, the lodges under the jurisdiction of the Supreme Council of Louisiana were told that they could no longer remain under its jurisdiction. Their choice was to return to the Grand Lodge or dissolve themselves. All three lodges returned to the jurisdiction of the Grand Lodge.

The following year, former Grand Commander and district court judge James Foulhouze announced legality issues with the concordat and that the Supreme Council of Louisiana had never ceased to exist. He invited the three lodges formerly under their jurisdiction to return.

Etoile Polaire and Disciples of the Masonic Senate voted to return to the supreme council, but Los Amigos Del Order voted to remain under the jurisdiction of the Grand Lodge. Why? No clear reason for their change in position was given.

James Foulhouze was made a Mason in Los Amigos Del Order and had served as its Worshipful Master. He seems to have viewed the refusal of the lodge to return to the jurisdiction of the supreme council as a personal insult. His upset at the lodge is open in his retelling of the account in his 1857 book, *Historical Inquiry into the Origins of the Ancient and Accepted Scottish Rite*. But, in his criticism of the lodge and its Worshipful Master, Foulhouze makes an interesting claim.

With no evidence to support or explain his statement, Foulhouze wrote that Los Amigos Del Order had joined "the Jacobite Rite."[2] For years, that charge puzzled me. What was the Jacobite Rite, and why would Foulhouze make this charge? It made no sense to me.

It turns out that the Jacobite Rite was a pseudo-Masonic Rite of questionable existence that was based on Roman Catholic membership or, at least, Roman Catholic of the more radical sort. It would seem more along the lines of the Jesuits. That information was of value but only of limited value as I saw nothing to explain *why* Foulhouze would make such a charge. I thought it might just be hard feeling and a desire to attack the lodge in some manner for the perceived insult of not returning to the supreme council.

Discoveries then started turning up. Several years ago, a fascinating discovery was made. The old Grand Lodge of Louisiana building on St. Charles Ave. in New Orleans had been sold a good number of years ago. It has changed hands several times since the sale and is now a hotel. The hotel's chief engineer petitioned a lodge and was an EA when he made a most interesting discovery.

Workers needed to cut a hole in the wall of one of the old lodge rooms to do some electrical work. They found wedged in the wall an old Jesuit Communion press from around the 1800s.[3] This was a hand press to form and make communion wafers for Roman Catholics. How in the world did it get there, who put it there, and *why* was it put there? No one had the slightest idea, and no records exist to explain the find.

On its own, the discovery of the Jesuit Communion press gives us more questions than answers. But it was not the only interesting discovery made.

From its creation in 1842, Los Amigos Del Orden was a Spanish-speaking lodge. In 1883, it merged with another

Spanish-speaking lodge, Silencio, to create Cervantes Lodge No.5. Cervantes remained a Spanish-speaking lodge for about another 125 years.

Around 2010, the lodge was having trouble finding Spanish-speaking officers and requested permission from the Grand Lodge to work in English until it could fill its chairs with Spanish-speaking members. A call was put out to non-Spanish-speaking Masons to plural with this lodge in order to save it. I was one of the Masons who answered this call and had the honor of serving as Worshipful Master of Cervantes in 2018.

Cervantes had always been known as having a unique nature, customs, and ritual. An effort was made to translate many of its early documents and records from Spanish into English. When this was completed, a very surprising discovery was made.

When one sought to join Cervantes in its Spanish-speaking days, a clear and open attempt was made in the ritual to identify candidates of the Roman Catholic faith. On its own, this raised more than a few eyebrows, as any question of a candidate's specific religious faith is not allowed. But, for a researcher, it was like finding gold.

The act of Cervantes seeking to identify Roman Catholic candidates could seem to support the charge by James Foulhouze that Los Amigos Del Orden (the original name of Cervantes) had joined the Jacobite Rite. It is certainly not clear proof, but it is interesting. But what would it have meant if Los Amigos Del Order had joined something known as the Jacobite Rite (even if only in philosophy)?

It could mean that the lodge had taken a decidedly Roman Catholic turn in its attitude. But it may also have meant that it was taking a clear "Creole side" in the "Masonic war" that existed in the state.

Records show that just following the 1850 takeover of the Grand Lodge, a number of new members came to a few of the older lodges from influential Creole families. These were Roman Catholic families. With this, the discovery of the Jesuit Communion press, hidden away in the lodge wall, creates a more complex picture.

If the Creoles were determined to reclaim the Grand Lodge (with maybe more of a Catholic flavor), then it does seem that, at least, this faction of them was organizing and developing a strategy to accomplish their aim with the Grand Lodge. Unfortunately, things soon changed in an unexpected and unfortunate way for both sides.

In 1853 and 54, yellow fever epidemics hit New Orleans, killing nearly 8,000. The entire Grand Lodge line from Grand Master to Grand Junior Warden died due to this epidemic. This was the English-speaking leadership.

But, also killed were many of the leading Creole Freemasons, including newly raised Gabrial Amie (a member of Perfect Union Lodge #1), son of Creole leader Valcour Amie who is reported to have been one of the wealthiest men in America and a most enigmatic figure. Following his son's death, a crushed Valcour is reported to have retreated from the world. All sides basically had their legs kicked out from under them.

The Grand Lodge's senior Past Grand Master, John Henry Holland, stepped up and, with questionable authority, assumed control of the Grand Lodge with the goal of bringing order to the deeply divided and broken Louisiana Masonry. He was only partially successful. While neither side could claim total success, enough of a compromise was created to allow the factions to continue to exist and maybe fight another day.

Today, there are significant holes in our understanding of many aspects of early Louisiana Freemasonry. But Light is coming into the dark corners that is our history. Discoveries are being made far more quickly than expected.

Things we have long believed to be facts in our history are now being proven to be simply incorrect. Many bits of our history are held as truth because they are emotionally accepted rather than proven by the evidence. We believe some things merely because we want to believe them or because the brother who brought us into Masonry told us something was so, and we accepted it as fact with no challenge.

If we care about Louisiana Freemasonry or any aspect of Freemasonry anywhere in the world, then it is time that we stop and take a reality check. The Almighty did not kiss His fingers and create Freemasonry. Men created it. We created it with all our talents and flaws. And guess what? We are not perfect. We make mistakes. Our ego may not like hearing it, but it's true.

Freemasonry is an inspired system of moral philosophy that can help anyone achieve a more spiritual, useful, and happy life. All we need to do is take advantage of what it has to offer.

The history of Louisiana Freemasonry is being rediscovered. The work must continue. Bit by bit, we are uncovering our past. If we attempt to edit our history, as was clearly done in the past, then we are neither honest with ourselves nor following the path of the enlightened. It does not matter if we rejoice in our history, dislike it, or wish it to be something else. We are who we are.

I am proud to be both a Louisiana Freemason and a Scottish Rite Mason because I understand who we are and what we are. Even if we are not quite "there" yet, I know enough of the past to know how important we are to the whole of our Order. I want to see us continue to grow in Light so that our lodges can return to their unique place in the new age of enlightenment.

Notes:

1. *The Sharp Documents, Volume IV* (Rennes, France: The Latomia Foundation, 1993).
2. James Foulhouze, *Historical Inquiry into the Origin of the Ancient and Accepted Scottish Rite* (New Orleans, LA: Cornerstone Book Publishers, 2012 reprint of 1859 edition.) 17.
3. The discovered Roman Catholic Communion press today resides in the Scottish Rite Valley of New Orleans.

James Foulhouze
A biographical study

> *Mr. Pike is altogether unknown to me, and I have never seen him, which is perhaps to be regretted, because in the event he spoke to me pursuant to the information which he has received from ill-disposed individuals, I suppose that he will be sorry for having allowed his pen to write what is neither correct nor rational.*
>
> ~ James Foulhouze, 1858.[1]

James Foulhouze was, unquestionably, the arch-nemesis of Albert Pike in Pike's early days as Grand Commander of the Supreme Council, Southern Jurisdiction, USA. Judge James Foulhouze, former Roman Catholic priest, Sovereign Grand Inspector General of the Grand Orient of France, and Sovereign Grand Commander of the Supreme Council of Louisiana in the pre-Concordat of 1855 period, along with some of the leading New Orleans Masons, including the very respected Judge T. Wharton Collens and the powerful United States Senator Pierré Soulé, almost destroyed the Concordat between the New Orleans and Charleston Supreme Councils — a Concordat which was the breath of life to the newly reorganized Charleston Supreme Council. Who was this man who could have caused such a disturbance? *Did* he cause the disturbance, or was he, himself, swept along in a tidal wave of events?

The following is a glimpse into the life and tumultuous Masonic times of a most significant but highly controversial figure in the history of the US Scottish Rite. It is to be regretted that no photograph or likeness of Foulhouze is known to exist. It is, also, unfortunate that some areas of his life are simply lost in the mists of time.

On 1 October 1800,[2] Jacques Foulhouze was born to Michel and Jeanne Cronier Foulhouze in Riom, France. The young Foulhouze received a Catholic education at the Seminary of St. Sulpice in Paris, culminating in his ordination as a Roman Catholic priest. The Reverend James Foulhouze traveled to the United States and labored in the Diocese of Philadelphia in 1834 and 35.[3] The next record of Foulhouze in the US comes in 1835 when his name appears in a Philadelphia court records book of aliens declaring their intention to take the oath of allegiance to the United States.[4] Foulhouze would not long remain a priest nor keep his domicile in Philadelphia. An 1858 New Orleans publication contains interesting comments about Foulhouze and his possible reasons for leaving the priesthood. The comments were written by Charles Laffon de Ladébat, who will be discussed further later in this paper. Ladébat says that Foulhouze might have remained a priest had not, "Mr. (now bishop) Hughes been appointed, *in his stead*, to the important rector ship of a northern parish, to which Mr. Foulhouze was, for his long service, justly entitled."[5]

John Hughes (1797-1864) was the fourth bishop and first Archbishop of the Roman Catholic Diocese of New York. Hughes served with Foulhouze in the Diocese of Philadelphia and founded the *Catholic Herald* newspaper there. Hughes was consecrated coadjutor to Bishop John Dubois of New York in 1838. He succeeded Dubois in 1842 and became Archbishop of New York in 1850.[6] Foulhouze, regardless of Ladébat's comments, could not have been affected

John Hughes

by the 1838 Hughes appointment as the *Journal Notes* of Philadelphia Bishop Francis Kenrick record Foulhouze's faculties being suspended on 5 February 1836.[7] As with many areas of Foulhouze's life, it is unclear what could have taken place causing his separation from the priesthood. Foulhouze graduated from the highly respected Seminary of St. Sulpice in Paris. Many Catholic dioceses consider such graduates to be a highly desirable prize. The accounts of Foulhouze for that time, however, tell a different story. The records of the Archdiocese of Philadelphia,[8] while confirming that Foulhouze was a priest assigned to them, show that he had "no specific assignment."[9] This is an interesting situation. Why would the Diocese of Philadelphia not take advantage of the quality education that Foulhouze received by using his abilities and education? Foulhouze, himself, may provide the answer. In 1843, Foulhouze was asked if he had taken the vows of the priesthood, and he replied: "No, but it is true that they were given to me, against my will."[10] Regardless of the philosophical point Foulhouze was trying to make, his statement reflects that he may not have ever wholly embraced the priesthood. If Foulhouze's work reflected the same lack of interest, then it is very likely that regardless of what seminary he attended, he would not have been given assignments or appointments to higher positions. All conjecture aside, Foulhouze left the priesthood, pursued a law career, and moved to New Orleans.

Foulhouze began his law career in Philadelphia after leaving the priesthood. In 1842, he published a book in Philadelphia that reflected the same interest in philosophy that he maintained throughout his life. The 200-page work was titled, *A Philosophical Inquiry Respecting the Abolition of Capital Punishment.*[11] It is possible that Foulhouze was in New Orleans when this book was released, but it is clear that he was in New Orleans the following year. Philadelphia Bishop Francis Kenrick (Foulhouze's former superior) writes in an 1843 letter:

> *Here affairs go on smoothly but at New Orleans an infidel faction are struggling to destroy or subjugate the Episcopal authority. A fallen French priest, Foulhouze, is the*

editor of an impious paper,[12] *the organ of the Marguillers. [...] The leaders in disorder are Freemasons, and they contrived to set apart a lot in the Cemetery for their Masonic brethren, and had it dedicated by a speech from their Grand Master who is a Marguiller.*[13]

The Marguillers were the wardens of the St. Louis Cathedral in New Orleans. The Grand Master that Kenrick spoke of was E. A. Canon, who was not only a Marguiller but the President of the Marguillers. The Marguillers (many of them being Masons) supervised the appointments of the priests for the St. Louis Cathedral during

St. Louis Cathedral

the early to mid-1800s. There was, of course, a great division within the congregation over Freemasons having a say in the appointment of their parish priests (regardless that these Freemasons were, themselves, Roman Catholic and members of the parish). In New Orleans, Masonry and the Roman Catholic faith were tightly intertwined in the early/mid 1800s in a love/hate relationship. It was a situation not without some hostile conflicts. An event that took place in 1842 is worth mentioning:

On the feast of All Saints, an incident took place in the Cathedral, which was in itself trivial, but which shows to what lengths the two factions[14] *would go. While Father Jamey was preaching, E. A. Canon, the president of the Marguillers, entered the sanctuary by way of the choir entrance, and made a tour of the altar towards that place assigned to the president of the wardens (side opposite the door of the sacristy by which he entered). He remained there for a few minutes, but not being able to hear very well, he advanced to the balustrade of a neighboring chapel, in order to hear better. He had only heard a few words, and then decided to retire by the way he had come in, that is, behind the altar. As he was going out he was greeted by Octave de Armas, a parishioner loyal to [Bishop] Blanc, (who was also seated in the sanctuary) with the words, "Get out; you are not in your place..." Canon answered this with apparent sharp disdain and was preparing to leave when he was pushed. He was near the door of the sacristy and fell on the steps. On getting up, he heard Armas distinctly cry, "I, I alone will get rid of the wardens." The services were interrupted for about five minutes, but the Mass was soon continued and all ended calmly.*[15]

The event may have ended "calmly" at that time, but the incident was far from over. As a result of his being pushed in the St. Louis Cathedral, Canon, following typical Creole custom, sought satisfaction from Armas by means of challenging him to a duel. Armas, however, refused the challenge on the grounds that he was a Roman Catholic.[16] Friends of Canon would not let the matter drop, and charges were filed against Armas with the City Recorder. Armas was found guilty of assault. The incident reflects the growing tensions between the factions within the New Orleans Catholic community. It was in this atmosphere and, likely, through the contacts with the Marguillers that Foulhouze was introduced to Louisiana Masonry. It obviously attracted him, and he sought to be a member.

From Priest to Freemason

The Marguillers may have introduced James Foulhouze to Louisiana Masonry, but it was not his first exposure to Freemasonry itself. Foulhouze stated in 1857:

Being a Grandson of Free-masons, I, in my early years, conceived and entertained a desire to enter the fraternity ... [17]

Foulhouze fulfilled that early desire by becoming a member of Los Amigos del Orden, a Spanish-speaking, New Orleans Scottish Rite Lodge.[18] Foulhouze also stated:

Within a year from my initiation I was made a Master Mason in the same Lodge.[19]

Unfortunately, there are no known records of the initiation of Foulhouze nor an exact date on his initiating, passing, or raising. Foulhouze did state in his *Historical Inquiry* that he was initiated by Antonio Costa.[20] Costa was Worshipful Master of Los Amigos del Orden in 1843. An 1843 initiation followed by an 1844 raising meant rapid advancement for Foulhouze. Foulhouze was, apparently, viewed as a Mason of promise. On 14 February 1845, he was appointed Grand Translator by the Grand Lodge. The office of Grand Translator did not exist prior to Foulhouze receiving the appointment. The office was created due to the growing need for French to English and English to French translations in Grand Lodge records and documents.

In the summer of 1845 (about a year after Foulhouze became a Master Mason), Foulhouze traveled to France carrying a letter of introduction from Robert Preaux, Grand Master of the Grand Lodge of Louisiana and Active Member of the Supreme Council of Louisiana. During his stay in Paris, Foulhouze received all the degrees of the AASR, culminating in the 33° on 27 September from the Grand College of Rites of the Grand Orient of France. The speed at which Foulhouze received the degrees is extraordinary and certainly was not normal procedure for the Grand Orient. There is no explanation yet found why this very rare honor was given to such a young Master Mason, nor has the contents of the letter from Preaux ever been revealed. Regardless of what activities Foulhouze later engaged in, he was, in the eyes of the US Masonic community, a legitimate Sovereign Grand Inspector General. Of this event, Foulhouze comments:

> *The Scotch Rite [...] pleased me on account of its truly philosophical principles, and the more I studied it, the more I felt anxious to take its superior degrees, when a fair opportunity so to do offered itself to me in 1845.*
>
> *I was in France, and on the recommendations and letters of my Scotch brothers here, the worshipful Lodge "Clémente Amitié" opened its door to me, and after a short stay among them I was made a Knight R∴ + and a Knight Kadosh, which I am bound to say, rendered still clearer to my eyes and intellect the views which I had long entertained on the merits of the Scotch Rite, and forever attached me to its admirable and useful tenets.*
>
> *The favors thus bestowed on me, were unexpected, and I certainly desired no others, when on a special and unasked resolution of the Supreme Council in the Grand Orient, I was called and raised in that body to the thirty third degree.*[21]

Following the death of Grand Commander Jean-Jacques Conte, New Orleans Judge Jean-François Canonge, an influential Past Grand Master of the Grand Lodge of Louisiana, became the Grand Commander of the New Orleans Supreme Council on 20 September 1845. [22] Foulhouze said of Canonge:

> *As long as he lived, I had but little to do, and contented myself with studying the rite ...* [23]

Foulhouze, who had affiliated with the Supreme Council of Louisiana in 1846, was, regardless of his comments, not idle during this period. Foulhouze was appointed Grand Secretary of the Supreme Council of Louisiana in 1847.[24] He, also, advanced through the chairs of Los Amigos del Orden serving as its Worshipful Master in 1847. Once serving his term as Worshipful Master, he was elected a life member of the Grand Lodge. It must also be pointed out that the invasion of the jurisdiction of the Grand Lodge of Louisiana by the Grand Lodge of Mississippi and the creation of the Louisiana Grand Lodge in 1848 would undoubtedly, have occupied a considerable amount of time with all the Worshipful Masters of New Orleans Lodges.

The Grand Lodge of Mississippi and the Union of 1850

A faction within the New Orleans English-speaking York Rite Masons felt that the 1844 Constitution of the Grand Lodge of Louisiana sanctioning the cumulating of the three rites worked by lodges in Louisiana (French, Scottish & York) altered the Grand Lodge into a body that was no longer a true York Rite Grand Lodge.[25] The decision was made by these Masons to sever their association with the Grand Lodge and organize themselves into what they felt was proper York Rite Masonry. A committee was formed, and a letter of grievance was brought before the Grand Lodge of Mississippi on 23 January 1845.[26] The Grand Master of the Grand Lodge of Mississippi was Mexican War hero and former governor of Mississippi, John Anthony Quitman. The Grand Lodge of Mississippi appointed a committee to go to New Orleans to examine the situation. On 21 January 1846, the committee from the Grand Lodge of Mississippi appointed to examine the charges presented by the York Masons from New Orleans presented three reports concerning the events. The first report was presented on behalf of the majority of the committee and concluded that there was "no Grand Lodge of Ancient York Masons within the limits of the State of Louisiana" and that the Grand Lodge of Mississippi had "the power, and it is its duty on proper application, to issue Dispensations and Charters to bodies of Ancient York Masons within the limits of the State of Louisiana, until the constitution of a Grand Lodge within that State."[27] Two "counter" reports were then presented which advised against the Grand Lodge of Mississippi issuing charters within the jurisdiction of the Grand Lodge of Louisiana. The outcome of the events of 21 January (despite the efforts of the two "counter" reports) was the chartering of George Washington Lodge in New Orleans and Lafayette Lodge in Lafayette [28] by the Grand Lodge of Mississippi on 22 February. Relations were severed between the Grand Lodges of Louisiana and Mississippi. The Louisiana Lodges chartered by the Grand Lodge of Mississippi were declared irregular by the Grand Lodge of Louisiana. In total, the Grand Lodge of Mississippi chartered seven Lodges in the New Orleans area by 1848.[29] These seven Lodges united to form the "Louisiana Grand Lodge of Ancient York Masons" on 8 March 1848. The Grand Lodge of Mississippi received an admonishment from most U.S. Grand Lodges, and the majority openly condemned its action.[30] While the future for this splinter group of the Grand Lodge of Louisiana may have looked bleak, several events took place to not only strengthen the position of the English-speaking New Orleans Masons but to assure them of total victory by the loss of French control over almost all forms of Louisiana Masonry.

One of the last official acts of Grand Commander Jean-François Canonge was a speech made on 3 November 1847 in Baton Rouge in which he is reported as stating that a circular issued by the Mississippi craft lodges in New Orleans was "unworthy of notice."[31] Canonge died on 19 January 1848. On 31 January 1848, James Foulhouze was elected Grand Commander of the New Orleans Supreme Council. The

Jean-François Canonge

Foulhouze election bypassed several senior members of the Council and clearly, established the popularity of Foulhouze with the Council. Foulhouze had brought with him various rituals from France[32] which he edited for the New Orleans Council.[33] During the same month as the death of Canonge and the election of Foulhouze, the Charleston Council was taking an action that significantly strengthened its position and further weakened the hold of the French-speaking New Orleans Masons. Albert Mackey (the Grand Secretary of the Charleston Council) sent a notice to the *Freemason's Monthly Magazine* [34] (Boston), which read:

> *At a special session of the Supreme Council ... for the Southern Jurisdiction of the United States of America, our Illustrious Brother, John A. Quitman ... Major General in the Army of the United States, was elected to fill a vacancy in this Supreme Council, and was duly and formally inaugurated a Sovereign Grand Inspector General of the 33d. All Consistories, Councils, Chapters and Lodges under this jurisdiction are hereby ordered to obey and respect him accordingly.* [35]

On 29 January 1849, the Grand Lodge of Louisiana published a report that Foulhouze wrote concerning the cumulation of the rites practiced by the Grand Lodge. On 26 February, the Grand Lodge published Foulhouze's report on the 1833 Concordat. Both reports upheld the positions of the Grand Lodge of Louisiana and encouraged the continued practice of the cumulation of the rites in Louisiana.

On 14 September 1849, Foulhouze and several other New Orleans Masons were honored by Friends of Harmony Lodge (whose Worshipful Master was elder Past Grand Master and Supreme Council of Louisiana Active Member, John Henry Holland) by being made honorary members. An excerpt from the Minutes of the Lodge reads:

> *Whereas by their great ability and impartiality our well beloved Brethren Joseph Walker, Jas. Foulhouze, P. Willman, John D. Kemper & R. Preaux have earned the destination of Honorary Membership, their services in the Masonic vineyard entitling them to some suitable token or tribute of appreciation of their worth, and of the high respect entertained for their estimable personal and Masonic character - they being Brethren to whom a burdened may pour out his sorrows, to whom distress may prefer its suit; Brethren whose hands are guided by justice and whose hearts are expanded by benevolence.*
>
> *Therefore be it now decreed, that the aforesaid distinguished Brethren be and they are hereby created Honorary Members of the Friends of Harmony Lodge of F & A Masons, this as a testimony of regard for the inestimable services as Masons, and their courtesy, affability and kindness as men - well worthy of initiation and the foregoing preamble and resolution being seconded and put is carried unanimously.*[36]

The Union of 1850

The 1848 Louisiana Grand Lodge obtained recognition from only one other Grand Lodge — the Grand Lodge of Mississippi. In 1849, John Gedge, a New Orleans attorney, was elected Grand Master of the Louisiana Grand Lodge. Despite what would seem to be the irregularity of the Louisiana Grand Lodge and the lack of support for this new Grand Lodge within the Masonic community, the Grand Lodge of Louisiana entered into negotiations and finally merged with this body in 1850. The Grand Lodge of Louisiana was left with little choice in this matter. The fact that the Grand Lodge of Louisiana was overwhelmingly considered the "regular" Grand Lodge was not sufficient to overcome the internal problems stemming from the cultural divisions in New Orleans. By mid-1849, it was likely realized that the English-speaking lodges that remained loyal to the Grand Lodge showed signs that continued loyalty would likely not happen. Realizing that the total collapse of the Grand Lodge of Louisiana was a real possibility, the Grand Lodge of Louisiana and the Louisiana Grand Lodge entered into talks designed to merge the two bodies.[37] That merger took place in June of 1850 with the approval of a new Constitution of the Grand Lodge of Louisiana of Free and Accepted Masons. Under the terms of the agreement of the merger, the Louisiana Grand Lodge members became recognized as "regular" by the Grand Lodge of Louisiana. All Lodges chartered by the Louisiana Grand Lodge (or by the Grand Lodge of Mississippi in Louisiana) passed under the jurisdiction of the new Grand Lodge of Louisiana. While the new constitution appeared to merge the two Grand Lodges, the Grand Lodge of Louisiana was, in effect, taken over by the Louisiana Grand Lodge. All non-York Rite Lodges were instructed to turn in their charters to receive York Rite charters from the new Grand Lodge. Three Scottish Rite Lodges, Etoile Polaire, Los Amigos del Orden, and

Disciples of the Masonic Senate, sought relief from the *New Orleans Supreme Council*. Of these events, Foulhouze wrote:

> *It was agreed that the Grand Lodge should no more cumulate the rites, that it would have and keep its own forms, but that each Lodge in the East might freely work according to its particular and more favorite rite and tenets.*
>
> *Had that agreement been faithfully observed, another series of quiet days might have ensued in Louisiana: but the newcomers in the Grand Lodge soon showed that far from being sincere, they had crept into our bosom with the only view to tear it to pieces and to build their powers on the ruins of ours. [...]*
>
> *They made as I had foreseen and foretold, a Constitution by which the Scotch lodges of the East were reduced to naught and the life members of the Grand Lodge expelled from it* [38] *the better to secure the triumph and power of those invaders.*
>
> *But from the moment that the constitution began to work, the Scotch lodges understood their mistake; and not withstanding the blame thrown upon them by the new Grand Lodge which was as it was expected, did not fail to say that they were bound by the vote of the majority at Baton Rouge, they all parted from it, averting and showing that they had been deceived, and could not thus be fetted and annihilated by a paltry trick.*
>
> *That event occasioned a good deal of rumor. The Mississippians who had snatched the power began promulgating their bulls of excommunication. John Gedge, like his imitators of this present Consistory, wrote his reports, made his speeches, sent his circulars, but it was to no purpose.*
>
> *The Supreme Council of Louisiana resumed its authority on the blue lodges of the Scotch rite, and the separation was consummated.* [39]

If the goal of the new 1850 Grand Lodge Constitution and the merger with the Louisiana Grand Lodge was to bring peace to all the Louisiana Masons, it was a total failure. If the goal was to remove the power base in the Grand Lodge from the French-speaking New Orleans Masons, it was a success. The French-speaking New Orleans Masons became split after 1850. Outraged at the turn of events, one faction wished nothing more to do with the Grand Lodge and saw the Supreme Council as the only hope of maintaining the French interests. The other French faction, most

Perseverance Lodge #4. Pre-1855 meeting place of the Supreme Council of Louisiana

likely very tired of the disputes, remained with the Grand Lodge in the hopes of possibly still bringing unity to the troubled Grand Lodge.

The 1850 Union of the Grand Lodge resulted in a perceived need for action in the New Orleans Council. Foulhouze believed he could strengthen the New Orleans Scottish Rite by expanding the number of 33rds in the Council beyond its nine Members. Foulhouze says of this:

> *Brother Canonge died and I was elected commander in his place. My first move was to promote to the 33d degree one or two members of each of the lodges then established and of some importance in the city of New Orleans, hoping that their initiation would be the best means to secure the masonic peace in our East, as it would contribute to carry light where it was most needed.* [40]

During Foulhouze's administration of the New Orleans Supreme Council prior to the Concordat, he elevated about 30

Masons to the 33° in the New Orleans Council.[41] Those elevated to the 33rd degree by Foulhouze included Charles Claiborne, Thomas Wharton Collens (22 June 1849), Claude Pierre Samory, and Charles Laffon de Ladébat (11 February 1852). The wisdom of expanding the membership of the Supreme Council was apparently recognized by Albert Pike on 25 March 1859 (Pike's first SC Session as Grand Commander) when he expanded the Membership in the Charleston Council from nine Members to thirty-three Members.

Charles Claiborne assumed the post of Secretary General for the New Orleans Council, and T. Wharton Collens that of Lt. Grand Commander. The Foulhouze/Collens relationship was a very close one which continued until Foulhouze's death in 1875 — years after both had resigned from Masonry. Foulhouze and Collens would, in the early 1850s, even share a law office.

The Lopez Expedition and James Foulhouze

If the Union of 1850 between the Grand Lodge of Louisiana and the Louisiana Grand Lodge, along with the many bomb shells from that event, were not enough to occupy the minds of the Louisiana Masons, an event took place at the same time that over-shadowed the Masonic events in Louisiana and was thrust into the forefront of the minds and thoughts of most all Americans. This disastrous event directly played a direct part in

Narciso Lopez

future New Orleans Masonic "battles."

In 1849 Narciso Lopez, a Venezuelan and former colonel in the Spanish Army, began a campaign to take control of Cuba and replace the Spanish government on the island with his own government. Lopez received limited support from various US politicians but was unable to raise a suitable sized army for his mission. Lopez found better luck in New Orleans, where he raised a small army of about 750 men, mainly veterans of the Mexican War, and sailed out of New Orleans in April of 1850 to capture the island. The mission was a complete failure. The US troops were slaughtered, and Lopez was eventually captured and executed. Reports quickly came to the US and the newspapers of the day reported the "murder" of the US troops along with the capture and execution of not only troops, but vacationing US tourists who happened to be on the island. New Orleans was an obvious "hot spot" for the Lopez Expedition as not only did the expedition leave from New Orleans, but the city contained many Spanish-speaking citizens from Cuba. The Grand Lodge of Louisiana had also chartered two Lodges in Cuba during the early years of the Grand Lodge.[42] The tie between New Orleans and Cuba was close for both the general and Masonic populations.

James Foulhouze became entwined in the Lopez Expedition when he traveled to Cuba at the height of the crisis. A New Orleans newspaper, the *Daily Delta,* ran a story on Foulhouze vehemently criticizing his trip and suggesting that he was, possibly, a spy for the Spanish government.[43] The very evening following the publication of the article concerning Foulhouze, T. Wharton Collens, and Robert Preaux published an article in the *Daily Picayune* explaining that Foulhouze's trip to Cuba was with the goal of, hopefully, securing the release of vacationing US citizens who were caught in the conflict.[44] Foulhouze, being made a Mason in a Spanish-speaking Lodge, had numerous interactions with New Orleans Masons from Cuba. In addition, Foulhouze had gained the confidence of various Spanish officials on the island of Cuba by acting as legal counsel for them several years earlier. Along with the article written by Collens and Preaux, the *Delta* article on Foulhouze received censure from a number of competing New Orleans newspapers. The *Delta* article was exposed to be a newspaper "thriller" story with little basis in fact. One newspaper entitled an article critical of the *Delta's* lack of support for its charges, "Newspaper Intolerance,"[45] and another newspaper calling the event of Foulhouze's trip "A Mission of Humanity."[46] The *Delta* ran one more article in defense of its position, claiming that the matter would be settled when Foulhouze returned to New Orleans and the entire event would be brought to the attention of the public.[47] Nothing more, however, was published on the matter by the *Delta*. The event passed from the public's attention. It was soon realized and attributed to a single newspaper's attempt to sensationalize anything concerning a recent event with the possible goal of increasing its sale of newspapers.

Enter the Charleston Supreme Council

John Gedge, who in 1849 was the Grand Master of the irregular Louisiana Grand Lodge, was elected Grand Master of the Grand Lodge of Louisiana for the year 1851. On 27 March 1851, the Supreme Council of Louisiana issued a manifesto in its own defense. This manifesto examined the New Orleans situation and was an appeal for the establishment of fraternal relations between the Supreme Council of Louisiana and other Masonic Bodies worldwide. With Louisiana Masonry in a state of turmoil and the once influential Supreme Council of Louisiana fighting for order and stability, the time for the Charleston Council to act was at hand.

At the invitation of John Gedge, Albert Mackey came to New Orleans in February of 1852 and established, for the Charleston Council, a Consistory of the 32°. Gedge served as Commander in Chief. The establishment of this Charleston Consistory in New Orleans resulted in a new wave of unrest and paved the way for the Concordat of 1855, merging the Charleston and New Orleans Councils.

The New Orleans Supreme Council responded to the Charleston Consistory in New Orleans by taking several measures. A notice critical of the new consistory was placed in the New Orleans Bee by the New Orleans Supreme Council on 27 February 1852.[48] The notice carried the names of the then 29 Active Members[49] of the New Orleans Council. The Supreme Council of Louisiana also incorporated itself under the official name of "Supreme Council of the Thirty-three [sic] and last degree of the Ancient and Accepted Scotch Rite for the United States of America, sitting at New Orleans, State of Louisiana." The act of incorporation was signed on 7 June 1852 and approved by the Secretary of State, the noted Charles Gayarre, on 13 January 1853.[50]

In July of 1852, Foulhouze traveled to New York to install Henry C. Atwood as Grand Commander of the "Supreme Council of the Thirty-third Degree of and for the Free, Sovereign and Independent State of New York" and then journeyed on to France in an attempt to enlist French support for his cause.

It is noteworthy that Foulhouze at this time embraced the concept that Supreme Councils should be limited to state jurisdictions just as Grand Lodges.[51]

The Concordat of 1855

The speed at which the total loss of the Grand Lodge of Louisiana by the French-speaking Masons occurred caused confusion and uncertainty about their future. James Foulhouze, as Grand Commander of the New Orleans Supreme Council, sought to unite the French-speaking Freemasons under his banner. Whether it was because of the rapid progress of Foulhouze (questions of his competence) or personality conflicts, Foulhouze was unable to unite all the French Masons. The conflict of opinions within the New Orleans Supreme Council as to the direction in which to proceed can reasonably be seen as a contributing factor to the resignation of Foulhouze on 30 July 1853 and nearly all the officers of the Supreme Council of Louisiana by December of 1853. The final break for Foulhouze appears to have occurred at the 22 June meeting of the New Orleans Council. At that meeting, T. Wharton Collens, the Lt. Grand Commander, had prepared a series of resolutions to present to the Council. After a reading of the resolutions, the floor was opened for comment, but instead of addressing the points of the various resolutions, Charles Claiborne apparently began a series of attacks on Foulhouze's clothing. The meeting fell into shouting matches, and the deep-rooted feelings of frustration from the events of the past years seemingly boiled up. Foulhouze, realizing that control of the meeting was lost, closed the Council, and departed.[52]

T. Wharton Collens

In the absence of the Minutes of the Supreme Council of Louisiana during the Foulhouze years,[53] it can only be presumed that T. Wharton Collens assumed the post of acting Grand Commander for the remainder of 1853 until his own resignation on 19 December of that year. The day following the resignation of Collens, the Grand Treasurer, Jean Baptiste Faget, turned in his letter of resignation, and an undated letter of resignation from Grand Secretary, J.J.E. Massicott, was also accepted by the Council.

On 7 January 1854, Charles Claiborne was elected Grand Commander of the Supreme Council of Louisiana. Claude Pierre Samory was elected Lt. Grand Commander, and Charles Laffon de Ladébat was appointed Grand Secretary. Samory and Ladébat were part of the French-speaking faction that split from Foulhouze during the 1850-53 turmoil. 1854 was devoted to negotiations with the Charleston Supreme Council. On 6 & 17 February 1855, the concordat merging the New Orleans and Charleston Supreme Councils was signed. Albert Mackey and John Quitman were present in New Orleans for the signing of the Concordat and representing the Charleston Council. John Gedge, who had spearheaded the drive of the Louisiana Grand Lodge and the 1852 Consistory, did not live to see the concordat

Grave of John Gedge in St. Louis #1 Cemetery

between the New Orleans and Charleston Councils — he died on 13 April 1854 during a yellow fever epidemic in New Orleans.

The death of John Gedge must have generated some concern for the future of the newly reorganized Scottish Rite

Masonry in New Orleans. Gedge had led a complete and total coup of the Grand Lodge, dramatically altering its nature. It was also Gedge who had written to Mackey to bring a Charleston consistory to New Orleans and took control of it as he did the Grand Lodge. The introduction of the Charleston consistory paved the way for the Concordat of 1855. His influence on the events of the times is unquestionable. It is reasonable to assume that Gedge might have taken some leadership position in the post concordat days had he lived. It is logical that Gedge would have become an Active Member of the Charleston Supreme Council and led the reorganized Grand Consistory of Louisiana. The death of Gedge made this impossible, yet the basic problem remained. An influential figure was needed to lead and unite the fragmented New Orleans Scottish Rite. Regardless of the fact that the Concordat had taken place, there were still quite a number of former Supreme Council of Louisiana 33rds unaffiliated with the Charleston Council — or any Council. The potential for uprising was undeniable. In a letter to Claude Samory, Albert Mackey suggested that the man to lead and unite the New Orleans Scottish Rite Masons had been found, and it was believed that only the formalities remained. Mackey wrote:

> *I hope to be present at the installation of that Bro∴ as S∴G∴I∴G∴ whose adhesion to us will heal all difficulties [...] The moment we receive your nomination, the nominated Bro∴ will be elected.*[54]

The man Mackey wrote of was James Foulhouze. The choosing of Foulhouze to join the Charleston Council and lead the New Orleans Scottish Rite for the Charleston Council is very reasonable and, given the situation, the only logical choice that could be made. Foulhouze was viewed as a regular 33rd from the Grand Orient of France. As Foulhouze was a former Grand Commander of the Supreme Council of Louisiana who resigned before the Concordat, he might have been viewed as a prominent "free agent." The fact that Foulhouze was a member (and even Grand Commander) of the Supreme Council of Louisiana was irrelevant from a regularity standpoint. The matter could be easily settled if he agreed to join the Charleston Council. Samory and Ladébat were also members of the Supreme Council of Louisiana (and both given the 33rd degree by Foulhouze), yet both became Active Members and officers of the Charleston Council. If James Foulhouze agreed to lead the New Orleans Scottish Rite under the Charleston Council banner, the Charleston Council would have a much easier road to travel in bringing the remainder of the New Orleans Scottish Rite Masons under their control. Foulhouze was approached by Albert Mackey and Claude Samory in the summer of 1856 and offered the position of Commander-in-Chief of the Grand Consistory and Active Membership in the Southern Jurisdiction, providing that he joined the Charleston camp.[55] Of this event, Foulhouze wrote:

> *About a year or fifteen months ago, M. Antonio Costa asked me whether I had any objection to converse with M. Claude Samory about the then state of affairs with regard to the Scottish Rite in Louisiana. I answered that I had none. On the following day M. Samory together with M. Costa called on me, and in his presence, told me that he had long been anxious to see me, that he was always my friend, that the course which he and other members of the Supreme Council of Louisiana had followed since I left it was with the only view of putting an end to any further contest and quarrel both with the Grand Lodge of our state and the Supreme Council of Charleston, that many a York mason of this east was now initiated to the high degrees of the Scottish Rite, that they all had heard of me as being well versed in its tenets and ceremonies, and were anxious to see me join the Consistory thereto assume the command of the Rite in*

Louisiana, that indeed I had just cause to complain of the conduct of some BB∴ towards me both in the Supreme Council and in the Polar Star Lodge, but that they all acknowledged it, and were ready on my joining the Grand Consistory, to offer me any apology I might wish, that there was a vacancy in the Supreme Council of Charleston which he had been offered to fill, and which he was ready to give up in my behalf if I would unite with them, that my presence in that Council would do immense good both here and at Charleston, and that the best I could do was to accept, if I desired to carry out my opinion and views with regard to the right which Louisiana has to its Supreme Council.

My answer to M. Samory was as follows:

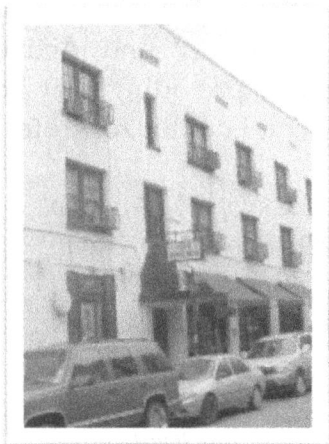

Present day 735 St. Louis Street was the residence of James Foulhouze when he met with Claude Samory and Albert Mackey. Today the building is the home of the Chez Bourbon Apartment Hotel.

I need no apology, for any thing which may have been done or said in any masonic body to hurt my feelings. Masonry, thank God, has taught me better desires, and it is enough for me to hear from you that all those who may have had an intention to offend me, do now regret it. As to your proposal, I can in no way or manner accept it. My position is clear and well defined. The Supreme Council of Louisiana was not founded by me. It existed before I was a mason. In 1845 I received, not in the Supreme Council of France founded by M. Grasse de Tilly, but in the Supreme Council of the Grand Orient, the 33d degree. That most Illustrious body treated me as a future member of the Supreme Council of Louisiana with which it corresponded, and I was

*commissioned by its Grand Commander and other members
to be the interpreter of their good feelings near our Supreme
Council. A short time after my return here, our Grand
Commander Jean François Canonge died, and I was elected
to replace him. On doing so, I bound myself to obey it and
protect its rights: and I must say that after a most serious
inquiry into its origin and the sources from which it
emanates, I am more than ever convinced that my opinion
with regard to the fundamental authority of the Scottish Rite
is correct, and that the views of Charleston thereon are
altogether erroneous. From the moment you and other 33rds
of this East judged fit to recognize the Council of Charleston
as your superior, I and two other members of our Supreme
Council, did immediately exercise what, in such case we
considered to be our right, and continued the work of our
Supreme Council. It is true that on account of the
momentary excitement which has prevailed, we have chosen
to be silent, but we exist nevertheless and have resolved to
safeguard our power and authority for any case of
emergency. I certainly feel much honored with the
proposition which you make me to accept an appointment as
an active member of the Supreme Council of Charleston and
as such to preside your Consistory here, but neither such a
flattering offer, nor any other consideration can make me
deviate from what I consider to be my duty towards a body
which I have sworn to protect. I have personally no
pretension whatsoever to power. I know that I am good only
to make an initiation, and I acknowledge that the privilege of
commanding should be better placed in other hands than
mine. Many a person, no doubt, will attribute my
determination to a spirit of opposition, but as I feel good will
towards all and even those who condemn me both in York
and Scotish [sic] ranks of Masonry, I will, happen what it
may, persevere following the line which I believe to be the
only correct one.*

Thereupon, M. Samory expressed his hope that I would change my mind, and asked me whether I would like to converse with M. Albert G. Mackey on that subject. I answered affirmatively and two or three days afterward, he called at my house with that Gentleman.

M. Mackey began by expressing a desire that his visit to me should not be considered as official. I replied that being both knights templars, we were authorized to meet as such and talk of the questions relative to the Scotish [sic] Rite, as if we were perfect strangers to it; and it being so agreed, he repeated to me all that M. Samory had said before with regard to the desire expressed by a large number of masons that I should join the consistory, and with regard to my being made an active member of the Council of Charleston and taking as such command of the Scotish rite in Louisiana. I answered him what I had already answered M. Samory. A few words where then exchanged between him and me, with regard to the origin of the council of Charleston, the constitutions of 1786, the authority which the Supreme Council of the Grand Orient of France claims on the Scotish degrees and the differences which exists between the York and Scotish rites. He admitted that difference and that the reasons which I gave upon all the other points presented a strong matter of consideration, but that he could not accept them as conclusive, which I immediately understood and acknowledged to be with him a matter of course.

He then insisted that I should again consider the proposition made by Mr. C. Samory, and confirmed by himself; and in conclusion he wished me to let him know what my determination would be after more mature reflection.

I promised to do so through Mr. Samory: and this Gentleman having called on me some weeks afterwards, and repeated all that he had been kind enough to say at his first interview with me, I again answered that I could not accept: and I remember having thus addressed him in the end:

'My dear Sir, in the same manner as the masons whom you now represent, express a desire to have me in your Consistory for their best interest, so a time may come when Scotish [sic] masons of this East, tired of a foreign dominion, shall be glad to know that there is in New Orleans a 33d of some value who has never varied, and can at any time be the strong hold around which they may gather as Louisianians.'

Thereon we parted good friends as I parted with Mr. Mackey, after due interchange of kindness and politeness. [56]

In 1858, Charles Laffon de Ladébat, while clearly bitter towards Foulhouze, commented on this meeting between Foulhouze, Samory, and Mackey:

Ill Bros. Mackey and Samory knew very well that with a few persons, amoung the weak minded and the ignorant, Mr. Foulhouze was "somebody," and that if they could prevail on him to join the Grand Consistory of Louisiana, peace would be finally restored, and it was solely for the purpose of securing that peace, that they paid him a visit, against the advice of many who knew Mr. Foulhouze better than they. [57]

With John Gedge dead and Foulhouze no longer in consideration, Claude Samory became the first New Orleans Mason to be elected an Active member of the Charleston Council. His election was on 20 November 1856. On 17 December 1856, the Grand Consistory filled the vacancy offered to James Foulhouze. The choice was a Mason of promise but little training in the Scottish Rite. The attorney from

Albert Pike

Arkansas, Albert Pike, was unanimously (and in his absence[58]) elected Commander in Chief of the Grand Consistory of Louisiana.

Prior to the election of both Samory and Pike, James Foulhouze took part in an activity that sealed his fate with the Charleston Council. Foulhouze, along with T.W. Collens, J.J.E. Massicott, J.B. Faget, and other former New Orleans Supreme Council members, declared, in effect, the Concordat of 1855 invalid and publicly resumed the activities of the New Orleans Council. The date that the Supreme Council of Louisiana was re-opened is sometimes disputed. Foulhouze stated in November of 1857:

> *From the moment I had noticed of that nameless act [the Concordat of 1855], I called upon some 33ds, whom I knew to be true to their obligations, and with them I immediately opened the Supreme Council and continued its work, in order that it might not even be said that it had slept a single instant ...* [59]

If such a meeting of 33rds did take place, it was still not until 9 October 1856 that J.J.E. Massicott would be elected Grand Commander of the reorganized Supreme Council of Louisiana, and their activities would become public. That action was the "shot" which started a new round of Masonic turbulence which dramatically altered the nature of the US Scottish Rite.

The Re-origination of the Supreme Council of Louisiana

The days/months/years following the concordat were a time of great uncertainty with many New Orleans Masons. The arguments made by all sounded somewhat reasonable. An examination of who chose to associate with the Charleston Council after the concordat, who chose to associate with the revived Supreme Council of Louisiana, and who chose to associate with neither body provides an interesting look into the divided, confused, and emotional state of affairs. Of the Grand Lodge of Louisiana officers who were Active Members of the Supreme Council of Louisiana in the pre-concordat days, two of the five Past Grand Masters[60] chose to affiliate with neither body. One PGM affiliated with the Charleston Council[61] and two with the revived New Orleans Council.[62] Of the eight senior Grand Lodge officers, two chose to affiliate with neither body,[63] two with the Charleston Council[64] and four with the revived New Orleans Council.[65] Of the non-Grand Lodge New Orleans 33°s in the pre-concordat days, eight chose to associate with neither body, fifteen with the Charleston Council, and four with the revived New Orleans Council. The total would be: twelve choosing to affiliate with neither body, nineteen with the Charleston Council, and ten with the revived New Orleans Council. These figures should not, however, be viewed as the final tally as they were, over the following years, modified as members moved from one body to the other in a most disconcerting manner. L. E. Deluzain, who was a participant in the 1855 Concordat affiliating with the Charleston Council, re-affiliated with the revived Supreme Council of Louisiana upon its revival. Joseph Lamarre, who was created a 33rd in the revived Supreme Council of Louisiana on 25 February 1858, was tried and expelled by that Council on 22 May 1858. He then affiliated with the Grand Consistory of Louisiana, becoming an Honorary 33rd. Neither side could truly claim clear victory as the severely bitter strife left both sides with ragged edges. Many of those who chose one side or the other eventually retired from any Masonic affiliation.

Possibly concerned over the reorganization of the New Orleans Council, the Grand Consistory of Louisiana sought to organize itself into a state corporation in early 1857. On 19 March 1857, the General Assembly of the Louisiana State Senate and the House of Representatives approved the incorporation of the Grand Consistory of Louisiana. Listed as members were two future Sovereign Grand Commanders of the Charleston Council — Albert Pike and James C. Batchelor. On 22 April 1857, Foulhouze was elected Grand Commander of the revived New Orleans Council. T. Wharton Collens resumed his former position as Lt. Grand Commander. With Foulhouze back in command, the Supreme Council of Louisiana began to grow in strength and size. 1858 was a pivotal year for Foulhouze and the reorganized New Orleans Supreme Council. In February, Albert Pike delivered a lecture before the Grand Lodge of Louisiana. His lecture was a sharp assault on Foulhouze and the New Orleans Council. The lecture by Pike, and arguments against it, occupied most of the March 1858 issue of the *Masonic Delta*.[66] Without question, the Charleston camp had found a Mason as capable of the "stinging pen" as Foulhouze. February of 1858 also saw a commanding new (really, returning) member to the New Orleans Council. The announcement in the *Masonic Delta* was sure to cause great concern in the Charleston/New Orleans camp:

Pierre Soulé

> *We are happy to say that our most Ill∴ and worthy Bro∴ Pierré Soulé has joined the Supreme Council of the 33d, in and for the Sovereign and Independent State of Louisiana. This eminent citizen and learned Freemason admits thus the State Rights masonically as well as politically.*[67]

The return of this fiery and powerful former United States Senator and US Minister to Spain to the rolls of the Supreme Council of Louisiana was the equivalent of a shot of adrenaline for the New Orleans Council. Soulé was created a 33rd on 8 March 1838 by Jean Jacques Conte and was, actually, a Member of the Supreme Council of Louisiana prior to the election of James Foulhouze as Grand Commander. Soulé apparently resigned from the Council at some point following the election of Foulhouze, as his name is nowhere to be found in any of the records concerning the Concordat of 1855. There is no known record giving the reasons for the resignation of Soulé from the Council nor his Masonic activities during, or thoughts of, the concordat. Soulé was elected a US Senator in 1847 and served in that office until 1853, followed by his appointment as Minister to Spain from 1853-55. Soulé was a vocal, resourceful and respected addition to the New Orleans Council.

The addition of Pierré Soulé as an Active Member of the Supreme Council of Louisiana would seem to be answered one month later by the addition of Albert Pike as an Active Member of the Charleston Council on 20 March 1858.[68] At the very session which elected Pike as an Active Member, Foulhouze was formally "expelled" from the Scottish Rite by the Charleston Council. Since Foulhouze was never a member of any of the bodies controlled by the Charleston Council, this action was more of a public statement of disapproval than an actual expulsion. What followed next was a series of "sledgehammer" verbal and written attacks from and upon both the New Orleans and Charleston Councils. The extremely bitter attacks surpassed even the Cerneau "war," which resulted in the death of all "High Grade" Scottish Rite Masonry in the US, with the exception of New Orleans. Foulhouze released his *Mémoire à Consulter* in French in 1858 and, then, in 1859, issued his *Historical Inquiry into the Origin of the Ancient and Accepted Scottish Rite* in English.[69] The book served as the platform from which Foulhouze stated his case, defined his actions and views on regularity, as well as his concepts of the history of the Scottish Rite. Foulhouze also used the *Masonic Delta* as a platform. This monthly publication was the official organ of the revived Supreme Council of Louisiana. Joseph Lamarre released his *A Masonic Trial in New Orleans* in French in 1858, and Charles Laffon de Ladébat translated and added notes to the work for an English edition. The next major New Orleans Masonic publication was a work designed to answer Foulhouze's *Mémoire à Consulter* and further state the position of the Charleston Council. *A Dissection of the Manifesto of Mr. Charles Bienvenu* was released in 1858 and opened a very regrettable door for the Charleston Council. The work, while originally issued as an anonymous publication, was later learned to be the work of Albert Pike and Charles Laffon de Ladébat. While the *Dissection* was as harsh in tone as Foulhouze's *Mémoire à Consulter*, it went back to the Lopez Expedition period and reprinted at the end of the booklet the article published on Foulhouze by the *Daily Delta* and the retort by T. Wharton Collens and Robert Preaux. What was not published, nor mentioned, was the response of nearly all of the competing New Orleans newspapers condemning the yellow journalistic style of the *Delta's* article on Foulhouze. The illusion created in the *Dissection* was that the *Delta's* article on Foulhouze was factual, and Collens and Preaux were only attempting to deny the obvious. In 1873, James Scot published his *Outline of the Rise and Progress of Freemasonry in Louisiana*. He revealed that the *Dissection* influenced his thinking and beliefs (and assuredly that of many others) of Foulhouze. Scot says of Foulhouze:

> *At this time [1850] he [Foulhouze] was charged with being a spy of the Spanish Government, and was afterwards denounced as such in the newspapers of the day when the*

news of the fate of the Lopez expedition reached New Orleans. During the excitement he was concealed by some friends to prevent his falling into the hands of the mob, until he was able to effect his escape to Havana. He afterward returned, and resigned his membership in the Supreme Council, July 30, 1853. [70]

The only newspaper which published such an opinion of Foulhouze was denounced by the balance of the newspapers in New Orleans. Foulhouze went to Havana to secure the release of American citizens *prior* to the article by the *Delta*. He did not "escape" to Havana. The statement by Scot is erroneous and very misleading. James Foulhouze became one who was not viewed as simply holding a very strong opposing Masonic opinion. He was now portrayed as a charlatan and spy of low moral character. It became character assassination. This was quite a different picture than the respected Mason Albert Mackey approached to become an Active Member of the Charleston Council. The Scot quotation is an example of the emotional and confused situation in Louisiana Masonry and that inaccuracies were, sadly, sometimes accepted as fact.

On 3 October 1858, Foulhouze informed the New Orleans Council, in Session, of a communication he received from the Grand Orient of France. Foulhouze, as a Grand Orient 33rd, was officially instructed to disassociate himself from the revived New Orleans Council. Foulhouze refused this mandate. On 4 February 1859, the Grand Orient of France struck Foulhouze's name from its list of 33rds.

Despite the actions taken and the decrees and publications written against Foulhouze and the New Orleans Council, there was no sign that the Council was weakening. In fact, the Supreme Council of Louisiana showed every sign of strengthening. By 1859, the Supreme Council of Louisiana was at its peak of power in the post concordat days. Twenty-five active lodges were under its jurisdiction[71] and the Council was composed of thirty-four Active Members.[72] Of the lodges under the jurisdiction of the New Orleans Council, seven were located outside of New Orleans in various regions of Louisiana. The makeup of the lodges reveal that the popularity of the Supreme Council of Louisiana was more than just with the French-speaking New Orleans Masons. Twelve lodges worked in the French language, seven in the English language, two in German, one in Italian, and one in Spanish. Remembering that the Louisiana Grand Lodge (with its "irregular" stamp) grew in power and took over the Grand Lodge of Louisiana in 1850 with no outside support, save the Grand Lodge of Mississippi, the matter of the Supreme Council of Louisiana had to be addressed. It was not simply a growing threat to the Charleston Council but also to the Grand Lodge of Louisiana.

With no real structure, rituals, or organization, the Charleston Council apparently began to realize that it was, indeed, in trouble. Of this time Charles S. Lobingier, 33°, G.C. writes in his 1931 *The Supreme Council, 33°:*

> *Both Pike and Mackey had, by this time, decided that the Supreme Council needed reform. On January 20, 1858, the former had written to the latter urging an increase in the membership and the introduction of the elective system.*[73]

For reasons that are, at best, ambiguous, Grand Commander John Honour resigned his office in the Charleston Council on 13 August 1858. It was not until 2 January 1859 that Albert Pike was proclaimed, by Albert Mackey, *elected* to the office of Grand Commander of the Charleston Council. It is logical that the actions of Foulhouze and the Supreme Council of Louisiana influenced the change of command and practice in the Charleston Council. Pike immediately began reforming the

Charleston Council and making the necessary changes for its survival.

In 1860, Foulhouze was elected Judge of the Second District Court in Plaquemines Parish. In 1861, Foulhouze moved his domicile from New Orleans to Plaquemines Parish. That same year former judge and Lt. Grand Commander T. Wharton Collens was elected Judge of the Seventh District Court in New Orleans. On 2 January 1861, the Supreme Council of Louisiana re-incorporated itself taking officially, for the first time, the name "The Supreme Council of Louisiana." Due to the pressures of his new legal positions, T.W. Collens resigned in 1861 as Lt. Grand Commander of the New Orleans Council. He was replaced by Sam Brown, who was created a 33rd by Foulhouze on 5 March 1860.

The Civil War

Arguably there has been no lower point in the history of the United States than the Civil War years of 1861-65. The divided country nearly destroyed itself in four years of devastating war, the effects of which plagued the county for a century to follow. While there have been numerous accounts of Masonic acts of charity during the Civil War years, the war weakened Masonry in the US due to the loss of life, property, and the economic hardship that followed the war years. There is no sign or record that any of the Supreme Councils in the US were active during the Civil Wars years. Pierré Soulé was imprisoned for a time upon the capture of New Orleans in 1862. Upon his release from prison, he lived out the remaining war years in Cuba. Albert Pike was charged with war crimes stemming from the *Battle at Pea Ridge* (his only war command) and was left out of the general amnesty afforded at the close of the war. Pike fled to Canada, awaiting a Presidential pardon allowing him to return to the US.

There are no known records of the Supreme Council of Louisiana during the war years, and it is unknown what events, if any, took place in the Council during this time. James Foulhouze, who prior to the war was a district court judge, is shown after the war as the Parish Attorney for Plaquemines Parish. There are no records of the exact date or reason that he left office as a judge. It is possible that the then 65-year-old Foulhouze retired from his judgeship, or the Union might have required his leaving office in the post war years. A series of events that can best be described as "amazing" then takes place concerning Foulhouze and the New Orleans Council.

On 3 May 1866, T. Wharton Collens, Pierré Soulé, and eight other 33rds of the Supreme Council of Louisiana signed an "oath of allegiance" to the New Orleans Council.[74] Foulhouze's name is not included in this apparent reorganization. On 10 May 1866, the Supreme Council of Louisiana obtained the oath of allegiance of Robert Preaux and created two 33rds. One of the 33rds created was a New Orleans music teacher, music shop owner, and composer of moderate note who corresponded with many of the artistic and literary figures in Europe, including Victor Hugo. His name was Eugene Chassaignac. On 7 January 1867, Chassaignac was elected Grand Commander of the New Orleans Council. It is unknown who was Grand Commander or "acting" Grand Commander at the time that Chassaignac was elevated to the 33rd degree or why Chassaignac was selected to lead the New Orleans Council. There is a full veil of mystery over the election of Chassaignac and the departure of Foulhouze.

The 1 May 1867 minutes of Liberty Lodge #19 (under the New Orleans Council's jurisdiction)[75] show that O.J. Dunn,

Grand Master of the Eureka Grand Lodge of Louisiana (Prince Hall) and five other Prince Hall Lodges in various locations in the US had officially accepted the invitation to attend Liberty Lodge and noted that this lodge admitted visitors with no regard to race. The Worshipful Master of Liberty Lodge was Eugene Chassaignac. The New Orleans Council, likewise, and that same year, officially announced that membership to its lodges was not based on race. That announcement seems curious as the Supreme Council of Louisiana (and the whole of New Orleans Masonry) had little concern over race prior to the Civil War.

In an amazing and dramatic move, the Grand Orient of France, ignoring its past action against James Foulhouze, re-recognized the Supreme Council of Louisiana on 5 November 1868. Eugene Chassaignac commented on James Foulhouze and the relations with the Grand Orient of France in the April-May 1869 issue of the *Bulletin:* [76]

> *It is true that in 1858, following the writings of Mr. J. Foulhouze, (writings that were not at all the acts of the Supreme Council) our relations with the Grand Orient were interrupted; but since I have had the honor of being the Grand Commander and Grand Master of the Scotch Rite, in Louisiana, I had the pamphlets disavowed by a solemn resolution; on the other hand, Mr. Foulhouze not being any longer a member of our order, there no longer exists a reason for the relations between the Grand Orient of France and the Supreme Council of Louisiana to be interrupted.*[77]

What could have happened? Without James Foulhouze, the reorganization of the Supreme Council of Louisiana would have failed before it started. The Chassaignac statement can only be viewed as incredible and shows an almost contempt for Foulhouze. Why? There is no clue as to what could have taken place during the Civil War years. Before the war, the Supreme Council of Louisiana was at its height of power. It could have, in a matter of a few years, realistically overpowered the Charleston Council and seriously threatened the Grand Lodge of Louisiana had the war not interrupted its growth. James Foulhouze was the power and the driving force of this movement. It simply could not have happened without him. There is no hint as to why Foulhouze left office, why Chassaignac was made a 33rd, why Chassaignac was elected Grand Commander, or why Chassaignac seemingly turned on Foulhouze. Just as perplexing as the Chassaignac statement on Foulhouze is the re-recognition of the Supreme Council of Louisiana by the Grand Orient. The Grand Orient had stripped Foulhouze of his 33rd Degree for his participation in reorganizing the New Orleans Council. Why would they now recognize that very same Body? The re-recognition of the Supreme Council of Louisiana by the Grand Orient of France unquestionably caused great concern in the Supreme Councils SJ and NMJ. In a bold move, relations between the Grand Orient and the SJ and NMJ were suspended by a joint resolution of the SJ and NMJ dated 2 May and 15 June 1870. The resolution included the following points (presumably written by Pike).

> *The Grand Orient of France well knew, for it had so decided in a sane interval, in 1858, that an Inspector-General created by itself could exercise no powers within the jurisdiction of another Supreme Council. It knew that the Chassaignac body was created by the sole authority of M. Jacques Foulhouze, whom it had denuded of his privileges as an Inspector-General, for "forfaiture d'honneur," in establishing it. And yet, without any new light upon the subject, without any reconsideration or reexamination, without restoring M. Foulhouze, and while in alliance with*

us, it recognized this spurious organization as a lawful Supreme Council. [78]

The Death of James Foulhouze

There is no suggestion found that Foulhouze had any association with Freemasonry following the Civil War years. In 1869 Foulhouze co-authored a book with William M. Prescott titled *The Ordinances of the Police Jury of the Parish of Plaquemines*. Foulhouze is listed as "Parish Attorney" and Prescott as "Parish Judge." Foulhouze apparently busied himself with legal matters and spent the remainder of his life in the river town of Pointe-a-la-Hache, Louisiana.

Headstone of James Foulhouze

On 21 December 1875, the following article appeared in the *New Orleans Bee*:

> *Deceased the 18th of December 1875 at Pointe-a-la-Hache, parish of Plaquemines, the Hon. James Foulhouze at the age of seventy-five. A native of Riom, Auvergue, France.*

Foulhouze was buried at St. Thomas the Apostle Church Cemetery in Pointe-a-la-Hache, Louisiana. T. Wharton Collens, who had resigned from all Masonic activities by then, handled the legal matters concerning Foulhouze's succession. Collens wrote of Foulhouze:

> *I was very intimately acquainted with the late James Foulhouze during the thirty years that preceded his death. He was a native of Riom in France, and during the*

thirty years that I knew him he frequently spoke to me of his relatives in that country, and showed me his correspondences with them. His father died previous to 1830, his mother a few years before he 'J. Foulhouze' did. He had a brother who died before he did - that brother left one heir a daughter. Foulhouze himself was never married. [79]

While Foulhouze did not seem to be a man of great wealth, he did own a home in Pointe-a-la-Hache and some property. Foulhouze's entire estate was willed to Odéalie Collens McCaleb, the married daughter of his longtime friend T. Wharton Collens and Odéalie's son, James Foulhouze McCaleb.

There are many unanswered questions concerning Foulhouze, and the events surrounding him may never be fully answered or understood. It is clear, however, that James Foulhouze followed a path that he felt was correct. Regardless of which side of the issue one takes, it must be objectively recognized that the impact that Foulhouze had on the whole of US Scottish Rite Masonry was substantial. It must also be pointed out that those who supported and held the same opinion as Foulhouze were neither "weak minded" nor "ignorant," as sometimes charged. Intelligent people frequently hold differing opinions. It is unfortunate when judgment is colored by emotion, and it is tragic when erroneous conclusions born of skewed judgment makes its way into accepted history.

Notes:

1. *The Masonic Delta* March 1858.
2. This date was obtained from the tombstone of James Foulhouze located in St. Thomas the Apostle Church Cemetery, Pointe a la Hache, Louisiana.

3. Personal letter: Christine McCullough, Assistant Archivist, Archdiocese of Philadelphia to Michael R. Poll, 23 April 1993.
4. *Passenger and Immigration List Index Vol. I* P. William Filby, Mary K. Meyer Editors. (Detroit, Michigan: Gale Research Co., 1981) 314.
5. Charles Laffon de Ladébat, translator, notes of *A Masonic Trial in New Orleans.* (New Orleans, LA: J. Lamarre, 1858) p. 62.
6. *Encyclopedia Britannica Vol. XI* (Chicago: William Benton, Publisher, 1965) 814.
7. McCullough to Poll, 23 April 1993. It should be noted that a priest having his faculties suspended is akin to a physician having his medical license suspended. The affected priest would no longer be able to carry out the duties of a priest, such as hearing confessions, performing weddings, baptisms, Mass, etc. While a priest who has had his faculties suspended is prevented from doing all that makes one a priest, only the Vatican can separate a priest from his vows as a priest. This would mean that Foulhouze might have, technically, remained a priest, without powers, until his death.
8. At the time that Foulhouze was a priest, Philadelphia was a "Diocese" and not yet an "Archdiocese."
9. McCullough to Poll, 23 April 1993.
10. Ladébat, notes, *A Masonic Trial in New Orleans* p. 62.
11. James Foulhouze, *A Philosophical Inquiry Respecting the Abolition of Capital Punishment* (New Orleans, LA: Cornerstone Book Publishers, 2019 reprint of 1842 edition.).
12. The paper that Bishop Kenrick mentions was *Le Penseur* (*The Thinker*).
13. *Records of the American Catholic Historical Society Vol. VIII*, 1896 Bishop Kenrick to Dr. Cullen 23 November 1843., 311-312.
14. Masonic and anti-Masonic.
15. *The Louisiana Historical Quarterly Vol. 31, No. 4 October 1948.* New Orleans, LA, 918.
16. Roman Catholic law forbids duels regardless of the fact that, for many years, the traditional site for duels was in the gardens directly behind and on the grounds of the St. Louis Cathedral.
17. *The Masonic Delta* November 1857 edition.
18. Ibid.
19. Ibid.
20. James Foulhouze, *Historical Inquiry into the Origin of the Ancient and Accepted Scottish Rite* (New Orleans, LA: Cornerstone Book Publishers, 2012 reprint of 1859 edition.) 17.
21. *Masonic Delta* November 1857.
22. Canonge served the Grand Lodge of Louisiana as Grand Master in 1822-24 & 1829 and also served as Commander in Chief of the Grand Consistory of Louisiana from 1843-46. Canonge had served as the Grand Senior Warden

of the Cerneau Grand Council of Princes of the Royal Secret, 32° in Philadelphia in 1818 and was an early member of the New Orleans Supreme Council, being appointed Grand Expert on 7 November 1839. It was during Canonge's administration as Commander in Chief of the Grand Consistory that this body passed under the jurisdiction of the New Orleans Supreme Council. Prior to his election to the office of Sovereign Grand Commander, Canonge served as the Lt. Grand Commander of the Supreme Council. Canonge had the reputation of being a "no nonsense" and "ready to act" individual with an amazing memory. As a criminal court judge, he once ordered the arrest of the entire state Supreme Court for interfering in one of his capital trials. *New Orleans Times Democrat* 8 January 1893 "Louisiana Families."

23. *Masonic Delta* November 1857.

24. Foulhouze, *Historical Inquiry* p. 62.

25. See: *The Elimination of the French Influence in Louisiana Masonry,* page 22 of this book.

26. *Report of the Committee on Foreign Correspondence of the Louisiana Grand Lodge of Ancient York Masons.* (New Orleans: Cook, Young & Co., 1849.) 5.

27. Ibid. 5.

28. The town of Lafayette was a suburb of New Orleans in the 1800s, located in what is now considered the "uptown" area of New Orleans.

29. George Washington, Lafayette, Warren, Marion, Crescent City, Hiram & Eureka.

30. *Grand Lodge of the State of Louisiana Report and Exposition* (New Orleans: J.L Sollée, 1849) 5-34.

31. James B. Scot, *Outline of the Rise and Progress of Freemasonry in Louisiana* 1873 (New Orleans, LA: Cornerstone Book Publishers, reprint 2008) 76.

32. Charles Laffon de Ladébat, *Ancient and Accepted Rite. Thirtieth Degree.* (New Orleans: 1857), xxvii.

33. Ladébat states in a footnote of his published 18° ritual: "The philosophical explanation of this and of all the other Degrees from the First up to the Thirtieth inclusive, is taken from the work of Ill.: Bro.: J. Foulhouze, 33d, with some slight alterations, of which, the author willingly assumes the responsibility." Ladébat, *Ancient and Accepted Scotch Rite. Eighteenth Degree* (New Orleans: 1856) 123. Foulhouze had also rewritten the 33° for the New Orleans Council. See: James D. Carter *History of the Supreme Council, 33° SJUSA (1861-1891).* (Washington, DC: The Supreme Council 33°, 1967). 37.

34. The title of this magazine is sometimes given as *Freemasons' Magazine.*

35. Charles S. Lobingier, *The Supreme Council , 33°* (Louisville, KY: The Standard Printing Co., Inc., 1931). 172; Ray Baker Harris, James D. Carter, *History of the Supreme Council, 33° SJUSA (1801-1861),* (Washington, DC: The Supreme Council 33°, 1964.) 236.

36. Minutes Book, Friends of Harmony Lodge #58 14 September 1849.

37. James Scot, *Outline of the Rise and Progress of Freemasonry in Louisiana.* New Orleans, LA: Cornerstone Book Publishers, reprint 2008. 78-80.

38. Prior to the Grand Lodge Constitution of 1850, Past Masters of the constituted lodges were made Life Members of the Grand Lodge with voting rights in the Grand Lodge. Following the Constitution of 1850, voting rights were only given to Grand Lodges Officers, the three principal members of each lodge, Past Grand Masters, and Grand Lodge Committee members.

39. *The Masonic Delta* November 1857.

40. *The Masonic Delta* November 1857.

41. The numbers vary according to the source. *The Annual Grand Communication of the Supreme Council,* 1859, VIII lists 26 new 33rds. Albert Pike, *Official Bulletin VIII,* 1886, page 571-572 lists 31 new 33rds.

42. Reunion Fraternal de Caridad in Havana 12 July 1815 and El Templo de la Devina Pastora in Matanzaz 12 July 1818, *Proceedings of the Grand Lodge of Louisiana* 1995 (A-2 & 3).

43. *New Orleans Daily Delta* 31 May 1850.

44. *The Daily Picayune,* New Orleans, Louisiana 31 May 1850.

45. *The Daily Crescent* New Orleans, Louisiana 1 June 1850.

46. *Daily Orleanian,* New Orleans, Louisiana 2 June 1850.

47. *New Orleans Daily Delta* 1 June 1850.

48. *New Orleans Bee* 27 February 1852.

49. James Foulhouze, T.W. Collens, Charles Claiborne, J.B. Faget, Felix Garcia, F.A. Lumsden, Joseph Walker, John L. Lewis, Robert Preaux, Charles Murian, S. Herriman , Jean Lamothe, Antonio Costa, A. P. Lanaux, G.A. Montmain, F. Correjolles, J.H. Holland, R.D. Fanis, J.E. Jolly, J. Bachino, Aug. Broué, M. Prados, F. Ricau, J.J.E. Massicott, François Meilleur, C.M. Emerson, H.G. Duvivier, C. Samory & Charles Laffon de Ladébat.

50. *The Masonic Delta* August 1857.

51. An interesting document resides in the New Orleans Scottish Rite Library and Museum. It is a handwritten copy of the 1846 General Regulations of the New Orleans Supreme Council. This document is of particular interest as it was used as a "working copy" for the 1848 General Regulations, which were approved on 20 July 1848. The document contains the notes and changes made by James Foulhouze with his signature. Clearly, the various changes were presented to the Council for approval. The official name *"The Supreme Council for the United States of America Sitting in New Orleans"* at the head of the Regulations has portions scratched out, leaving only *"The Supreme Council sitting in New Orleans."* In addition, the side margins contain the proposed changes. In addition to the official name being altered to remove "for the United States of America," the proposed change

to "for the State of Louisiana" was also scratched out in the margin. Presumably, the new title did not pass the vote of the Council, or Foulhouze decided not to propose this name change — at that time. It is significant, however, to realize that Foulhouze, from the early days of his administration, considered the Supreme Council structure as possibly being limited to state boundaries just as Grand Lodges.

52. This account cannot be confirmed in totality by any existing official record. But it is recounted in an old unsigned handwritten paper in the New Orleans Scottish Rite Library and Museum. In the notes of the 1859 *A Masonic Trial in New Orleans*, Charles Laffon de Ladébat writes of the event: *"... An opportunity offered and that was the address of Ill∴ Bro. Chas. Claiborne who, instead of arguing the point at issue, that is, the merits and demerits of the 20 articles, amused himself by ridiculing the masonic costumes of Mr. Foulhouze. Mr. Foulhouze was stung to the quick and swore, in leaving the hall, that he had done with Masonry! He sent in his letter of resignation on the 30th of July 1853." P. 43.*

53. Alain Bernheim located the Minutes of the New Orleans Supreme Council from its creation to 15 February 1847 in the BN in Paris in 1987. This writer located the Minutes of the New Orleans Supreme Council from the election of Charles Claiborne to the Concordat of 1855 in the Library of the New Orleans Scottish Rite Bodies in 1994.

54. *Official Bulletin VIII* 1886 p 536.

55. Foulhouze, *Historical Inquiry* 78. *The Masonic Delta*, August 1857 & March 1858. Charles Laffon de Ladébat, Translator, *A Masonic Trial in New Orleans (Lamarre's Defense)* (New Orleans, J. Lamarre, 1858) 43-44. Note: *A Masonic Trial in New Orleans* was written by Joseph Lamarre and originally published in French. The work was translated into English and republished that same year. The name of the translator is not given in this work. Charles Laffon de Ladébat states on page 83 of *Dissection of the Manifesto of Mr. Charles Bienienu* (New Orleans: privately published, 1858) that he was the translator for Lamarre's work and author of the notes in that book.

56. *The Masonic Delta* August 1857.

57. Ladébat, *A Masonic Trial in New Orleans* page 43.

58. *Albert Pike's Address Before the Grand Consistory of Louisiana,* page 175 of this book.

59. *The Masonic Delta* November 1857.

60. Felix Garcia, Lucien Hermann.

61. John Henry Holland.

62. Jean Lamothe & Robert Preaux.

63. Ramon Vionnet & Stephen Herriman.

64. François Meilleur and Charles Murian.

65. Jean B. Faget, Jean J.E. Massicott, Romain Brugier and Joseph Lisbony.

66. The revived New Orleans Council's monthly publication.

67. *The Masonic Delta* February 1858.
68. Although Pike was elected an Active Member in March, it was not until 7 July that Mackey would send the official general notification of his election. Harris, Carter *History* 260. Mackey would, however, inform Claude Samory of Pike's election on 8 May 1859. *Official Bulletin VIII*, 544.
69. Foulhouze's *Historical Inquiry* cannot be viewed as an English translation of his *Mémoire à Consulter.* Upon examination by Alain Bernheim, it has been determined that the *Historical Inquiry,* while closely following *Mémoire à Consulter,* has enough significant changes to consider it a rewrite rather than a translation.
70. Scot, *Outline.* 4.
71. *The Masonic Delta* September 1859.
72. The *Masonic Delta* April 1860.
73. Lobingier, *Supreme Council*, 249.
74. Original document in the George Longe Collection in the Amistad Research Center at Tulane University, New Orleans, Louisiana.
75. Photocopy reproduction of the minutes in *The Perfect Ashlar* (current publication of the Supreme Council of Louisiana) October 1969.
76. The *Bulletin* replaced *The Masonic Delta* in 1869 as the official publication of the Supreme Council of Louisiana.
77. Eugene Chassaignac *Bulletin* (New Orleans, A. Simon, 1869) 28.
78. Carter, *History* 431.
79. *Foulhouze Secession Papers*, 1875, Court House Pointe a la Hashe, Louisiana.

The Supreme Council Session in New Orleans

When talking about the Scottish Rite, two of the most popular questions asked are when Albert Pike received his 33° and where. The answers can be found in the Supreme Council, Southern Jurisdiction's rare *1857 Proceedings*. (A reproduction of these *Proceedings* follows this paper.) The short answer is that he received the 33° on April 25, 1857, *"in the Grand Council Chamber, Grand Lodge Buildings, Corner of St. Charles and Perdido streets, City of New Orleans, State of Louisiana."* (p. 3) As so often is the case when studying historical events, the short answer hardly tells the whole story.

From just this one amazing booklet, we can pick up some most interesting facts. For example, Pike's degree took place just two years following the Concordat of 1855 between the Supreme Council, Southern Jurisdiction, USA (Charleston Supreme Council), and the Supreme Council of Louisiana — or, really, about half of it. The Concordat of 1855 was an attempt to unite the Supreme Councils of Charleston and New Orleans. It was not wholly successful, with only about half of the 33rds in New Orleans agreeing to participate. What followed was an unfortunate and damaging period of conflict.

At the time of these *Proceedings* (as well as from its creation), the Southern Jurisdiction accepted and followed the Grand Constitutions of 1786 as their "rules of order" for governing a Supreme Council. Article V of these Constitutions states that "Each Supreme Council is to be composed of nine Inspectors General..."[1] Accordingly, the Southern Jurisdiction had no more than nine Sovereign Grand Inspectors General as its Active Members. However, the Supreme Council of Louisiana had disavowed the Grand Constitutions a few years earlier and increased their number of Active Members. It would not be until the time of Albert Pike as Sovereign Grand Commander that the Southern Jurisdiction would expand the number of its Active Members to 33. The result was that at the time of the Concordat (and with only about half of the Active Members of the Supreme Council of Louisiana), the 33rds formally under the Supreme Council Louisiana outnumbered the 33rds in the Southern Jurisdiction. When the time came to bring everyone together, the Southern Jurisdiction simply could not accommodate all these additional 33rds as Active Members.

In the summer of 1856, Albert Mackey would offer the first available Active Membership following the Concordat (as well as head of the Grand Consistory of Louisiana) to former Supreme Council of Louisiana Sovereign Grand Commander, James Foulhouze.[2] Upon Foulhouze's refusal, the Active Membership would be offered to, and then accepted by, Claude Samory. The leadership of the Grand Consistory of Louisiana would soon pass to a relatively new Scottish Rite Mason by the name of Albert Pike.

In an attempt to somehow find a place for as many as possible of the former Active Members of the Supreme Council Louisiana, the Southern Jurisdiction created what became known as the "Chamber of Deputies," consisting of nine former Active Members of the Supreme Council Louisiana. The members of this Chamber would serve as Deputies of the Southern Jurisdiction. You will note on page 33 of the 1857 Proceedings that it was the Deputies (with the blessing of Albert Mackey) who elected Albert Pike to receive the 33rd degree. You will also note that at the April 25, 1857, Session where Albert Pike received the 33°, the only Active Member present was Claude Samory. In fact, *every* 33rd listed as attending was a former Active Member of the Supreme Council Louisiana. It is noted with interest and irony that Albert Pike received his 33° from 33rds formally under the Supreme Council of Louisiana. Claude Samory was, at the time of the Concordat, the Lt. Grand Commander of the Supreme Council of Louisiana, Charles Claiborne, the Sovereign Grand Commander, and Charles Laffon de Ladébat (who would give up his seat in the "Chamber of Deputies" in favor of Albert Pike, the Secretary General. It would be interesting to know if they used a Supreme Council of Louisiana 33° ritual for Pike.[3]

The *1857 Proceedings* is filled to the brim with interesting tidbits that provide more information on the times and events as well as the positions/beliefs of the players involved in the drama of the mid-1800s in Louisiana.

One very interesting aspect of this document is the Address given by Claude Samory. The Address was given in French with an English translation provided by Albert Mackey. This is important as, at that time, there were New Orleans Masons who spoke only French and those who only spoke English. It is also noteworthy that the Address is directed to "all Masons, irrespective of Rites...." Clearly, there was a desire to make this Address available to everyone and for everyone to understand what was said.

In this *Address*, Samory gives his explanation why some half of the Active Members of the Supreme Council of Louisiana moved to the Southern Jurisdiction. By this time, the Supreme Council of Louisiana had reorganized itself and was a serious threat to the stability of the Southern Jurisdiction and, maybe, the new Grand Lodge of Louisiana. Not only does this *Address* present the case of the Southern Jurisdiction, but it is a most valuable look into what seems to have been their mindset.

The *Address* begins with a general "they are wrong" and "we are right" preamble. The divisions in Louisiana Masonry were emotionally based on whatever they knew and believed. Masons on both sides acted on what they had read or had been told. The arguments in this *Address* are presented with all the authority, conviction, and clear desire for possible peace and unity. Not for a moment do I believe that either side was anything but sincere in their desire to bring a stop to the fighting in Louisiana Masonry. It is simply the case that their emotions seemed to have gotten out of control, and they lost their balance in Masonry. Egos were injured, and everyone became fixed on one position rejecting the possibility that they could be in any way wrong or that "the other side" could in any way be right.

It is also clear that, like today, many of the rank and file Masons had no interest in digging out information for themselves. It was far easier to accept what someone in any position of authority said rather than to dig the factual information out for themselves. I believe that all of them held sincere beliefs, but that none on either side had all the facts of today available (and we are still missing much). They did the best that they could with what they had. It is to be deeply regretted that they could not find a way to work out their issues in a more Masonic manner.

The problem faced by Masons today is while much in this *Address* is presented as official sounding, fact-based, and logical, much of it is today known to be incorrect. For example, considerable space was given to prove that the 33-degree AASR is directly linked to the earlier so-called Rite of Perfection (properly known as Order of the Royal Secret). That may be true for the rituals but not the organization. We know today that the *organization* of the 33-degree AASR was created in 1801 in Charleston, SC. It dates no earlier. It is also claimed that because of the belief that the "first" high-grade Rite of Perfection body was located in Charleston, SC then, this somehow established the regularity of the Charleston Council. Today, we know that this is simply factually incorrect. It was not until late in the administration of Albert Pike that it was learned that Albany, New York had an older body of this rite, and then not until after WWI, and with the discovery of the *Sharp-Bordeaux Documents,* that the oldest known Rite of Perfection body in the US was located in New Orleans.[4] Yes, we know today that New Orleans, not Charleston, had the senior body. But does that matter?

Another problem with the *Address* is the very clear position that the Grand Constitutions of 1786 are 100% legitimate and are the law for all bodies of the Scottish Rite. The *Address* offers (as it did with attempting to trace back the *AASR* to the Rite of Perfection) a lengthy and complex (to the point of being unclear) argument on these Constitutions. But, today, I know of no serious Scottish Rite historian who will say that the Grand Constitutions are anything but a self-creation with no legitimate claim of being authentic.

The argument in this *Address* that nothing has ever been shown to prove that the Grand Constitutions is a forgery is not an attempt to discover the truth. It is an attempt to control the narrative. It's *nonsense.* You don't *prove* a negative. If the Grand Constitutions of 1786 were in any way legitimate, then you can bet your bottom dollar that after all the many years of fighting about them, someone would have come up with proof that they *are legitimate.* Nothing has ever been shown to prove them as legitimate. That is why today no one accepts them as anything but a made-up set of rules that have been *accepted* as the rules and then modified.

Another interesting aspect of the argument concerning the Grand Constructions of 1786 is the claim that the Supreme Council of Louisiana was not legitimate at their creation in 1839. The argument seems to be that only two Supreme Councils were allowed in the "United States of America" (page 16) per Article V of the French version of the Constitutions. The Supreme Council of Louisiana was claimed to be the third Supreme Council and, therefore, irregular. That is a most interesting argument because of several factors. Let's put aside, for the moment, that Scottish Rite historians today hold that the Constitutions are *not* legitimate (as well as the fact that other Supreme Councils were floating around in the US in various stages of existence at that time[5]) and look only at the argument presented in this *Address*.

As noted in the first paper in this book, the oldest known version of the Grand Constitutions of 1786 is the copy made by Frederick Dalcho. This version of the Grand Constitutions has become known as the "French Version." Interestingly enough, the Supreme Council, SJUSA has historically embraced the Latin version while the Supreme Council, NMJ has embraced the French Version. In this *Address*, the French or Dalcho version is used. I have to wonder if the version Samory used was from the Supreme Council of Louisiana prior to their denunciation of the Grand Constitutions or from Albert Mackey and the SJ. The French Version allows for only two Supreme Councils in the United States. The Latin Version allows for only two in North America.

It is claimed in the *Address* that the Supreme Council of Louisiana was irregular at its creation due to it being the third or "odd man out" in the number of allowed Supreme Councils existing in the United States in 1839. But what does that mean for us today? Should we reconsider our relations with the PHA Supreme Councils because they violate the "two Supreme

Councils in the US" limit? If we use the Latin Version, then does it mean that we need to reconsider, in addition to the PHA Supreme Councils, the Supreme Councils of Canada and Mexico? Clearly, just like Grand Lodges and the concept of Exclusive Jurisdiction, exceptions to the "rule" have always been made for no other reason than because there was a desire.

But to further examine the several claims made in this *Address*, let's continue to look deeper. The apparent assumption was that there were three Supreme Councils of the AASR existing in the United States at the time of the creation of the Supreme Council of Louisiana in 1839. It is further assumed that the Supreme Council of Louisiana was the third of these three Supreme counsels existing in 1839, the other two being the SJ and NMJ. But did they exist?

Over the years, much has been written about the "slumber years" of the Supreme Councils SJ and NMJ. These were the years when they were not active or barely active. Generally, this time is accepted as being between the early/mid-1830s to early/mid-1840s — about 10-15 years. It can even go to 20 years by some accounts. But what is the difference between "not being active" and "being dead"? If we turn to the Grand Constitutions of 1786, there is no clear answer as to when a Supreme Council can be declared dead. But maybe there are some clues.

Neither the French nor Latin version of the Grand Constitutions of 1786 provides for the election of officers. The first elected Grand Commander of the Supreme Council, SJUSA was Albert Pike in 1859. Prior to that time, the Lt. Grand Commander, per the Grand Constitutions, *automatically* assumed the office of Sovereign Grand Commander upon the Grand Commander dying, resigning, or for any other reason leaving office. A new Grand Commander would then appoint a new Lt. Grand Commander. But who was the Lt. Grand Commander of the Southern Jurisdiction during the so-called "slumber years" or the administration of Moses Holbrook?

Moses Holbrook was Sovereign Grand Commander of the Supreme Council, Southern Jurisdiction from October 1826 until his death in September 1844. In his book, *History of the Supreme Council 33° (Mother Council the World) Ancient and Accepted Scottish Rite of Freemasonry, Southern Jurisdiction, USA 1801 to 1861*, Ray Baker Harris writes of the Active Members of the Southern Jurisdiction. He cites a list Holbrook had written in April 1830. Of this list, Harris writes:

> *This list is of interest on a number of counts. It shows the complete Council of nine, not counting Sebring, who is designated under remarks as "Removed." McDonald's title indicates him still to be "Acting Lieutenant Grand Commander, pro tem," showing that nearly four years as Grand Commander, Dr. Holbrook had not yet appointed a Lieutenant Grand Commander who, under the grand constitutions, would automatically succeed to the office of Grand Commander.*[6]

Holbrook moved to Florida about a year or so before his death. Ray Baker Harris states: *"There is no record of any actions Dr. Holbrook may have taken as Grand Commander before leaving Charleston."*[7] Harris also states that after Holbrook's move to Florida, the Charleston Council consisted of only four members, with only two living in the Charleston area.[8] Upon Holbrook's death, the Lt. Grand Commander would have *automatically* become the new Grand Commander. Harris, however, is anything but clear on who had been appointed as the Lieutenant Grand Commander by Holbrook and succeeded him as Grand Commander. Harris does offer a few speculations but then adds:

>   *All this, however, is conjecture in the absence of more revealing evidence.* [9]

In his valuable, *Scottish Rite Ritual Monitor & Guide*, Arturo de Hoyos provides a record of the Sovereign Grand Commanders of the Southern Jurisdiction from 1801 until 2016.[10] A list of Southern Jurisdiction Grand Commanders is offered on page 133 and reads in part:

1. John Mitchell: 1801-1816
2. Frederick Dalcho: 1816-1822
3. Isaac Auld: 1822-1826
4. Moses Holbrook: 1826-1844
   Jacob De La Motta (Acting Grand Commander) 1844-1845
5. Alexander McDonald: 1845-1846
6. John H. Honour: 1846-1858
   Charles M. Furman (Acting Grand Commander) 1858-1859
7. Albert Pike: 1859-1891

But wait, is this a typographical error? Why would Jacob De La Motta not be listed as the 5th Grand Commander and McDonald as the 6th? Maybe because De La Motta was the "Acting Grand Commander" (the same being true of Charles M. Furman in 1858-59 according to this list[11]). But why would that be necessary? If De La Motta were the Lt. Grand Commander under Holbrook, he would have "automatically" become the Grand Commander upon Holbrook's death as per the Grand Constitutions of 1786. He would not have been listed as the "Acting Grand Commander." We must ask that if De La Motta had not been appointed Lt. Grand Commander by Holbrook, then who was appointed? Alexander McDonald? He was listed as "Acting Lt. Grand Commander, pro tem" by Holbrook. But, if Holbrook had appointed De La Motta (or anyone) as the Lt. Grand Commander, he would have been the one who "automatically" became Grand Commander upon the death of Holbrook. Why does there seem to be confusion about who the Grand Commander was upon Holbrook's death? Why is there only an "Acting Grand Commander" for a solid year? Maybe because there was no official meeting of the Supreme Council where the Lt. Grand Commander could have been officially installed as Grand Commander? No. Both versions of the Grand Constitutions of 1786 are quite clear. The Lieutenant Grand Commander *automatically* becomes Grand Commander upon there no longer being a Grand Commander. If the Lt. Grand Commander is home eating dinner and the Grand Commander drops dead 100 miles away, then in between his bites of pot roast (and before he even knows of it), the Lt. Grand Commander becomes the Grand Commander. That's it. That's the way the Grand Constitutions are written. The simple fact is that no evidence exists that Holbrook did appoint a Lt. Grand Commander in the months before his death in Florida.

Did the Supreme Council of Louisiana Active Members who supported the Concordat of 1855 know about this situation? I can't believe that they did. If they had known of it, then they would have had to have realized that under this situation, the Charleston Council would have had their Grand Commander die with no Lt. Grand Commander in office. The only way to overcome that situation would be to have an SGIG (Active Member) act on his authority *as* an SGIG and create/recreate the Supreme Council in 1844 or 1845 following the rules as laid down in the Grand Constitutions of 1786 — meaning, they would need to do this in an unoccupied area. The problem, of course, was that the area was no longer unoccupied. The Supreme Council of Louisiana had existed since 1839.

But is any of what I have written provable fact? No, it's not. I can't prove a negative. But then again, the burden of proof is on the Supreme Council, Southern Jurisdiction, to prove their valid, continuous existence since 1801. Their history books have yet to prove any of this by their accounts. It seems probable that the records that are needed to *prove* this matter, one way or the other, no longer exist.

But let's move on.

There are also other very interesting elements to this *1857 Proceedings*. Note on page 8 that on February 15, 1857, Albert Mackey "opened the Supreme Council in the first Degree of Masonry." I find the information presented in just this one line extremely significant to the story of the times. Because this Supreme Council Session was being held in New Orleans with every single 33rd present, save one, being a former SGIG of the Supreme Council of Louisiana, it would seem highly irregular (and yet possible) that they would have used a York Rite EA ritual for the opening of this *Scottish Rite* Supreme Council. It is difficult to imagine that they would have used anything but one of the New Orleans AASR Craft lodge rituals to open the Southern Jurisdiction Supreme Council Session. But this is only a guess on my part. Mackey may have provided a Charleston Scottish Rite Craft ritual (if one existed). I have no information at all on the ritual that they used.

But let's go back to that Samory's Address for a minute. On Page 10 of the *Proceedings* (the second page of the Address), Samory writes:

> From the year 1839, V∴E∴, till February 1855, V∴E∴, There existed in Louisiana a Supreme Council, which had arrogated to itself rights exclusively belonging to the Grand Lodge. The Supreme Council not only pretended to administer the higher degrees of the Ancient Accepted Rite but also the three Symbolic Degrees. The Concordat which took place in February, 1855, V∴E∴, Between that Supreme Council and our own, put an end to that state of things and

since then the M∴W∴G∴ Lodge of Louisiana has, without opposition, exclusively held all the Symbolic Lodges under its jurisdiction, and the Supreme Council retained its authority over the higher bodies of the Ancient Accepted Rite.

Let's look at this statement. Samory seems to be saying, in error, several incredible things. First, the Supreme Council of Louisiana did not have jurisdiction over any Symbolic Lodge (York or Scottish Rite) prior to 1850. From their creation in 1839 until 1850, they worked only in the 4th to 33rd degrees. This was because they honored the Concordat entered into between the Grand Consistory of Louisiana and the Grand Lodge of Louisiana in the early 1830s (before their existence). The Grand Consistory agreed not to take jurisdiction over any Scottish Rite Craft (Symbolic) Lodge, and the Grand Lodge agreed to accommodate Scottish Rite Craft Lodges. They only began accepting Craft lodges under their jurisdiction because the "new" Grand Lodge of Louisiana violated the agreement and announced that they would no longer allow any lodge to work in the Scottish Rite or French Rite rituals. Three lodges applied to the Supreme Council for relief based on this violation, and the Supreme Council accepted them. To suggest otherwise is factually incorrect. Samory should have well known these events.

However, we need to step back and look again at page 8 of these *Proceedings*. Albert Mackey opened the Supreme Council, Southern Jurisdiction, USA, on the "first Degree of Masonry." Think about that. Claude Samory and Albert Mackey harshly criticized the Supreme Council of Louisiana for its actions. Yet, they were using Craft rituals, a *Symbolic Degree*, and opening an EA lodge in the Supreme Council, SJ. How can this not be defined as hypocrisy? It is also important to note that they clearly wanted their *Address* to be delivered in two languages and distributed to *"all Masons, irrespective of Rites...."* Did they also inform them that the Supreme Council Session was opened in the First Degree of Freemasonry?

But not everything contained in these *Proceedings* is so problematic. When we look at days gone by, we sometimes apply today's customs and practices to the past. This will often lead us to misunderstandings. The way things are done today offers no guarantee that this was the practice long ago. As an example, today the term "Illustrious" is reserved for those who have received the 33rd degree. On page 33 of these *Proceedings*, you will note that Albert Pike and Willis P. Coleman, both (at that time) 32nds, are given the title "Illustrious." This is because, in the 1800s, "Illustrious" applied to both 32nds and 33rds. A 32nd was considered to be one of considerable rank and standing. You will also note that no mention of anyone being a Knight Commander of the Court of Honour. This is because the KCCH, as well as the Grand Cross of the Court of Honour investitures, were not invented then. It would not be until Albert Pike became Sovereign Grand Commander and after his discovering and obtaining the ritual of the old *Ceremony of the Fiery Heart* (an old New Orleans Scottish Rite investiture for 32nds and 33rds) that he would create the KCCH (for 32nds) and the Grand Cross (for 33rds).

As to where the 1857 Session was held, the location was 333 St. Charles Ave or the then current and today former home of the Grand Lodge of Louisiana. While the location is the same, the building is not. The present building was constructed in 1921. The old Masonic Temple Building was torn down for the new one. But why there? The Grand Consistory met in the hall of Etoile Polaire Lodge #1. They chose not to meet in Etoile Polaire. Prior to the Concordat of 1855, the Supreme Council of Louisiana met in the hall of Perseverance Lodge #4. The Session was not held there either. Maybe they felt it inappropriate to meet there.

The election of Albert Pike as a 33rd was also a new practice for the Southern Jurisdiction. Just a short time before Pike received the degree, the Southern Jurisdiction changed how they advanced someone to the 33rd. It was the beginning of what is today known as the "White Cap." Before this time, when one received the 33rd degree, he would also become an Active Member of the Supreme Council. The 33rd degree and the office of Sovereign Grand Inspector General were received at the same time. With the change in practice, one would receive the 33rd degree but not the office of SGIG (Active Member of the Supreme Council). He would become an *Honorary* Member of the Supreme Council or *Honorary* Sovereign Grand Inspector General. He would have no voice or vote in a Supreme Council session. It is sometimes written that Albert Pike made this change in practice. That is incorrect. While Pike did make many changes, this was not one of them. He was one of the first to receive the 33°, but not the office of Sovereign Grand Inspector General. Pike would, however, be elected an active member (Sovereign Grand Inspector General) of the Southern Jurisdiction on March 20, 1858. On January 2, 1859, he would be the first one *elected* as Sovereign Grand Commander of the Southern Jurisdiction.

The past can be just yesterday or an incredible story in need of telling. The history of the Scottish Rite in Louisiana is such an incredible story. The complete details of our amazing development and unique practices are, for a great part, still a mystery to us. So much is just unknown. This small paper on the 1857 Supreme Council Session in New Orleans cannot hope to do justice to the whole story of what we know as the Ancient and Accepted Scottish Rite in Louisiana. All the why's, when's, how's, and more are simply not fully understood. The most we can hope for is to whet the appetite to learn and research why we are so unique and important. It is a journey available to us all, and we only need to take the first historical step.

Notes:

1. There have been two historically accepted versions of the *Grand Constitutions of 1786*, the "French" and the "Latin" versions. Neither is accepted by most Scottish Rite historians today as legitimate. While the general meaning of the two versions is basically the same, they do vary somewhat in wording. The oldest known copy of these Constitutions (the "original" has never been found) is in the handwriting of Frederick Dalcho. The text given is from the Dalcho copy, which seems to have been the basis for the text of the "French" version. A copy of the Dalcho copy is reproduced in: Ray Baker Harris, James D. Carter *History of the Supreme Council, 33° Southern Jurisdiction, USA (1801-1861)* Washington, DC: The Supreme Council, 33° 1964) 335.

2. James Foulhouze, *Historical Inquiry into the Origin of the Ancient and Accepted Scottish Rite* (New Orleans: Cornerstone Book Publishers, 2012. Reprint of 1859 edition.) 78. *The Masonic Delta*, August 1857 & March 1858. Charles Laffon de Ladébat, Translator, *A Masonic Trial in New Orleans (Lamarre's Defense)* (New Orleans, J. Lamarre, 1858) 43-44. Note: *A Masonic Trial in New Orleans* was written by Joseph Lamarre and originally published in French. The work was translated into English and republished that same year. The name of the translator is not given in this work. Charles Laffon de Ladébat states on page 83 of *Dissection of the Manifesto of Mr. Charles Bienienu* (New Orleans: privately published, 1858) that he was the translator for Lamarre's work and author of the notes in that book.

3. James Foulhouze rewrote the 33° ritual for the Supreme Council of Louisiana. See: James D. Carter, *History of the Supreme Council, 33° SJUSA (1861-1891)* (Washington, DC: The Supreme Council 33°, 1967) 37-38.

4. *Sharp Document #40* is located in the Archives of the Supreme Council Northern Masonic Jurisdiction USA in Lexington, Massachusetts. See also: *The Sharp Documents, Volume IV* (Rennes, France: The Latomia Foundation, 1993).

5. In 1839, the United Supreme Council of the Western Hemisphere existed, even if it was in the process of dying.

6. Ray Baker Harris, James D. Carter *History of the Supreme Council, 33° Southern Jurisdiction, USA (1801-1861)* Washington, DC: The Supreme Council, 33°1964), 210.

7. Ibid., 221.

8. Ibid., 221.

9. Ibid., 222.

10. Arturo de Hoyos *Scottish Rite Ritual Monitor & Guide* Third Edition Washington, DC: The Supreme Council, 33° 2016) 133.

11. Like Jacob De La Motta, Charles M. Furman is not listed in the sequence of Grand Commanders, and also, like De La Motta, he is listed as an "Acting Grand Commander." Following Furman, Albert Pike is listed as the 7th Grand Commander. Pike was the first Grand Commander to be elected to this office in a break with the Grand Constitutions of 1786. The situation of Furman and his listing may or may not be exactly the same as De La Motta. If the Charleston Council voted to move away from the Grand Constitutions of 1786 and towards the election of officers *before* the death of John Honour, then Furman may have been "Acting Grand Commander" until the elections. That seems reasonable. But, if Charleston did not take this action until *after* the death of Honour, then Furman would have become Grand Commander upon Honour's death. He would not have been "Acting" Grand Commander at any time. Furman was the Lt. Grand Commander under Honour and would have, per the Grand Constitutions, become the Grand Commander at the moment of Honour's death. This writer is under the impression that the Minutes of the SJ meetings before and following the death of John Honour do not exist. This is a subject for another paper.

ORDO AB CHAO.

AD UNIVERSI TERRARUM ORBIS SUMMI ARCHITECTI GLORIAM.

DEUS MEUMQUE JUS.

PROCEEDINGS

OF THE

ANNUAL SESSION

OF THE

SUPREME COUNCIL

OF

Sovereign Grand Inspectors General,

33d and Last Degree of the Ancient and Accepted Rite,

FOR THE SOUTHERN JURISDICTION OF THE U. S. A.

HELD AT THE VALLEY OF NEW ORLEANS,

on the 20th, 21st and 23d days of the month called "Sebat," A∴ M∴ 5617, corresponding to the
14th, 15th and 17th days of February, in the Vulgar Era, 1857.

NEW ORLEANS:

PRINTED AT THE BULLETIN BOOK AND JOB OFFICE.

1857.

ORDO AB CHAO.

AD UNIVERSI TERRARUM ORBIS SUMMI ARCHITECTI GLORIAM.

DEUS MEUMQUE JUS.

PROCEEDINGS

OF THE

ANNUAL SESSION

OF THE

SUPREME COUNCIL

OF

Sovereign Grand Inspectors General,

33d and Last Degree of the Ancient and Accepted Rite,

FOR THE SOUTHERN JURISDICTION OF THE U. S. A.

HELD AT THE VALLEY OF NEW ORLEANS,

On the 20th, 21st and 23d days of the month called "Sebat," A∴ M∴ 5617, corresponding to the 14th, 15th and 17th days of February, in the Vulgar Era, 1857.

NEW ORLEANS:

PRINTED AT THE BULLETIN BOOK AND JOB OFFICE.

1857.

PROCEEDINGS.

———•━━●━•———

SATURDAY, 20th "Sebat," A∴ M∴, 5617. ⎱
February 14th, 1857, V∴ E∴. ⎰

The Supreme Council was this day convened at half-past six o'clock, P.M., pursuant to a Decree from Charleston, S. C., in the Grand Council Chamber, Grand Lodge Buildings, Corner of St. Charles and Perdido streets, City of New Orleans and State of Louisiana, the avenues being, as usual, duly guarded by a body of K∴ K-H∴.

WERE PRESENT :

The following Ill∴ BB∴.

ALBERT G. MACKEY, C. SAMORY,	⎱ Sov∴ G∴ Insp∴ Gen∴ 33rd D∴ ⎰ and active Members of the Supreme ⎰ Council, at Charleston.
CH. LAFFON DE LADEBAT, A. R. MOREL, J. L. TISSOT, P. M. CHASSANIOL, CHARLES CLAIBORNE,	Sov∴ G∴ Insp∴ Gen∴ 33rd D∴ and Honorary Members and Deputies of the aforesaid Supreme Council for the State of Louisiana.
A. COSTA, P. D. FORMEL, A. P. LANAUX, G. COLLIGNON,	Sov∴ G∴ Insp∴ Gen∴ 33rd D∴ and Honorary members of the afore- said Supreme Council.

The Supreme Council was opened in ample form by Ill∴ Bro∴ Albert G. Mackey, 33rd, acting as M∴ P∴ S∴ G∴ C∴ by special authority of a Decree, dated Charleston, 20th Hesvan, A∴ M∴, 5617; after which, Ill∴ Bro∴ C. Samory, 33rd, took the Chair as M∴ P∴ S∴ G∴ C∴, *pro tem.*

The M∴ P∴ S∴ G∴ C∴ then informed the Ill∴ BB∴ present, that by virtue of the authority vested in the Deputies of this Supreme Council for the State of Louisiana, they held a meeting on the 7th " Sebat," instant, and selected the following K∴ K-H∴ and Sub∴ P∴ of the R∴ S∴, viz.,

ALBERT PIKE	32d	T. F. BRAGG	32d
HARMON DOANE	"	C. WOLTERS	"
J. Q. A. FELLOWS	"	J. B. ROBERTSON	"
J. C. BATCHELOR	"	A. SCHREIBER	"
EDWARD BARNETT	"	L. LAY	"
L. H. PLACE	"	R. F. McGUIRE	"
C. B. CLAPP	"	F. H. KNAPP	"
WM. M. PERKINS	"	J. T. MONROE	"

to be initiated into the 33d and last Degree of the A∴ and A∴ Rite.

And the M∴ P∴ S∴ G∴ C∴ further observed that he was happy to state that, at the aforesaid meeting of the Deputies of this Supreme Council, it was unanimously resolved that, considering the services rendered to the cause of the A∴ and A∴ Rite, in this State, by Ill∴ Bro∴ Edw. Barnett, 32d, at the time of the Union of the two Consistories then existing, the 33rd D∴ be conferred on him as a special token of regard and esteem.

The M∴ P∴ S∴ G∴ C∴ then informed the Supreme Council that, should no objection be made, the above named Ill∴ BB∴ would, at once, be exalted to the 33rd and last D∴ of the A∴ and A∴ Rite.

No objection having been made, said K∴ K-H∴ and Sub∴ P∴ of the R∴ S∴

HARMON DOANE	32d	T. F. BRAGG	32d
J. Q. A. FELLOWS	"	C. WOLTERS	"
J. C. BATCHELOR	"	J. B. ROBERTSON	"
L. H. PLACE	"	L. LAY	"
C. B. CLAPP	"	F. H. KNAPP	"
WM. M. PERKINS	"		

were duly initiated into the 33rd and last D∴ of the A∴ and A∴ Rite, constituted and proclaimed Sovereign Grand Inspectors General and Honorary Members of this Supreme Council.

Ill∴ BB∴ Albert Pike, Edward Barnett, A. Schreiber, R. F. McGuire, John T. Monroe, having been unavoidably prevented from attending, it was unanimously resolved that they should be initiated on Tuesday next, February 17, 1857, V∴ E∴

The Deputies of this Supreme Council having suggested the necessity of holding a General Grand Communication for the purpose of addressing Brethren of all Rites and Degrees of Masonry on matters of the greatest importance to the welfare of the Order in this Jurisdiction, it was unanimously—

Resolved, That a General Grand Communication of this Supreme Council be holden the next day, 15th February, 1857, V∴ E∴, at ten o'clock, A. M., at the Grand Lodge Hall, and that the Brethren of all Rites and Degrees of Masonry be fraternally invited to attend.

Resolved, That Ill∴ Bro∴ C. Samory, 33rd, be respectfully requested to deliver an Address in the French Language, to the General Grand Communication, and that Ill∴ Bro∴ Albert G. Mackey, 33rd, be invited to deliver to the same a translation of said Address in the English language.

To which these Ill∴ BB∴ kindly consented.

Ill∴ B∴ Laffon de Ladébat, 33rd, on leave being granted, informed the M∴ P∴ S∴ G∴ C∴ and the Members of this Supreme Council, that he had received a balustre from Ill∴ Bro∴ Albert Pike, 32d, one of the members elect to receive the 33rd D∴, and now at Washington, whereby it appeared that he would be unable to be in New Orleans before the month of March next, and said Ill∴ Bro∴ Laffon de Ladébat moved that the Deputies of this Supreme Council be authorized to confer the 33rd and last D∴ on said Ill. Bro∴ Albert Pike, on his return to this City.

Ill∴ Bro∴ L. also moved that the Deputies of this Supreme Council be authorized to fill the vacancies among themselves, by appointing new members of the 33rd and last D∴, the appointment, in all cases, to be approved by the Supreme Council, at Charleston.

Both motions were duly seconded and unanimously adopted.

The Supreme Council then adjourned till the next day, at 10 o'clock A. M., and the Members retired in peace, glorifying the name of God.

CH. LAFFON DE LADEBAT, 33RD,

Sec∴ G∴ H∴ E∴, pro tem.

SUNDAY, 21st "Sebat," A∴ M∴, 5617. }
February 15th, 1857, V∴ E∴ }

The Supreme Council was opened in ample form, by Ill∴ Bro∴ C. Samory, 33rd, acting as M∴ P∴ S∴ G∴ C∴.

WERE PRESENT:

ILL∴ BB∴ ↓ALBERT G. MACKEY..............................33d
" " C. SAMORY................................... ..... "
" " A. R. MOREL.. .... "
" " C. LAFFON DE LADEBAT .... "
" " J. L. TISSOT... "
" " P. M. CHASSANIOL.............................. "
" " A. COSTA... "
" " R. PREAUX................................,........... "
" " P. D. FORMEL... "
" " M. PRADOS.. "
" " H. DOANE... "
" " J. Q. A. FELLOWS .... "
" " THOMAS F. BRAGG.............................. "
" " J. C. BATCHELOR................................. "
" " C. B. CLAPP... "
" " F. H. KNAPP... "

The minutes of the last session were read and approved.

The consideration of business was postponed until after the General Grand Communication.

Whereupon, the M∴ P∴ S∴ G∴ C∴ ordered the Supreme Council to move in procession, duly escorted by a body of K∴ K-H∴ to the Hall of the M∴ W∴ Grand Lodge of Louisiana, for the purpose of holding the General Grand Communication.

GENERAL GRAND COMMUNICATION.

Ill∴ Bro∴ Albert G. Mackey, 33rd, acting as M∴ P∴ S∴ G∴ C∴ opened the Supreme Council in the first Degree of Masonry.

After which, the M∴ P∴ S∴ G∴ C∴ informed the meeting that, at a special session of this Supreme Council, holden at Charleston, on Tuesday, 20th Hesvan, A∴ M∴, 5617, November 18th, 1856, V∴ E∴, Ill∴ Bro∴ C. Samory, 33rd, was unanimously elected an active Member of the Supreme Council for the Southern Jurisdiction of the U. S. A., to supply a vacancy occasioned by the death of late Ill∴ Bro∴ J. C. Norris.

After some appropriate remarks on this happy selection, which were warmly responded to by Ill∴ Bro∴ C. Samory, 33rd, the M∴ P∴ S∴ G∴ C∴ proclaimed said Ill∴ Bro∴ in due form, and commanded the members and bodies under this jurisdiction, to acknowledge and obey said Ill∴ Bro∴ in his aforesaid capacity.

The M∴ P∴ S∴ G∴ C∴ then informed the Members of the General Grand Communication of the object of the meeting, and requested their kind attention to the Address to be delivered by Ill∴ Bro∴ C. Samory, 33rd.

This Ill∴ Bro∴ then took the floor and delivered, in the French language, an Address, of which the following is a correct translation, as given on the spot, by Ill∴ Bro∴ Albert G. Mackey, 33rd.

ADDRESS.

MY BRETHREN OF ALL RITES AND DEGREES :

Under ordinary circumstances, the Supreme Council of the 33rd and last Degree of the Ancient and Accepted Rite, for this jurisdiction, would have been content to have called a meeting of such Brethren as were exclusively under its immediate jurisdiction ; but present circumstances require that we should make an appeal to all Masons, irrespective of Rites, and should point out those dangers which seem to threaten the Order. In pursuance of this duty, we now declare, that such dangers exist, and call upon you as Masons devoted to our sacred cause, to take these dangers into serious consideration and to apply the proper remedy.

Whatever the Rite may be to which we belong, whatever may be the jurisdiction which we obey, we must at all hazards maintain peace and harmony among ourselves. One of the fruits of the peace which has existed in this jurisdiction since the Concordat of February, 1855, V. E., has been the initiation of a large number of Brethren of other Rites into the sublime teachings of Scotch Masonry.

Many of our Brethren, misled we know not by what fatal influence, would again create a new schism and encroach upon the prerogatives of the M∴ W∴ Grand Lodge of this State, and in like manner upon those of our Supreme Council. Hence you perceive the nature of our danger, and understand somewhat of the object of this Grand Communication.

Our desire is to let the truth be known at once by those who are in doubt, and to place our Supreme Council and the Grand Lodge of this State in an impregnable position, that those who may conspire to interrupt the harmony which now prevails, may be compelled to refrain from pursuing their evil design, and may return to the path of duty. You will perceive that those who assail our Supreme Council, by the very same act attack the Grand Lodge of this State. It is indeed a happy coincidence that the interest of these two Sovereign Bodies is identically the same, and that the adherents to each are thus bound to act in unison when peace and harmony are to be maintained.

2

From the year 1839, V∴ E∴, till February, 1855, V∴ E∴, there existed in Louisiana, a Supreme Council, which had arrogated to itself rights exclusively belonging to the Grand Lodge. This Supreme Council not only pretended to administer the higher degrees of the Ancient and Accepted Rite, but also the three Symbolic Degrees. The Concordat which took place in February, 1855, V∴ E∴, between that Supreme Council and our own, put an end to that state of things, and since then the M∴ W∴ G∴ Lodge of Louisiana has, without opposition, exclusively held all the Symbolic Lodges under its jurisdiction, and the Supreme Council retained its authority over the higher bodies of the Ancient and Accepted Rite.

We now understand, however, that a new schism is about to break forth, and that trampling under foot the most sacred obligations, certain disturbers of public tranquillity contemplate proclaiming and acknowledging the authority of the so-called Supreme Council of New Orleans, and design thereby to repudiate not only the jurisdiction of our Supreme Council, but that of the M∴ W∴ Grand Lodge of the State. That Supreme Council, which has no authority, and which is not recognized by any of the existing Supreme Councils, claims jurisdiction over the first three Symbolic Degrees, as well as over the higher Degrees of the Ancient and Accepted Rite.

A few weeks ago the so-called Supreme Council constituted in this valley a spurious Chapter of Rose-croix, under the name and title of St. Andrew Chapter of Rose-croix, No. 5, and at this very moment that Supreme Council constitutes a Symbolic Lodge, " Le Foyer Maçonnique," which, no later than yesterday, was under the jurisdiction of M∴ W∴ G∴ Lodge. Let us hope, however, that the members of that Lodge will soon discover that they are strangely deceived.

Let us here warn those who receive Degrees in Masonic bodies not recognized by the M∴ W∴ Grand Lodge of this State, and by our Supreme Council, that they shall not be recognized by, nor admitted as visitors in, any of the bodies of the Ancient and Accepted Rite in both Hemispheres, as said bodies have no authority whatsoever to confer any of the Degrees of our Rite, and as they will be denounced throughout the World by the Grand Consistory of Louisiana, and by our Supreme Council.

And here we may state a very curious exemplification of the reckless and restless spirit of these disturbers of the public tranquillity. In 1850 and 1851, V∴ E∴, they seceded from the Grand Lodge and joined the so-called Supreme Council; in 1853 and 1854, they seceded from the so-called Supreme Council, and joined the Grand Lodge again, and now it seems they are about to recede once more from the Grand Lodge to join again the so-called Supreme Council. This battle-door and shuttle-cock game is most assuredly unworthy of intelligent Masons. But we know not which is the greater subject of wonder, those who can thus deceive, or those who allow themselves to be used as tools for the gratification of the vanities and whims of the deceivers.

The object of those deceivers is plain ; they wish to substitute error for truth, wrong for right ; they wish to avail themselves of the ignorance of some Brethren, and of the indifference of others, who are always ready to act without examination.

We, therefore, can hesitate no longer; the interest, as well as the welfare and prosperity of the Masonic Order, make it a law for us to enforce the rights of the M∴ W∴ Grand Lodge of this State over the three Symbolic Degrees, and to demonstrate that the authority of our Supreme Council to administer the higher Degrees of the Ancient and Accepted Rite of Masonry from the 4th to the 33rd Degree, inclusively, rests on an impregnable basis. If we prove, on the one hand, that there can be but one Supreme Council for the Southern Jurisdiction of the United States, and that one sitting now in Charleston, S. C. ; and if, on the other hand, whatever our rights may be, we disclaim and waive all authority over the first three Symbolic Degrees, we trust no one having the due exercise of reason will repudiate the authority either of the Grand Lodge or of our Supreme Council, thus defined.

For that purpose, we propose to give a sketch of the Ancient and Accepted Rite, and to lay before you the Masonic events which took place in Louisiana since 1839, V∴ E∴ We have, therefore, obtained authentic documents, which, we have no doubt, will clearly convince all who act in good faith of the truth of what we assert, that we are in the right, and that the present organization of Masonry, in Louisiana, is the only means of securing peace and harmony among us. We may thus restrain those who are tempted to listen to the fraudulent assertions of these disturbers of Masonic peace, and we boldly challenge them to controvert the facts we are about to lay before you.

The Scotch Rite, or Rite of Perfection, also called the Ancient and Accepted Rite, was brought to America, in 1761, by a French Jew, Bro∴ Stephen Morin, in accordance with the powers with which he had been invested by the Grand Consistory of Sublime Princes of the Royal Secret, convened at Paris under the Presidency of Chaillou de Joinville, Substitute General of the Order. The Scotch Rite was then composed of twenty-five Degrees only, the last of which was that of Sublime Prince of the R.·. S.·.

When Morin arrived at St. Domingo, agreeably to his patent and according to his instructions, he appointed Brother M. M. Hayes, as a Deputy Inspector General, for North America, with the power of appointing others, wherever necessary. Brother Morin also appointed Brother Frankin as a Deputy Inspector General for Jamaica and the British Islands, and Brother Col. Provost for the Windward Islands and the British Army.

On the 25th October, 1762, V.·. E.·., the Grand Masonic Constitutions were finally ratified in Bordeaux, and proclaimed for the government of all the Lodges of Sublime and Perfect Masons, Councils, Colleges and Consistories of Sublime Princes of the Royal Secret, over the two Hemispheres. This was done with the consent and approval of the G.·. Consistory at Berlin. These Constitutions were transmitted, the same year, to Stephen Morin, who furnished with an authentic copy of the same all the Deputy-Inspectors appointed by him and by his Deputies. These Constitutions, of which we possess an authentic copy, duly signed by Isaac Long, one of Morin's Deputies, are still in force, as far as they are not modified or repealed by those of 1786.

Brother Hayes appointed Brother Da Costa, Depury Inspector General for South Carolina, who, in 1783, and in accordance with the Constitutions of 1762, established a Sublime Grand Lodge of Perfection in Charleston. This body was the first of the Rite that was constituted in the United States.

After the death of Brother Da Costa, Brother Joseph Myers was appointed to succeed him by Brother Hayes, who also appointed Brother Solomon Bush, Deputy Inspector General for Pennsylvania, and Brother Berend M. Spitzer, for Georgia, which appointments were confirmed by a Council of Inspectors General that convened at Philadelphia, on the 15th of June, 1781, V.·. E.·. On the second of August, 1795, V.·. E.·., Ill.·. Bro.·. John Mitchell, was appointed Deputy Inspector General, for the State of South Carolina, *vice* Ill.·. Brother Berend M. Spitzer. These facts are incontrovertible, and are substantiated by all Masonic writers, and the researches which have been made in the Annals of the Order, go to prove, that notwithstanding the appointment of Inspectors General for the several

States, the Scotch Rite was worked in Charleston only. In that City only was established, in the year 1783, V.·. E.·., a Sublime Grand Lodge of Perfection, wherein, for the first time in America, were conferred the Degrees of our Rite above the first three Symbolic Degrees. On the 20th of February, 1788, V.·. E.·., a Council of Princes of Jerusalem was duly installed, also in Charleston, by Ill.·. BB.·. J. Myers, Berend M. Spitzer, and A. Frost. To the zeal, therefore, of our Brethren of Charleston, to their constant application to the Scotch Rite, are we indebted for the foundation of the first Body of our Rite in America. This Body is, therefore, the basis, the parent of all Bodies of the Scotch Rite now in existence.

And now, my Brethren, that we have stated the introduction of the Scotch Rite, the foundation of the first Body of the Rite in the United States, let us go back to the year 1786, when the Grand Constitutions of the 33rd Degree were ratified and promulgated.

Trusting to the opinions of certain authors hostile to our Rite, some have attempted, and still attempt, to show that the Constitutions of 1786 are not the proper act of Frederick the Second, and of those Illustrious Brothers who composed the first Supreme Council, opened in Berlin ; that this instrument is a forgery and deserves no credit, and that, consequently, it cannot be regarded as the supreme organic law of our Rite.

The Brother who has proclaimed and still proclaims this doctrine, and who continues to do all in his power to inculcate it, has not always entertained this opinion. He is the author of a Decree, dated Dec. 3rd, 1851, the 10th Article of which reads as follows: "The Free, Ancient and Accepted Scotch Rite is now founded upon the Constitutions of 1762, the new Institutes of Frederick, in the year 1776, the Grand Constitutions, approved the same year by the said Frederick, and the Treaty of Alliance and Confederation, signed on the 22nd day of February, 1833, of the Christian Era."* It is true that, at that time, these Constitutions not being in his way, he had no scruples in admitting their validity. But two years after, in 1853, having other purposes to accomplish, he apparently changed his mind, and without any previous deliberation, and without asking the authorization of the late Supreme Council of New Orleans, he altered and modified the text of the Article just quoted, in the French

---

* By referring to the original document in our hands, it will be seen that it is not in the year 1833, but in the year 1834, that this Treaty was signed. This error is insignificant, and we will rectify it hereafter in this Address.

translation which he made of that Article. This new version, as it appears in the French translation, reads as follows: "The Ancient and Accepted Scotch Rite is principally founded upon the Constitutions of 1762, and on the usages and Decrees of the Grand Orient of France, in all that relates to the nomenclature."

The late Supreme Council of New Orleans, which had adopted and sanctioned the Decree of 1851, admitting the Constitutions of 1786, never anthorized the alteration made in 1853 in that Decree. The body, and all its members, were strangers to this change made in its solemn declaration of 1851, and which was never cancelled; and hence, it necessarily follows, that the Supreme Council of New Orleans, up to the time of its dissoluton, constantly recognized the Constitutions of 1786; and it was only with a view to act in accordance with them, that the late Supreme Council transferred its powers to our Supreme Council, in order that both bodies should form but one: therefore, when you are told that the Supreme Council of New Orleans did not admit the validity of the Constitutions of 1786, you can safely deny the statement, by referring to the English text of the Decree of 1851, printed by Brother J. Lamarre, in that year, and to the 3rd paragraph of page 4, for a corroboration of your denial.

The Constitutions of Frederick are authentic and genuine, and the evidence we are about to offer must satisfy you and completely disprove the assertions of those who maintain the contrary. The evidence of their authenticity is to be found in the Treaty of Masonic Union, Alliance and Confederation, made in Paris on the 23rd of February, 1834, signed by Illustrious Brothers Fréteau de Pény, Count Ste. Rose de St. Laurent, General Lafayette, Charles N. Jubé, Philip Dupin, Dupin the Elder, Duke de Choiseul-Stainville, and others, who assert that these Constitutions are real and genuine, and after having compared the copy, which was annexed to the above named Treaty, *with the original* in the hands of Illustrious Brother Count de St. Laurent.

No one can doubt the testimony of these witnesses, whose names we have just given, nor can any faith after this be placed in the words or opinions of those who hesitate not to alter authentic documents whenever their purposes require it. To doubt the genuineness of the Constitutions of 1786, is, therefore, impossible, and equally impossible is it to prove that they are fraudulent or forged, as has been asserted, and if the least doubt is entertained by any of our Brethren, we have an authentic copy of the Treaty of 1834, and thus the truth of our assertion can be easily established.

The Grand Constitutions were ratified and signed at Berlin, on the first of May, 1786, by Frederick II, King of Prussia, who, as Grand Commander of the Order of Princes of the Royal Secret, was the Supreme Chief of the Scotch Rite. By these Constitutions, Frederick resigned his authority, and his Masonic prerogatives were deposited with a Council in and for each nation, consisting of nine Brethren. By these Constitutions, also, the number of our Degrees, which, heretofore, consisted of 25 only, was extended to 33,—the last of which is that of Sov∴ G∴ Inspector General.

It is, therefore, self-evident that the Dignity of Sov∴ G∴ Inspector General of 33rd Degree was created, and the formation of Supreme Councils authorized, by the Constitutions of 1786. It is also certain that no Sov∴ G∴ Inspectors General of the 33rd Degree, nor any Supreme Council, can exist, except by the authority of those Constitutions.

Now, if our opponents deny those very Constitutions, how can they claim the right of being Sov∴ G∴ Inspectors General of the 33rd D∴ and of forming Supreme Councils?

This, we believe, is a question which they will most assuredly find very difficult to solve.

The first Supreme Council, now existing, which was formed agreeably to the Constitutions of 1786, is our own, and was founded at Charleston, on the 31st of May, 1801, by BB∴ John Mitchell and Frederick Dalcho, the former a Colonel in the American Army, and the latter a Protestant Clergyman and most distinguished writer.

As a proof of the priority of our Supreme Council, we have the testimony of the best Masonic authors, and for proof of what we assert, we hold at the disposition of our BB∴ all the documents we possess on the subject.

It is then a positive fact which every one must admit, even among our opponents, that the first Supreme Council which appeared in the Masonic World is our Supreme Council. It is, consequently, the parent of all the other Supreme Councils which were established after its foundation ; all spring from it. Its priority, legality and authority are, consequently, beyond all doubt.

But in order to prove that this conclusion is correct, we may state further, that BB∴ de Grasse-Tilly, Hacquet, and de la Hogue, received the 33d Degree from our Supreme Council in 1802, and that those BB∴ established the Supreme Council of France, and those of the French and

English Colonies. The Supreme Council of France was duly installed by Ill.·. Bro.·. de Grasse-Tilly, on the 22d of December, 1804, V.·. E.·., at Paris, in the Hall known as the Gallery of Pompeii, situated in the Rue Neuve des Petits Champs, by virtue of Letters Patent to that effect from our Supreme Council, dated February 21st, 1802, V.·. E.·. This Supreme Council was the first and only one established in France, and it was afterwards divided into two branches, one called the Supreme Council of France, and the other the Supreme Council of the Grand Orient of France. These two bodies are still in existence. Ill.·. Bro.·. de-Grasse also established the Supreme Councils of Italy, Naples, Spain, and the Netherlands.

Thus the two Supreme Councils of France, as well as all the other Supreme Councils of the world, derive their being, either directly or indirectly, from our Supreme Council, and no Brother possessed of the 33d Degree can repudiate or overlook the authority by virtue of which he has been invested with his dignity, without, at the same time, resigning said dignity and all his prerogatives.

Article V of the Constitutions of 1786 provides that there shall be only one Supreme Council of the 33d Degree in each Nation or Kingdom; two in the United States of America, as distant as possible one from the other; one in the British Islands of America, and one also in the French Colonies.

As already stated, the first Supreme Council which was created by virtue of those Constitutions, is our own. It began its labors on the 31st of May, 1801, and its jurisdiction extended over the whole of the United States of America, until the 5th of August, 1813, when it established and constituted a Supreme Council in the City of New York, through its special proxy and representative, Emmanuel de la Motta. This Supreme Council, whose M.·. P.·. S.·. G.·. Commander was Ill.·. Brother D. D. Tompkins, Vice President of the United States of America, replaced the Grand Consistory of Sub.·. P.·. of the R.·. S.·., 32d Degree, which had been established in that city by our Supreme Council, on 6th of August, 1806, V.·. E.·. The seat of this Supreme Council has been lately removed to Boston; its jurisdiction is distributed over the Northern part of the United States of America, whilst that of Charleston is now confined to the Southern part of this country. The Supreme Council for the Northern Jurisdiction of the United States of America, created the Supreme Council of England and Wales; and this Body, in its turn, created the Supreme Council of Scotland and Ireland, with both which Bodies we are in correspondence.

The labors of the two Supreme Councils of the U. S. A. have never been interrupted, and, from the first day of their creation, up to this time, both have enjoyed the rights and privileges belonging to Supreme Councils, as the constituent and administrative heads of the Ancient and Accepted Rite, each in its respective jurisdiction; and whenever an attempt has been made to invalidate their authority and prerogatives, it has been met with a denunciation of the individuals or bodies encroaching upon their rights.

For instance, on the 21st of September, 1813, V∴ E∴, they denounced Cerneau, who had the pretension to establish a Supreme Council at New York, and the consequence of this denunciation was to unmask an impostor, trading in Masonry.

The denunciation of Cerneau by our Supreme Council, was approved and sanctioned by a Decree of the Supreme Council of France, dated December 24th, 1813, V∴ E∴, and this Decree shows that a third Supreme Council of the 33rd Degree cannot exist in the United States of America.*

The Supreme Council of Cerneau had but a short existence, but his numerous victims have not forgotten his impostures, even at this day.

In 1827, another attempt to revive the Supreme Council of Cerneau was made by Henry C. Atwood; this did not succeed. However, this usurpation of the rights of the Supreme Council for the Northern jurisdiction of the United States of America was immediately denounced in a protest, under date of August 6th, 1827, and signed by J. J. J. Gourgas, M∴ P∴ S∴ G∴ Commander.

The Supreme Council of Atwood, which appointed J. Crosse to succeed him, was unable to resist this denunciation, and ceased its labors.

Another Supreme Council sprung up also in New York, under the presidency of Elias Hicks; it had but a nominal existence. It was, likewise, denounced as having no legal authority.

When the Supreme Council of New Orleans brought itself into notice through its antagonism to the Grand Lodge of the State of Louisiana,

---

* See in the proceedings of the Supreme Council of France, the very interesting trial of the M∴ P∴ S∴ G∴ Commander, Count de Grasse-Tilly. We propose to publish this trial in the English and French languages for the information of all concerned.

3

its illegality and spuriousness were also denounced to the Masonic world by the circulars issued on the 18th and 26th April, 1851, by the Supreme Councils for the Southern and Northern jurisdictions of the United States of America.

Since, therefore, the 5th of August, 1813, the provisions of Article V. of the Constitutions of 1786 have been complied with; and there are in the United States of America, consequently, but two Supreme Councils. They have ever preserved and enforced their authority, and they have never failed to discountenance all attempts against an authority which belongs to them.

It was impossible for a third Supreme Council to be established in the United States of America without violating the Constitutions of 1786, without which, as already stated, neither the 33rd Degree nor Supreme Councils can exist. Nevertheless, on the 27th October, 1839, BB∴ O. de Santangelo, R. Perdreauville, Roca Santi Petri, J. F. Canonge, F. Verrier, A. Montmain, and others, established in New Orleans a Supreme Council, which was pompously called "Supreme Council for the United States of America."

In the act of foundation of this Supreme Council, the signers declare that they form and constitute themselves into a Supreme Council of the 33rd Degree, by virtue of the Constitutions of 1786, which they proclaim to be authentic and genuine; and they declare, besides, on behalf of this Supreme Council, that they agree to the Treaty of Masonic Union, Alliance and Confederation, made at Paris, on the 23rd of February, 1834.

It is evident that the Constitutions of 1786, by virtue of which the late Supreme Council of New Orleans claimed to be established, prohibited, instead of authorizing the creation of any such body, as the fifth Article of the same provides that there shall be but two Supreme Councils in the United States of America, and as in 1839 there had already existed one of said bodies at Charleston, since 1801, and another at New York, since 1813.

Thus the late Supreme Council of New Orleans never had a legal existence, as it could not be created nor exist without violating the Constitutions of 1786, which their founders had declared to be the supreme organic law of the A∴ and A∴ Rite.

Those who established the late Supreme Council of New Orleans, acknowledged also the Treaty of Masonic Union, Alliance and Confederation of 1834, and sanctioned the same, as above stated.

In order to become parties to said Treaty, and to clothe their Supreme

Council with the required legality, and thereby cause it to be recognized, they addressed, on the 26th of February, 1840, a baluster to the Supreme Council of France, notifying the latter body of their adhesion to said Treaty of Alliance of 1834, and demanding the recognition of their Supreme Council, and its admission to the Treaty.

We are in possession of the above-mentioned baluster, which has been returned to us by our BB.·. in France: it bears the names, all signed *manu propriâ*, of BB.·. De Santangelo, De Perdreauville, Santi Petri, Dubayle, Pichot, Montmain, Faget, and Canonge; and we have also been favored with the Decree of the Supreme Council of France, under date of July 25, 1845, and by which that Sovereign Body declines to recognize said Supreme Council, and to admit it in the Masonic Alliance of 1834; and further declares said Supreme Council to be spurious, clandestine, and illegal.

Thus the so-called Supreme Council for the United States of America, otherwise, the late Supreme Council of New Orleans, has never been recognized by the Supreme Council of France, nor by the Masonic bodies who were parties to the Treaty of 1834.

You have now the reason why an alteration was made in the text of paragraph 10 of the Decree of December 3d, 1851.

In 1851, the late Supreme Council of New Orleans declared "that the Free, Ancient and Accepted Scotch Rite was founded upon the Constitutions of 1762, the new Institutes of Frederick, in the year 1786, the Grand Constitutions given and approved in the same year by the said Frederick, and the Treaty of Alliance and Confederation signed on the 22d day of February, 1833, C.·. E.·."

This declaration, which, however, was similar to the one made in 1839, at the time of the formation of the late Supreme Council of New Orleans, and the refusal of the Supreme Council of France to recognize, and, consequently, to admit, said body as a party to the Treaty of 1834, gave the death blow to the Supreme Council of New Orleans. It was necessary to get out of this awkward position, the error of which was detected only in 1853, V.·. E.·., and it was for that purpose that the Decree of 1851, V.·. E.·., was altered.

Once provided with this Decree, thus altered, the members of the late Supreme Council of New Orleans believed themselves to be in a good and regular position; and, indeed, by means of this very alteration, they succeeded in procuring the recognition of their Supreme Council by that of the Grand Orient of France. But this Illustrious Body would never have granted their sanction, if they had known the truth, that is, the declaration of adhesion to the Treaty of 1834, as contained in the Decree of the late Supreme Council of New Orleans, under date December 3d, 1851, and for this reason : as already stated, there are two Supreme Councils in France, one in opposition to the other. The late Supreme Council of New Orleans first recognized one of them, as per their declaration of December 3d, 1851 ; and remember that this declaration has never been repealed ; and it was only when their demand to be recognized was defeated, that, after clandestinely altering the text of their declaration, they applied to the other Supreme Council, which they, at first, had virtually declared to be the spurious Supreme Council.

All the foregoing shows plainly that there never existed any legal and lawful Supreme Council in New Orleans, and that there cannot exist any as long as the Constitutions of 1786 shall remain unchanged, or as long as the Supreme Councils of Boston and Charleston shall exist.

These considerations convinced the members of the late Supreme Council of New Orleans, of the illegality of their position, and prompted them to negotiate and to sign the Concordat of the 6th and 17th of February, 1855, V∴ E∴, the consequence of which was the dissolution of that body, and its merging into our Supreme Council.

By this Concordat, all the rights, privileges and prerogatives possessed or claimed by our BB∴ during the existence and under the authority of the late Supreme Council of New Orleans, were guaranteed to them, and we have the satisfaction to state that those of our BB∴ who wished to enjoy the rights stipulated in said Concordat, met with no obstacles whatever, and we may here assure those who have not yet fulfilled the required formalities, that they will be welcomed when they desire to do so.

Let us come now to the period when the late Supreme Council of New Orleans, whose existence was unknown, since it had never been recognized, as already stated, by any of the Supreme Councils with which it had sought an intercourse ; let us, I say, come to that period when the late Supreme Council of New Orleans attempted to encroach upon the rights of the M∴ W∴ Grand Lodge of the State of Louisiana.

Up to that period, peace and harmony had prevailed among the Masons of this East : the Symbolic Lodges were working under the jurisdiction of the Grand Lodge of the State of Louisiana, whilst the late Supreme

Council of New Orleans administered all the Degrees of the Ancient and Accepted Rite from the fourth up to the last. In June, 1850, V∴ E∴, a Convention of Representatives of all the Symbolic Lodges of the State was held at Baton Rouge, under the authority of the Grand Lodge of the State of Louisiana. This Convention adopted a Constitution, wherein it was declared, " That the Grand Lodge of Free and Accepted Masons for the State of Louisiana recognized none other than Ancient Masonry, consisting of three Symbolic Degrees only, and that it was forbidden to tolerate any distinction derogatory to its character."

The late Supreme Council of New Orleans pretended that this declaration had been made witth a view to proscribe the Ancient and Accepted Scotch Rite. But this was not correct, and we all know that the declaration of 1850 was intended to establish the fact that all Masons of the three Degrees of all Rites were to unite together and to form but one and the same family.

The Supreme Council of New Orleans made use of this frivolous pretext to proclaim that, henceforth, it would constitute and administer the Symbolic Lodges of the Ancient and Accepted Rite, and that it would admit to the Degrees above the third, only the members of the Lodges under its jurisdiction, and called upon the Symbolic Lodges to recognize its authority.

This usurpation of the rights of the Grand Lodge, together with the contempt evinced for the solemn expression of the will of the Masons of Louisiana, as stated in the Convention of 1850, caused general discontent, created a schism and became a firebrand of discord among the Masons of this jurisdiction.

Of the thirty Lodges which, at the time of the declaration, were working under the jurisdiction of the Grand Lodge of the State of Louisiana, only three repudiated the authority of the Grand Lodge and recognized the jurisdiction of the Supreme Council.

These three Lodges were denounced and proclaimed to be spurious and clandestine by the Grand Lodge of this State, and by the Grand Lodges of the United States of America. All Masonic papers and publications thundered against them.

The position of the BB∴ who composed those Lodges was indeed painful and unenviable; they were everywhere shut out; the Masonic Temples of the United States of America were closed against them; in one word, they were denied admittance by all the Lodges of their own country.

The profanes who were initiated in those Lodges had a right to complain, and did complain when they discovered that, instead of acquiring the rights and privileges of Masons, their hopes were frustrated; and they declared unhesitatingly that they had been deceived.

Such was the mournful state of things after the strange proclamation of the Supreme Council, which never succeeded in procuring the approbation of the majority of the members of the Craft, and the proof is, that it never exercised jurisdiction over any other bodies than the three Lodges above named, and one of them afterwards abandoned the Supreme Council; whilst the number of Lodges under the jurisdiction of the Grand Lodge, which was only 30 at that time, increased to 70 in 1851, and is now 102.

This is the most conclusive proof that the attempts of the Supreme Council to exercise jurisdiction over the Symbolic Degrees, were discountenanced by an overwhelming majority.

All the efforts of this Supreme Council to enlist our American BB.·. were defeated. In 1850, this Supreme Council adopted the English language, although the great majority of the same were French, and did not understand that language.

But it was of vital importance to secure our American BB.·. Their influence was necessary. It appears, however, that a change has taken place; those who in 1850 had decided to use the English language exclusively, wish us now to use the French language alone, and blame us for speaking English to those who do not understand French.

On the 21st of September, 1853, Brother J. Foulhouze resigned his membership in the Supreme Council. On the 21st December, same year, BB.·. J. J. E. Massicot, Thomas Wharton Collens, and J. B. Faget resigned also. On the 7th of January, 1854, Bro.·. Stephen Herriman resigned. BB.·. Lisbony, Lamothe and others, were stricken off the Rolls on the 5th October, 1854, for non-payment of dues.

Consequently, the Supreme Council was composed of the following BB.·. only: C. Claiborne, C. Samory, C. Laffon de Ladébat, G. Collignon, A. Costa, L. E. Deluzain, P. D. Formel, John H. Holland, J. L. Tissot, A. P. Lanaux, John L. Lewis, F. A. Lumsden, C. Maurian, F. Meilleur, A. R. Morel, H. Peychaud, M. Prados, F. Ricau, P. M. Chassaniol, R. Preaux, E. Barthe, F. Garcia, Samuel Ward, and Joseph W. Walker. The four last named BB.·. were absent, at that time, and have not yet returned.

These BB.·., true to their duty, and sincerely devoted to the welfare of the Order, could not overlook the position of their BB.·. who, on account of their faithfulness to the late Supreme Council, were ostracized every where, and they resolved by all honorable means to restore them to the rights and privileges to which they were entitled.

For that purpose, these BB.·. of the late Supreme Council examined carefully :

1st. The act by which the late Supreme Council of New Orleans was established in 1839.

2d. The act by which its founders recognized the Constitutions of 1786 and the Treaty of Masonic Union, Alliance and Confederation of 1834.

3d. The Decree of this very Supreme Council under date of December 3d, 1851.

4th. The Decree by which, on the 26th July, 1845, the Supreme Council of France refused to recognize the late Supreme Council of New Orleans, and to admit it as a party to the Treaty of Masonic Union, Alliance and Confederation of 1834.

A Report was made and unanimously adopted, the consequence of which was a Resolution decreeing that the late Supreme Council had never had a legal existence, and that, in accordance with the ratification given by it, in 1839 and 1851, to the Constitutions of 1786, it could continue no longer to exercise a power which did not belong to it, without committing an act of usurpation, unless its authority were recognized and sanctioned by the Masonic authorities which contested its rights, and which alone could render its acts legal and lawful; those Masonic authorities were the Supreme Councils for the Southern and Northern jurisdictions of the United States of America, and to obtain that sanction, a memorandum was addressed to those Sovereign Bodies, who, after mature consideration, decreed that a third Supreme Council could not exist in the United States of America, inasmuch as the 5th Article of the Constitutions of 1786 forbade it, and that, consequently, the petition of the Supreme Council of New Orleans could not be granted.

This refusal gave birth to the Concordat of 1855, by which the late Supreme Council of New Orleans transferred its powers and jurisdiction to that of Charleston, so that now those two bodies form but one body; the bodies constituted by said late Supreme Council were recognized and maintained in all their rights and privileges, and all BB.·. having received degrees and dignities from said body, have been acknowledged as legally possessed of the same, after the necessary formalities.

Since this Concordat, all the Symbolic Lodges were united under the jurisdiction of the Grand Lodge of the State; their position is prosperous; peace, union and harmony prevail, and are evidences of the wisdom of said Concordat, and each and every good Mason must do all in his power to maintain that act.

As regards the bodies under the jurisdiction of our Supreme Council, they are in a very flourishing condition. Never has our beloved Rite been extended and appreciated as it is at the present day; never did it possess as many disciples, especially among our American BB.·., who profess towards it a most sincere and deserved enthusiasm.

In this district, we have five Chapters of Rose-croix, four Councils of Kadosh, and one Grand Consistory of Sub.·. P.·. of the R.·. S.·., and we are receiving, from several points, petitions for the establishment of similar bodies.

We are thus enabled to state that the Ancient and Accepted Rite, which had been heretofore neglected, slandered and proscribed, is in the way of accomplishing its grand and noble mission in a country which is its real fatherland.

To the Concordat of 1855, and to the distinct and separate administration of the three Symbolic Degrees and of the higher Degrees of our Rite, are we indebted for this happy state of things.

Your duty, my BB.·., is then to assist us in preserving and maintaining our present position. We make an appeal to your zeal and faithfulness to the Order of Masonry.

To you, my BB.·., to you, who once were under the jurisdiction of the late Supreme Council, to you, I say : remember the time when discord prevailed among us, remember that all Masonic Temples were closed against you, and that your title was no longer for you a universal passport. Most assuredly you do not wish to replace yourselves in the same awkward position ! Stand, therefore, by us; be faithful to the M.·. W.·. Grand Lodge of the State, and to our Supreme Council; those two bodies alone can maintain peace, union and concord among us; they alone can maintain you in the enjoyment of all your rights throughout the world.

Listen not to empty words of promise; look to facts and justice only; take no notice of what is not actually authentic. You have been, and you are still told that the Supreme Council of the Grand Orient of France acknowledges the right of certain Brethren, and has given them the proper authority to open a Supreme Council in New Orleans; but this is entirely erroneous, for we have in our possession the material proof of the contrary, and this is a balustre or letter, dated Paris, November 28th, 1856, V∴ E∴, signed "Heulant," Assistant Grand Master of the Order in that country.

And if our opponents, as they have done lately, should, as a proof of the recognition of their so-called Supreme Council by that of the Grand Orient of France, adduce the Masonic Calendar of 1856, V∴ E∴, yearly published by that Ill∴ Body, and in which is inserted the name of the so-called Supreme Council of New Orleans, we will show them a balustre, dated Paris, December 10th, 1856, V∴ E∴, and signed also "Heulant," Assistant Grand Master, as aforesaid, and in which that Ill∴ Brother states that the insertion is a typographical error, to be found in the first copies only, the proper measures having been taken to erase it from subsequent copies.

Remember that once already your hopes have been deceived, and that the promises held out to you were never fulfilled.

Our authority in this country has been in existence for more than half a century. We have ever protected and guaranteed the rights of the members and bodies under our jurisdiction; they have always enjoyed their rights and privileges. We, therefore, are entitled to your confidence. We hope that it will never fail us, and that you will participate with us in the honor of having forever secured the reign of Truth, Justice and Peace.

We may observe, that according to the Decree of the late Supreme Council of New Orleans, under date of December 3d, 1851, the Treaty of Alliance took place on the 22d of February, 1833, whilst the original, in our hands, shows that it was on the 23d of February, 1834, V∴ E∴. We intend to publish also this Treaty and the Grand Constitutions of 1786.

And while we are engaged in proving the authenticity and legitimacy of the Supreme Council at Charleston, it will be proper and necessary to call the attention of our BB∴ of all Rites, to many gross errors and misrepresentations contained in a historical sketch of the Ancient and Accepted Rite, in a book entitled "The Templar's Chart," by Jeremy L. Cross, published in New York in 1852, V∴ E∴, of the existence of which book we were not aware until a short time since, or we would have noticed it at an earlier period.

4

In a Supplement of said book, entitled "The Ineffable Degrees," the author attempts to explain the Degrees of our Rite, from the 4th to the 33d, inclusively, the perusal of which, by any of our BB.·. regularly initiated in any of said Degrees, will convince them of Mr. J. L. Cross' total ignorance of our Rite,—of its ceremonies, and of its philosophy and object. He concludes with what he terms "A history of the Scotch Rite in America," in which he asserts that a Supreme Council was established at New Orleans in 1795, V.·. E.·., by the Grand Orient of France. This is a gross and palpable error. The first Supreme Council constituted by virtue of the Constitutions of 1786, V.·. E.·., was that of Charleston, which was opened 31st May, 1801, V.·. E.·.; said Supreme Council conferred the 33d Degree on Count de Grasse-Tilly, and he was the founder of the first Supreme Council of France, which was formed on the 24th December, 1804, V.·. E.·.

There was no Supreme Council in France previous to said date, and therefore there existed no Masonic authority in that country to create a Supreme Council in New Orleans in 1795, V.·. E.·. Besides, there never existed any Supreme Council in New Orleans previous to the 27th of October, 1839, V.·. E.·., at which time a body of that Degree was established.

Mr. Cross further asserts that a quarrel occurred in 1807, V.·. E.·., between the Supreme Council of Louisiana and that of Charleston, that they *appealed* to the Grand Orient of France, which declined to interfere, and deputized Jos. Cerneau, the notorious Masonic impostor, to form a Supreme Council in the city of New York.

It is, indeed, difficult to conceive of such gross ignorance, or so bold an attempt to mislead. The published proceedings of the Grand Orient and Supreme Council of France, and numerous authentic documents, show that the denunciation of Jos. Cerneau, as an impostor, and of his Supreme Council, as a spurious and clandestine body, was approved and sanctioned by a Decree of the Grand Orient and Supreme Council of France, under date of 24th December, 1813, V.·. E.·., and that his Supreme Council was never recognized by any of the legal Masonic authorities in either hemisphere.

As to the allegation that an appeal was made in 1808, V.·. E.·., by the Supreme Councils of Charleston and New Orleans to the Grand Orient of France, it is the boldest attempt at deception which has ever been made. There could be no appeal made in 1808, V.·. E.·., by the Supreme Council of New Orleans to the Grand

Orient of France, for the best of all reasons, to wit: that it was not until thirty-one years after that date that a Supreme Council was formed in said City. Authentic documents are in our possession to sustain the facts we assert, and to contradict the errors and misrepresentations of Mr Cross.

The object of these very incorrect statements of Mr. Jeremy L. Cross, was to announce that he was the Grand Commander for the Northern Jurisdiction of the United States of America, and to show, as he says, " that the existence of a regular Supreme Council in the city of New York is not a fable." Now, we not only assert, but we are prepared to prove, that the greater portion of Mr. Cross' history of the Scotch Rite, and the existence of a Supreme Council in New York, of which he is the Grand Commander, are " *but fables*," fabricated for the purpose of deceiving our Brethren.

The M∴ P∴ S∴ G∴ C∴ afterwards invited the Members present to take the floor, if they had any observations to offer for the interest of the Order.

Whereupon, Ill∴ Bro∴ S. P. Auchmuty, 32d, made some very appropriate remarks on the foregoing Address, which, he said, could not fail to throw full light on matters hitherto almost unknown to the majority of Masons in this Valley, and the consequence of which would be forever to remove not only all attempts at disturbance and even certain prejudices resulting only from ignorance, but above all, to draw closer the bonds of friendship between the Members of all Rites of Masonry. This Ill∴ Brother concluded in moving that said Address, together with all the necessary vouchers, be printed in the French and English languages and distributed among the fraternity.

Which motion was duly seconded and unanimously adopted, and the M∴ P∴ S∴ G∴ C∴ was respectfully requested to submit the same to the Supreme Council.

The General Grand Communication having no further business to act upon, the M∴ P∴ S∴ G∴ C∴ closed the

Supreme Council in the first degree of Masonry, and the
Sov∴ G∴ Inspectors General returned in procession, duly
escorted by a body of Knights Kadosh, to the Grand Council
Chamber.

On resuming the Chair, Ill∴ Brother Albert G. Mackey,
33d, offered the floor to any Members who might desire to
address the Supreme Council.

Whereupon, Ill∴ Brother C. Samory, 33d, offered the
following Preamble and Resolutions, which were unanimously adopted :

WHEREAS, The members of this Supreme Council consider the suggestion of Ill∴ Bro∴ Chas. W. Vigne, Sec∴ Gen∴ H∴ E∴ of the Supreme
Council for England and Wales, as contained in his letter of 21st January,
1856, V∴ E∴, to Ill∴ Brother Charles W. Moore, respecting a General
Grand Conference of all the existing Supreme Councils, as highly important and necessary for the welfare of the Order, and as the best means of
uniting said bodies into an alliance which would produce harmony and a
better understanding :

Resolved, That the suggestion of a General Grand Conference be respectfully submitted to the Supreme Council, at Charleston.

WHEREAS, By the Constitutions of 1786, all the rights, powers and
prerogatives of Frederick II, as Supreme Chief of the Ancient and Accepted Rite, are conferred on a Supreme Council of nine Brethren in each
nation, who *possess,* IN THEIR OWN DISTRICT, *all the Masonic prerogatives
that his Majesty individually possessed, and are* " SOVEREIGNS OF MA-
SONRY : "

WHEREAS, By said Constitutions, " *the Sovereigns of Masonry,*" in the
United States of America, are the Supreme Councils for the Southern and
Northern Jurisdictions; and as such, have the right to make such amendments to said Constitutions as they may deem necessary for the better
administration of the Order in their jurisdiction :

WHEREAS, The spirit of our American institutions, the ideas, opinions,
customs, usages of the age, and the extension of our territory, require that
amendments should be made to the Constitutions of 1786, as far as regards
the administration of the Ancient and Accepted Rite in our *own district*
or jurisdiction :

Resolved, That the members of this Supreme Council respectfully suggest that a Conference be held between the Southern and Northern Councils, for the purpose of making such amendments to the Constitutions of 1786, as said bodies may deem necessary and proper.

WHEREAS, Information has been given to this Supreme Council of the existence in this Valley of a body styling itself St. Andrew Chapter of Rose-croix, No. 5, of which J. Lamarre is Secretary, and Jos. Lisbony is said to be the presiding officer :

WHEREAS, Said body, styling itself St. Andrew Chapter of Rose-croix, No. 5, is an illegal, spurious and clandestine body, having no legal authority to sit as a Chapter of Rose-croix, or to confer any of the Degrees of the Ancient and Accepted Rite :

WHEREAS, Said spurious and clandestine body, styling itself St. Andrew Chapter of Rose-croix, No. 5, has been denounced and proclaimed in both Hemispheres by this Supreme Council, in circulars addressed to all existing Masonic bodies :

Resolved, That all Brethren under the obedience of this Supreme Council, or of bodies under its jurisdiction, are forbidden to hold any Masonic intercourse relating to any Degrees of the Ancient and Accepted Rite above the third or Master's Degree, with the members of said body styling itself St. Andrew Chapter of Rose-croix, No. 5; to visit said body, or to admit any of its members as visitors in any of the bodies under the jurisdiction of this Supreme Council, under the penalties provided in the Statutes, Rules and Regulations of this Supreme Council.

Resolved, That all bodies under the jurisdiction of this Supreme Council are enjoined strictly to enforce the provisions of the preceding resolve.

On motion of Ill.·. Bro.·. Charles Laffon de Ladébat, duly seconded—

Resolved, That, in compliance with the unanimous vote of the General Grand Communication, the Address of Ill.·. Brother C. Samory, 33d, together with all the necessary vouchers, be printed in French and English, and distributed to the Fraternity.

The Supreme Council having no further business to act

upon, adjourned till Tuesday evening, 17th February, inst., and the Members retired in peace, glorifying the name of God.

CH. LAFFON DE LADEBAT, 33RD,

Sec.·. Gen.·. H.·. E.·., pro tem.

TUESDAY, 23rd "Sebat," A.·. M.·., 5617, ⎱
February 17th, 1857, V.·. E.·.   ⎰

The Supreme Council met pursuant to adjournment, and was opened in ample form, by Ill.·. Bro.·. Charles Laffon de Ladébat, 33rd, acting as M.·. P.·. S.·. G.·. C.·.

WERE PRESENT:

ILL.·. BB.·. ALBERT G. MACKEY...........................33d
"   "   C. LAFFON DE LADEBAT .... "
"   "   A. R. MOREL................................... "
"   "   J. C. BATCHELOR.............................. "
"   "   C. B. CLAPP.................................. "
"   "   L. H. PLACE.................................. "
"   "   P. M. CHASSANIOL............................ "
"   "   H. DOANE.................................... "
"   "   J. Q. A. FELLOWS .... "
"   "   C. WOLTERS .... "
"   "   P. D. FORMEL................................ "

The M.·. P.·. S.·. G.·. C.·. stated that the object of the meeting was to confer the 33d and last Degree on Sir Knights K-H.·. and Sub.·. P.·. of the R.·. S.·., Edward Barnett, A.

Schreiber, R. F. McGuire and John T. Monroe, who had been prevented from attending the ceremony of initiation on the Saturday previous, and invited the Ill.·. BB.·. to state their objections, if any they had, against the advancement of the aforesaid Ill.·. Brethren Candidates. No objection was made.

Ill.·. Brother A. R. Morel, Sec.·. Gen.·. H.·. E.·., *pro tem.*, begged leave to propose Sir Knight K-H.·. and Sub.·. P.·. Ezekiel Salomon, 32d, for initiation into the 33rd and last D.·., and he gave his reasons for making this proposition, which met with the unanimous approval of all present.

Ill.·. Bro.·. E. Salomon was, consequently, elected to receive the 33rd and last D.·. of the A.·. and A.·. Rite.

Whereupon, the M.·. P.·. S.·. G.·. C.·. proceeded, forthwith, with the initiation ceremonies, and the Members elect were duly constituted and proclaimed Sovereign Grand Inspectors General, 33rd D.·. of the A.·. and A.·. Rite, and Honorary Members of this Supreme Council.

And none of the Members present expressing a desire to address the meeting, and all the business on hand having been transacted, the M.·. P.·. S.·. G.·. C.·. adjourned the Supreme Council till the return of Ill.·. Bro.·. Albert Pike, 32d, and the Members retired in peace, glorifying the name of God.

A. R. MOREL, 33rd,

Sec.·. Gen.·. H.·. E.·., pro tem.

•

SATURDAY, "Yiar" 1st, A.·. M.·. 5617, }
April 25th, 1857, V.·. E.·. }

The Supreme Council met pursuant to orders issued by
Ill.·. Bro.·. C. Samory, 33d, Active Member of the Supreme
Council for the Southern Jurisdiction of the U. S. A., sitting
at Charleston, S. C., at seven o'clock, P. M., in the Grand
Lodge Hall, corner of St. Charles and Perdido streets, City
of New Orleans, and State of Louisiana, the avenues being,
as usual, guarded by a detachment of Knights Kadosh.

WERE PRESENT:

ILL.·. BB.·.	C. SAMORY	33d.
" "	CHARLES CLAIBORNE	"
" "	C. LAFFON DE LADEBAT	"
" "	A. R. MOREL	"
" "	P. M. CHASSANIOL	"
" "	THOMAS F. BRAGG	"
" "	J. Q. A. FELLOWS	"
" "	JOHN H. HOLLAND	"
" "	H. DOANE	"
" "	C. B. CLAPP	"
" "	C. WOLTERS	"
" "	P. D. FORMEL	"
" "	F. H. KNAPP	"

The Supreme Council was opened in ample form by Ill.·.
Bro.·. C. Samory, 33d, acting as M.·. P.·. S.·. G.·. Commander.

The M∴ P∴ S∴ G∴ Commander informed the Ill∴ BB∴ present that at a meeting of the Deputies of the Supreme Council at Charleston, held on the 14th February, 1857, V∴ E∴, authority had been given by Ill∴ Bro∴ Albert G. Mackey, 33d, Special Representative and Proxy of the aforesaid Supreme Council, to confer the 33d and last Degree of the A∴ and A∴ Rite on Sir Knight K-H∴ and Sub∴ P∴ Albert Pike.

The M∴ P∴ S∴ G∴ Commander further stated that the Deputies of the aforesaid Supreme Council had received a balustre from Sir Knight K-H∴ and Sub∴ P∴ Willis P. Coleman, showing that, in consequence of circumstances over which he had no control, he had been prevented from receiving the 33d Degree, to which he had been elected by said Deputies, on the 7th of February last, and that he had received from Ill∴ Bro∴ Albert G. Mackey, then in this Valley, the assurance that he would be initiated as soon as this Supreme Council would meet again for conferring the 33d Degree on Ill∴ Bro∴ Albert Pike, 32d.

The M∴ P∴ S∴ G∴ Commander also observed that the Deputies of this Supreme Council had acknowledged the rights of Ill∴ Bro∴ Willis P. Coleman, 32d.

Whereupon, the M∴ P∴ S∴ G∴ Commander informed the Members present, that if no objections were made, he would proceed at once with the ceremony of initiating Sir Knights and Sub∴ P∴ Albert Pike and Willis P. Coleman into the 33d and last Degree of the A∴ and A∴ Rite.

No opposition being made, Sir Knights and Sub∴ P∴ Albert Pike and Willis P. Coleman were duly initiated into the 33d and last Degree of the A∴ and A∴ Scotch Rite,

5

and proclaimed Sov.·. G.·. Inspectors General, and Honorary Members of the Supreme Council, at Charleston.

After which, Ill.·. Bro.·. C. Laffon de Ladébat, on leave being granted, proposed that the Deputies of this Supreme Council be invited to appoint a Deputy in the stead of Ill.·. Brother C. Samory, 33d, elected active Member of the Supreme Council, at Charleston—which was adopted.

Whereupon, Ill.·. Brother Harmon Doane was unanimously elected to fill the vacancy occasioned by the promotion of Ill.·. Brother C. Samory, 33d.

The M.·. P.·. S.·. G.·. Commander then read a balustre from Ill.·. Brother J. L. Tissot, 33d, tendering his resignation as Deputy of this Supreme Council, and respectfully suggesting that Ill.·. Brother J. Q. A. Fellows, 33d, be appointed in his stead. The resignation and request of Ill.·. Brother J. L. Tissot, 33d, were unanimously granted, and Ill.·. Brother J. Q. A. Fellows was appointed a Deputy of this Supreme Council.

The M.·. P.·. S.·. G.·. Commander read also a balustre from Ill.·. Brother Charles Laffon de Ladébat, 33d, tendering his resignation as Deputy of this Supreme Council for the purpose of enabling this Supreme Council to appoint Ill.·. Brother Albert Pike, whose election was better calculrted to promote the prosperity of the Order, in America. The motives of Ill.·. Bro.·. Laffon de Ladébat were duly appreciated by this Supreme Council; his resignation was, consequently, accepted, and Ill.·. Brother Albert Pike, 33d, appointed as Deputy of the Supreme Council, at Charleston, in his stead.

And none of the members present expressing a desire to

address the meeting, the M.·. P.·. S.·. G.·. Commander adjourned the Supreme Council *sine die*, and the Members retired in peace, glorifying the name of God.

CH. LAFFON DE LADEBAT, 33ᴅ,

Sec.·. Gen.·. H.·. E.·., pro tem.

A LIST OF THE MEMBERS

COMPOSING THE

𝕲𝖗𝖆𝖓𝖉 𝕮𝖔𝖓𝖘𝖎𝖘𝖙𝖔𝖗𝖞 𝖔𝖋 𝕾𝖚𝖇.∴ 𝕻.∴ 𝖔𝖋 𝖙𝖍𝖊 𝕽.∴ 𝕾.∴

32d Degree of the Ancient and Accepted Scotch Rite,

IN AND FOR THE STATE OF LOUISIANA,

All Sov.∴ G.∴ Insp.∴ Gen.∴ being Active Members "de Jure."

———•◄►•———

FIRST CLASS.

C. SAMORY, 33d, Active Member of the Supreme Council at Charleston.

SECOND CLASS.

P. M. CHASSANIOL, 33d, Hon.∴ Member and Dep.∴ of the Sup.∴ C.∴ at Charleston.
CHAS. CLAIBORNE, 33d,   "   "   "   "   "   "   "
HARMON DOANE, 33d,   "   "   "   "   "   "   "
J. Q. A. FELLOWS, 33d,   "   "   "   "   "   "   "
JOHN L. LEWIS, 33d,   "   "   "   "   "   "   "
F. A. LUMSDEN, 33d,   "   "   "   "   "   "   "
CHARLES MAURIAN, 33d,   "   "   "   "   "   "   "
A. R. MOREL, 33d,   "   "   "   "   "   "   "
ALBERT PIKE, 33d.   "   "   "   "   "   "   "

THIRD CLASS.

EDW. BARNETT, 33d, Hon∴ Member of the Sup∴ C∴ at Charleston.

J. C. BATCHELOR, 33d, " " " " " " "

J. BEUGNOT, 33d, " " " " " " "

THOS. F. BRAGG, 33d, " " " " " " "

C. B. CLAPP, 33d, " " " " " " "

W. P. COLEMAN, 33d, " " " " " " "

G. COLLIGNON, 33d, " " " " " " "

A. COSTA, 33d, " " " " " " "

L. E. DELUZAIN, 33d, " " " " " " "

P. D. FORMEL, 33d, " " " " " " "

JOHN H. HOLLAND, 33d, " " " " " " "

F. H. KNAPP, 33d, " " " " " " "

C. LAFFON DE LADEBAT, 33d, " " " " " "

A. P. LANAUX, 33d, " " " " " " "

L. LAY, 33d, " " " " " " "

R.′F. McGUIRE, 33d, " " " " " " "

F. MEILLEUR, 33d, " " " " " " "

JOHN T. MONROE, 33d, " " " " " " "

W. M. PERKINS, 33d, ·" " " " " " "

H. PEYCHAUD, 33d, " " " " " " "

L. H. PLACE, 33d, " " " " " " "

M. PRADOS, 33d, " " " " " " "

R. PREAUX, 33d, " " " " " " "

F. RICAU, 33d, " " " " " " "

JOHN B. ROBERTSON, 33d, " " " " " " "

E. SALOMON, 33d, " " " " " " "

A. SCHREIBER, 33d, " " ·" "· " " "

J. L. TISSOT, 33d, " " " " " " "

S. WARD, 33d, " " " " " " "

C. WOLTERS, 33d. " " " " " " "

38   MEMBERS OF THE GRAND CONSISTORY OF LOUISIANA.

FOURTH CLASS.

S. P. AUCHMUTY, 32d,   Active Member.
J. S. BEERS, Jr., 32d,   "   "
JOS. CHELLET, 32d,   "   "
C. DE CHOISEUL, 32d,   "   "
P. DEVERGES, 32d,   "   "
A. F. ELLIOT, 32d,   "   "
J. A. FERGUSON, 32d,   "   "
JOHN GALPIN, 32d,   "   "
JUAN GOMILA, 32d,   "   "
F. LEVASSEUR, 32d,   "   "
H. T. LONSDALE, 32d,   "   "
F. L. K. LUDWIGSEN, 32d,   "   "
M. MEILLEUR, 32d,   "   "
G. MINIERI, 32d,   "   "
N. J. PEGRAM, 32d,   "   "
JOHN PEMBERTON, 32d,   "   "
C. RAYMOND, 32d,   "   "
D. I. RICARDO, 32d,   "   "
JUAN RICO, 32d,   "   "
S. G. RISK, 32d,   "   "
ALFRED SHAW, 32d,   "   "
JOHN C. SMITH, 32d,   "   "
A. TEXIER, 32d,   "   "
S. M. TODD, 32d,   "   "
B. P. VOORHIES, 32d,   "   "
R. WATSON, 32d,   "   "
J. C. WILNER, 32d.   "   "

MEMBERS OF THE GRAND CONSISTORY OF LOUISIANA.   39

FIFTH CLASS.

WILLIAM R. BELL, 32d,   Honorary Member.
JOHN CLAIBORNE, 32d,   "   "
S. G. FABIO, 32d,   "   "
J. C. GORDY, 32d,   "   "
JOSHUA JACKSON, 32d,   "   "
S. MEILLEUR, Sr., 32d,   "   "
B. DA SILVA, 32d,   "   "
WM. STEFFENS, 32d,   "   "
JOHN STRENNA, 32.   "   "

OFFICERS

OF THE

𝕲𝖗𝖆𝖓𝖉 𝕮𝖔𝖓𝖘𝖎𝖘𝖙𝖔𝖗𝖞 𝖔𝖋 𝖙𝖍𝖊 𝕾𝖙𝖆𝖙𝖊 𝖔𝖋 𝕷𝖔𝖚𝖎𝖘𝖎𝖆𝖓𝖆,

FOR THE YEAR 1857, V∴ E∴

————◆————

ALBERT PIKE, 33d.........Ill∴ Commander-in-Chief.

L. H. PLACE, 33d.............Dep∴ Ill∴ Commander-in-Chief, *vice* Edw.
[Barnett, resigned.

C. B. CLAPP, 33d..............First Lieutenant Commander.

F. A. LUMSDEN, 33d........Second Lieutenant Commander.

THOS. F. BRAGG, 33d.......G∴ Chanc∴, *vice* C. Laffon de Ladébat,

A. SCHREIBER, 33d.........G∴ Treasurer.   ·[resigned.

J. Q. A. FELLOWS, 33d......G∴ M∴ of State.

C. WOLTERS, 33d.............G∴ Arch∴

D. I. RICARDO, 32d..........G∴ Steward.

F. H. KNAPP, 33d.............G∴ M∴ of Ceremonies.

JOHN GALPIN, 32d..........G∴ Standard Bearer.

J. H. HOLLAND, 33d........G∴ Captain of the Guards.

JUAN RICO, 32d..............G∴ Tyler.

C. RAYMOND, 32d............Assist∴ G∴ Tyler.

SUPREME COUNCIL
OF
SOVEREIGN GRAND INSPECTORS GENERAL
OF
THE ANCIENT AND ACCEPTED RITE,

For the Southern Jurisdiction of the United States.

FROM THE GRAND EAST OF CHARLESTON.

At a special session of this Supreme Council, holden in their Council Chamber, at the Grand East of Charleston near the B.·. B.·. and under the C.·. C.·., on the 23d day of the month "Sivan" A.·. M.·. 5617, corresponding to the 15th of June, A.·. L.·. 5857, it was ordered that the following balustre or proclamation be signed by the most Puissant Sovereign Grand Commander and the Illustrious Secretary General of the H.·. E.·. and that it be published for the information of all whom it may concern.

Extract from the records,

ALBERT G. MACKEY, M. D. 33d.

Secretary General.

AD UNIVERSI TERRARUM ORBIS SUMMI ARCHITECTI GLORIAM.

To all Illustrious Princes and Knights, Grand, Ineffable and Sublime Free Masons of all Degrees, ancient and modern, over the surface of the two Hemispheres to whom these presents shall come,

GREETING.

WHEREAS it has been made known to us that a body has lately been organized or attempted to be organized in the City of New Orleans,

2

calling itself the *"Supreme Council of Sov.·. Grand Inspectors General of the Ancient and Accepted Scotch Rite of the State of Louisiana"*, whereof the following persons are declared to be officers and members, namely : James Foulhouze, G.·. C.·.—T. Wharton Collens, L.·. G.·.C.·. — Louis Dufau, Sec.·. Gen.·. — Joseph Lisbony, G.·. Or.·. — J. B. Faget, G.·. Tres.·. and J. J. E. Massicot, G.·. C.·. of the G.·.

NOW KNOW YE, that the Supreme Council for the Southern Jurisdiction of the United States deeming it derogatory to its dignity to repeat the many arguments and reasons by which it has, on former occasions, conclusively shown the illegality of any such organization in contravention of its acknowledged constitutional prerogatives and the Statutes and Regulations of the Rite, and which, for the last time, were must ably and unanswerably presented by our FAITHFUL and ILLUSTRIOUS Brother C. Samory, in the address delivered by him on the 15th day of February last before the Masons of New Orleans, will content itself by declaring, on the present occasion, that the so called *"Supreme Council of Louisiana"* of which James Foulhouze is represented as the Grand Commander, is but a new attempt to revive a claim long since abandoned, as being in direct violation of the CONSTITUTIONS OF 1786, which are the FUNDAMENTAL LAW of the Ancient and Accepted Rite. And the Supreme Council for the Southern Jurisdiction, in grand convocation assembled, does hereby denounce the said *"Supreme Council of Louisiana"* of which James Foulhouze is represented as the Grand Commander, as SPURIOUS, ILLEGAL and CLANDESTINE ; and it forbids all Masons under its own Jurisdiction and fraternally warns all Masons under every other Jurisdiction, from holding any masonic communication with the said SPURIOUS body, or with any councils, chapters or lodges which it may organize, under the most rigorous pains and penalties of disobedience.

And as a *spurious* and *irregular* organisation deficient, as this is, in all the elements of vitality, UNSUPPORTED by Constitutional Law and UNRECOGNIZED by ANY of the Supreme Councils of the World, can expect to prolong its existence only by the stimulus of an active and continued opposition, the Supreme Council for the Southern Jurisdiction requests and advises its Brethren of New Orleans especially, in the midst of whom this VISIONARY SCHEME has sprung forth, to enter into no arguments with its abettors, but to treat its organization and that of any subordinate bodies which it may establish, with that silent contempt which is justly due to so stupid an attempt to impair the peace and harmony of the Masonic Jurisdiction of Louisiana.

By Order of the Supreme Council,

JOHN H. HONOUR.

SEAL.

R.·. †.·., K–H.·.,S.·. P.·. R.·. S.·., S.·.G.·.I.·.G.·., 33D,
M.·. P.·. S.·. G.·. Commander.

ALBERT G. MACKEY, M. D.
R.·. †.·., K–H.·., S.·. P.·. R.·. S.·., S.·. G.·. I.·. G.·., 33D,
Secretary General H.·. E.·.

SPES MEA IN DEO EST.

AD UNIVERSI TERRARUM ORBIS SUMMI ARCHITECTI GLORIAM.

RESURGENS TENEBRAS VERA LUX DIMOVET.

Grand Consistory of S∴ PP∴ R∴ S∴, 32d D∴ of the Ancient and Accepted Scotch Rite in and for the State of Louisiana, under the Jurisdiction of the Supreme Council for the Southern Jurisdiction of the United States of America, sitting at Charleston, S. C.

WHEREAS, by advertisements published in the "New Orleans Bee," and in the "Picayune," of the 26th, 27th and 29th June, 1857, and to which the name of *S. G. Fabio, 32d*, is affixed as *Secretary*, a meeting is called of a certain body styling itself *"Polar Star Chapter of Rose-Croix No. 3*, under the jurisdiction of the SO--CALLED *Supreme Council of Louisiana:*

4

WHEREAS, the so-called *Supreme Council and Chapter* are SPURIOUS, IRREGULAR and CLANDESTINE Bodies, not recognized by any of the Masonic authorities of the Ancient and Accepted Scotch Rite in the U. S. A., or in any other part of the World :

WHEREAS, there exists in this Valley, under the Jurisdiction of this Grand Consistory, a chapter of Rose-Croix, bearing the same name and number as the SPURIOUS, ILLEGAL and CLANDESTINE Body above denounced :

AND WHEREAS, said *S. G. Fabio*, lately EXPELLED from this Grand Consistory, is no longer possessed of any Masonic qualification whatever:

NOTICE is hereby given to all whom it may concern, that the only REGULAR and LAWFUL Chapter of Rose-Croix, in this valley, bearing the name and number of POLAR STAR CHAPTER OF ROSE-CROIX No. 3, is that under the Jurisdiction of this Grand Consistory, and of which Ill.·. Bro.·. Charles Laffon de Ladébat, 33d, is M.·. W.·. and Ill.·. Bro.·. Michel Meilleur, 32d, Secretary.

Given under my hand and seal, at the Valley of New Orleans, this 7th day of "Tamuz," A.·. M.·. 5617—June 29th, 1857, V.·. E.·.

L. H. PLACE, 33d,
Deputy Ill.·. Com.·. in chief
Grand Consistory of Louisiana.

By Order

THOS. F. BRAGG, 33d,
Grand Chancellor.

SPES MEA IN DEO EST.

AD UNIVERSI TERRARUM ORBIS SUMMI ARCHITECTI GLORIAM.

RESURGENS TENEBRAS VERA LUX DIMOVET.

Grand Consistory of S∴ PP∴ R∴ S∴, 32d D∴ of the Ancient and Accepted Rite in and for the State of Louisiana, under the Jurisdiction of the Supreme Council for the Southern Jurisdiction of the United States of America, sitting at Charleston, S. C.

Sitting of " Ab " 3d, A∴ M∴ 5617—July 24 1857, V∴ E∴

WHEREAS, by advertisements in the " Bee " and in the " Picayune " of the 22d inst., this Grand Consistory is informed of the existence, in this Valley, of a certain body styling itself " Grand Council of Kadosh Polar Star No. 3," *under the jurisdiction of a body assuming the title of Supreme Council for the Independent State of Louisiana* ;

2

WHEREAS, the above so called *Grand Council and Supreme Council* are *clandestine, spurious* and *illegal* bodies, NOT RECOGNIZED BY ANY OF THE LEGAL AND LEGITIMATE MASONIC BODIES of the Ancient and Accepted Rite in either hemisphere;

And WHEREAS, there exists in this Valley A REGULAR AND LAWFUL COUNCIL OF KADOSH, bearing the same name and number as that assumed by the ILLEGAL AND SPURIOUS COUNCIL above denounced;

NOTICE is hereby given to all whom it may concern, that the only LEGAL and LAWFUL Council of Kadosh in this Valley, bearing the name and title of POLAR STAR ·COUNCIL OF KADOSH; No. 3, is that under the jurisdiction of this Grand Consistory, and of which Ill.·. Bro.·. C. Samory, 33d, is T.·. P.·. G.·. M.·., and Ill.·. Bro.·. Michel Meilleur, 33d, the Chancellor.

By order of the Grand Consistory :

{ SEAL }

THOS. F. BRAGG, ·'3d,

G.·. Chancellor.

Albert Pike's Address Before
The Grand Consistory of Louisiana

I believe readily that you did not want the office, but the office wanted you.

~ Charles Laffon de Ladébat to Albert Pike [1]

The passage of years can sometimes elevate a historical figure into a legend. This is not always beneficial when a study of the individual is desired. A historical figure can be examined, and their actions evaluated from a more human perspective. A legend, however, can take on near supernatural qualities, and the whole of their activities are sometimes not expected to be understood or completely recounted. Such is, at times, the case with Albert Pike. It is often difficult to imagine Albert Pike as *a* player (rather than as *the* player) in American Scottish Rite events of the 1800s. Pike's monumental mark on the Southern Jurisdiction can mask the fact that his influence was not always as profound as it was in his later years. Regardless of his many accomplishments, there was a time when Illustrious Brother Pike was but an inexperienced yet promising Mason with a blank book before him upon which it was unknown exactly what would be written.

This address, the first ever given by Pike as the presiding officer of a Scottish Rite body, gives us a rare look at the early Albert Pike. While in his later years, many viewed Pike as a true Master of the Scottish Rite, this address clearly calls into notice his immaturity in the Rite, and he asks for "lenient judgment"

Albert Pike

upon his "shortcomings." In his address, Pike is clearly humble and seems sincerely appreciative of his election. He notes that his election to the position of Commander in Chief was politic in nature and due to "circumstances that surround us." What could have caused a political election of the untried Albert Pike as the presiding officer of the Grand Consistory of Louisiana? Let's take a look at the "circumstances."

Just seven years prior to Pike's assuming the leadership of the Grand Consistory of Louisiana, the whole of Louisiana Masonry underwent a dramatic shift in direction, leadership, and character. Louisiana was the most "foreign" Grand Lodge (as well as state) in the U.S. Over time, many did not view this as an acceptable situation. There was a desire to "be like everyone else." Albert Pike, however, played no part in the troubled events in Louisiana Masonry before the merger of the two Grand Lodges in Louisiana and the Concordat of 1855.

Albert Pike was an attorney by profession and a Mason of only five years when he moved his law practice to New Orleans in 1855.[2] Three years earlier, Pike received the Scottish Rite degrees up to the 32° from Albert Mackey in Charleston. Mackey saw a unique quality in Pike and recruited him to be on the ritual committee of the Charleston Supreme Council. Mackey lent Pike a collection of Scottish Rite rituals for his review and study. It was through the examination and transcription of these rituals that Pike received his first understanding of the AASR. Busy with setting up his law practice and studying the rituals lent to him by Mackey, Pike did not concern himself with the momentous developments taking place in New Orleans at the time of his arrival.

One of Pike's earliest Masonic acquaintances in New Orleans was Charles Laffon de Ladébat. Over the years (even after Pike became Grand Commander), these two would maintain a "love/hate" relationship that was founded on a basic respect for each other. Ladébat was made a 33° by James Foulhouze in the Supreme Council of Louisiana on February 11, 1852, and served as its Grand Secretary at the time of the Concordat of 1855. Ladébat would later be elected an Active Member of the Charleston Supreme Council in 1859. Pike's time in New Orleans put him in close contact with many competent New Orleans 33rds who were quite capable of completing Pike's education, and understanding of the AASR Ladébat was, clearly, one of Pike's early mentors.

Just as he had done with Albert Mackey, Pike greatly impressed the New Orleans Scottish Rite Masons. Pike's talent and raw abilities made him a candidate for any Masonic office. The fact that Pike played no part whatsoever in the Concordat of 1855 may have made Pike even more attractive and a prime candidate for leading the Grand Consistory of Louisiana. Pike did not carry baggage with him from the Louisiana Masonic turmoil. While he was under the jurisdiction of the Charleston Supreme Council at the time of the Concordat, he was not an Active Member and played no part in any of the decisions concerning the Concordat. No one could blame Pike for any of the events. Albert Pike was the only serious candidate for leading the Grand Consistory who could be seen as potentially objective as well as extraordinarily promising. Next to James Foulhouze, no one had a better chance of appeasing the French Masons and unifying all the factions. Once the Supreme Council of Louisiana was reorganized, Pike's value to the Charleston cause was even more evident.

This address, given by Pike four days after he received the 33°,[3] is valuable to Scottish Rite researchers not only because it is a rare piece of early Pike literature, but because of the significant information provided. From this address, we get a better feel of the early Albert Pike and have the opportunity to develop a more detailed understanding of the events that were taking place at the time Albert Pike arrived on the Scottish Rite stage. Within two years from the time of this address, Pike was elected an Active Member of the Southern Jurisdiction (over the apparent objections of the Grand Commander and Lt. Grand Commander),[4] and then on January 2, 1859, with the very first SJ election of officers (a dramatic change in practice), be elected to the position of Sovereign Grand Commander.

Pike's address was ordered to be recorded in the handwritten Minutes of the Grand Consistory of Louisiana. A typed transcript of this address was made by an unknown Brother sometime between the 1940s and 1950s, and a copy of the transcript was acquired by this writer. The accuracy of the transcript has been verified by a comparison of the transcript with the original Minutes located in the Scottish Rite Bodies of New Orleans.

ADDRESS BEFORE THE
GRAND CONSISTORY OF LOUISIANA

By ALBERT PIKE
April 29, 1857

Th∴ Ill∴ Bros∴ and Sublime Princes of the Royal Secret:

I pray you to accept my most sincere thanks and profoundest gratitude for the great and unexpected honor which you conferred upon me, when, in my absence, you selected me to fill the most honorable and very responsible station of Grand Commander of this Grand Consistory and for your present ratification of that choice. I will earnestly endeavor to have myself not wholly undeserving of your good opinion; so that, although it must now be said that when elected I was not worthy either by service or qualification, it may not hereafter be said that when I cease to serve, you repented of your selection.

I can bring to your service, Princes, little more than good intentions, kind feelings, and a zealous devotion to the interest of Masonry of all Rites — when you find me deficient (and wherein shall I not, alas, be found, Bros∴?) I entreat of you in advance lenient judgment upon my short-comings, and that you will kindly aid me with your sympathy, support and advice. For I must be ever embarrassed by the reflection that I have been by your too favorable judgment preferred to many eminent and distinguished Brethren, whose longer service and greater familiarity with the work gave them far higher claims than any I could have preferred to the post of honor and command. If I supposed that personal consideration or a belief in my superior fitness and capacity had led you to this choice, I should sink under a sense of my feebleness, not ever have succeeded in overcoming my repugnance to accept a post where so much was to be expected. But, amass that there were other reasons, which acted upon you, and made your selection seem politic and for the interest of Masonry in this Valley, reasons not personal to me, but growing out of the conditions of things and the circumstances that surrounded us. I am encouraged to hope that I may in some degree aid in attaining the result which you all desire, and that your just expectations may not be disappointed.

I have accordingly accepted the post which you have tendered me, and will endeavor to perform its duties. Most important private business will compel my absence for some months. I shall return as soon as practicable, and remain thereafter permanently in the city.[5]

Should the interest of the Order at any time be likely to suffer by my temporary absence, I shall be prepared at once to surrender up my office, faintly imitating the lofty magnanimity, of which so beautiful an example has been set me by an Ill∴ Bro∴ whose genius and labors have done so much to restore the splendors of the Ancient and Accepted Rite[6] in this Valley, and whose name will not be forgotten among us, while the order of Knights Rose Croix continues to exist, or the Kadosh to war against tyranny and usurpation.

But I shall most sensibly feel how great will be the contrast between myself, with my slender experience, and the Th∴ Ill∴ Prince and Sovereign whose place I come to take, but not fill.[7] Eminent in Masonic learning and more illustrious by long and faithful service than even by his high rank and lofty station, the new and supreme dignity recently conferred upon him was a most just and appropriate acknowledgment of his worth. This Consistory must most sensibly feel its loss, as he, Ill∴ Gr ∴ Commander, crowned and laureled with the highest honor, and with the grateful thanks and recollections of his brethren, most gracefully retires from this distinguished post, to yield it of his own choice to another. I beseech him not to withdraw from me his counsel and advice, and I pray him and our Ill∴ Bro∴ Laffon,[8] and the other eminent brethren who surround me, to aid me, to advise me, to support me in my inexperience, that, guided by them I may not despair of rendering some little service to the cause of humanity, to the cause of truth, of liberty, of philosophy, and of Masonic progress.

My brethren, I see around me the representatives of more than one race,[9] and the disciples of more than one Masonic Rite — I rejoice at this reunion, and it gives me happy augury of the prosperity, health, and continuance of Masonry in this Valley. I am especially glad that here and in other bodies of this Rite, I see by the side of the children of the first generous and gallant settlers of Louisiana, many of another land, and who not long since for the first time passed beyond the boundaries of the York Rite.

We are all aware, my brethren, how little among Masons of the latter Rite is known of the Ancient & Accepted Rite, and how great and general a prejudice has obtained those against it. It has been imagined that there was antagonism between the two: Scottish Masonry has been deemed almost spurious, and its degrees, at the best, no more than mere side degrees; and the York Mason who has entered into our sanctuaries has been regarded in the estimation of many, as untrue to his allegiance and disloyal.

Those of you, my brethren, who lately have known only the York Rite, are already aware how unfounded is this prejudice, how erroneous this opinion, how chimerical these apprehensions and alarms. It shall be my study to make you more fully to know this hereafter.

The Ancient and Accepted Rite is, when itself fully developed and understood, when itself what it should be and can be, a great, harmonious and connected system, all the degrees and lessons, embody the philosophy, the history, the morality and the essential meaning of Masonry, and are to us what the Ancient mysteries were to the initiate of Eleusis, of Egypt, and of Samothrace.

The degrees of this Rite are commentaries on the Master's Degree, which itself is essentially the same in all Rites. They interpret instead of being at variance with that degree. They ultimately make it known to the Initiate the true word and the true meaning and inner sense of the True Word of a Mason. They teach the great doctrines that God taught the Patriarchs, and which are the foundations on which all religions repose.

We do not undervalue symbolic Masonry, nor love it the less because we also love the Ancient & Accepted Rite, we but learn justly to value the Master's degree, by coming to understand its full meaning and to appreciate the sublime and lofty lessons which it teaches. Masonry is one everywhere and in all its Temples of whatever Rite; as it has been one in all times. Everywhere it teaches the same great lessons of morality and philosophy, or should do so, if faithful to its mission, and if its apostles are properly informed and true to the duties which it imposes on them. If anywhere it has excluded from even the inmost Sanctuaries of its Temples men of any faith who believe in Our Supreme God, Creator and Preserver of all things that become, and in the immortality of the Soul-if it has anywhere assumed the garb of religious exclusion and intolerance, of Jesuitism, of political vengeance, of Hermetic Mysticism, there most assuredly it has ceased to be Masonry.

It would not be true to say, however, that even Scottish Masonry has adequately fulfilled or been equal to its missions. While by the irresistible influence of time, by innovations and by mutilations and corruptions of ignorance, the degrees of the York Rite have long since ceased to be what they should be, and what they were in the beginning, when they succeeded to those ancient academies of science, philosophy and morality, the mysteries; while the practice of confirming everything contained in them to the memory has by the silent lapse of time caused more and more both of ceremony and substance to be forgotten, much to be intentionally dropped, and the field of each degree to be made more and more narrow; while the true meaning of very many of their most valuable symbols have faded away and disappeared, and been replaced by commonplace, and the inventions of ignorance, and the lofty science and profound teachings, of the Ancients have too much given way to unimpressive phrases and valueless formulas, — the Scottish Rite also has not enjoyed immunity from the ravages of the biting tooth of time, universal destroyer of all human beings.

For even here, where over the Temples of our Degrees stood perfect and complete in all the splendor and Majesty of their beautiful and harmonious proportions, we are like strangers from a far land who wander amid the shattered columns and wrecked glories of Thebes and Palmyra, and union over the ruins that track the steps of time, and over the instability of all earthly things. From many of our degrees everything has dropped out except the signs and words, and they remain half effaced and corrupted. From more, all is lost except these and some unimportant formulas; in still more, useless repetition arrives at impressiveness, but cannot renunciate us for the old science and the noble philosophy whose place it endeavors to supply. Those huge chasms have been created in the work, and the connections between the degrees have been broken; so that each has become a fragment instead of being, as at first part of one consistent, regularly progressive and harmonious whole.

Thus it has come that of the degrees from the fourth to the thirty-second inclusive, which we retain and apply to ourselves the sounding titles, four only are habitually conferred, which all the residue remain in a great measure, and part of them altogether unknown.

It had become so obvious that this Rite needed reformation, and that either its degrees should all be made worthy to be conferred and of value to be attained, or else those which were not so ought to be abandoned and their titles disused, that more than two years ago the Supreme Council at Charleston appointed a Committee of five Brethren to revise the whole ritual of the degrees; on which Committee I had the distinguished honor to be placed. While my Brother Laffon, both before and after he was also placed there in the stead of my Brother Samory, who to the general regret found himself compelled to decline the act.[10] While my Brother Laffon labored, more particularly on the 18th Degree, but not alone on that, I also, undertaking at first a few degrees, continued my labors during two years, until I completed a revision of all; which that it may be thoroughly examined and sanctioned, I have printed in a volume and submitted to the Supreme Council. Whether that August Body will stamp it or any part of it with its approval, is wholly unknown to me. I have endeavored to restore the effaced or faded lineament of many of the degrees to develop and elaborate the great leading idea of each, to correct the whole together as a regular series, and to make of them our harmonious and systematic whole, ascending by regular graduations to the highest moral and philosophical truth — I have endeavored to prime away all commonplaces and puerility's, all unmeaning forms and ceremonies, all absurd interpretations, and everything useless or injurious with which time and ignorance had overloaded the degrees. I have endeavored so to restore, to retouch and to supply, retaining all that was valuable and working up all the old material, as to make every degree worth to be conferred: that there should be no longer any empty tile, or barren honors in the Ancient & Accepted Rite.

This I have attempted; but I am only too well aware that the undertaking was too great for my furios; and that what I have done will be found full of imperfections, as the work of the painter, the sculpture, the creator, and the poet ever falls short of his own ideal.

Still I have endeavored to do somewhat; and it is my desire, at some appropriate future time, and with your consent and assistance, to confer upon some suitable candidate such of the degrees, as I have revised them, as have not been already revised by other and more competent hands.

I congratulate you, my brethren, on the advancement and progress of the Ancient & Accepted Rite in this Valley: The Concordat by which the Supreme Jurisdiction of the Supreme Council at Charleston was acknowledged and under which the two Consistories then existing became one, laid broad and deep the strong foundations of the prosperity of our Rite. The walls of our Temple, solidly and squarely built, bid defiance to the storms of faction; and if we are true to ourselves, peace will dwell within our gates.

And in the Realm of Masonry, if anywhere on earth, there ought to be peace and quiet and harmony. No where are schism and faction, and disunion and discontent so lamentably out of place as here. Here there should be no lust for power and no eagerness for rank or distinction. If discontented men should in this valley have established, or if any shall hereafter establish, under a foreign authority which has no jurisdiction here and act only by usurpation, any body or bodies, claiming to administer the Ancient & Accepted Rite, we shall, I think, be prepared to show that the Supreme Council at Charleston, to which we owe allegiance, is the only legitimate authority in the Rite that can exist in our country south of the River Potomac; and that the Grand Orient of France and the Supreme Council within its bosom offered against Masonic Law and Masonic

Comity where they made another jurisdiction and erect their banners on the soil of Louisiana.

It is time that this question should be receive the fullest consideration; and that the authentic history of the creation of the Grand Orient itself and of that of the Supreme Council of France, of the disputes between those two bodies and their temporary alliance should be made known to the order in the United States. Supplied with the emissary documents on both sides, it is every intention to translate them and make them public, that all may judge where is the right and where the usurpation.

The time when fables would pass for history has gone by; and that has come when criticism and investigation will deal with the history of Masonry as with other histories, separating the truth from the error, and after reducing great pretensions to the narrowest proportions. Let us examine the history the Ancient & Accepted Rite and the Grand Orient in that spirit and by the rules and canons of sound criticism, never forgetting that courtesy, moderation, and kindness ought to inspire all Masonic discussions, hoping to find a like tone and spirit on the other side, and that those who may array themselves against us will, if Right and Truth be found with us, candidly admit it, and uniting with us acknowledge the same allegiance and so cause peace ever and ever to reign in this valley.

My Brethren, let me impress it upon you, that there is much to do, if we would have Masonry adequately fulfill its mission. It is not sufficient merely to receive three or four of the degrees, and then, imagining the rest, to live in contented indolence, without an effort to know the high science and philosophy of the system. The time has come when one who would be truly and really be a Scottish Rite Mason must study and reflect. It shall be my earnest endeavor to aid you in penetrating to the inmost heart of Masonry and in unveiling its profound secrets, which are that light towards which all Masons at least profess to struggle, that knowledge of the True Work which is the great remuneration of a Mason's labor. But if I should fall short of the performance of this duty, be not you, my brethren, disheartened nor discouraged. Masonry must be true to itself, or it will find in numbers weakness only, and its walls will be crushed to the ground with its own might. In this intellectual and practical age. Masonry must it from merited disaster and dissolution.

It is time for it to assume a higher ground; and here, if any where, the effort to elevate it must be made. Here, I believe, we can commence and successfully carry onward the indispensable work of reformation, that shall in time end the reign of puerility's and trivialities, and make masonry what it should be. The great teacher of moral and philosophical truth; the teacher of the primitive religion known to the first men that lived; the defender of the right of free thought, free conscience and free speech; the apostle of rational and well regulated liberty; the protector of the oppressed, the defender of the common people, the asserter of the dignity of labor and the right of the laboring man; the enemy of intolerance, fanaticism and uncharitable opinion, and of all idle and pernicious theories that arraign providence for its dispensations, and endeavor to set their notions of an abstract justice and equality above the laws by which God chooses to rule all human affairs.

In this great work I wish your co-operation, and I ask, for myself and for those eminent brethren who are to act with me and in my place, your countenance, your assistance, and your encouragement. I am sure my brethren that I shall not ask this in vain; and that grateful, deeply grateful as I now am for your confidence and kindness, I shall be far more so, and with far greater reason, when I am allowed to surrender into your hands the trust which you have so generously confided to me.

Notes:

1. Charles Laffon de Ladébat to Albert Pike, June 24, 1860. Archives of the Supreme Council, 33°, SJ, Washington. Photocopy in possession of the author.
2. Pike's law office was located in downtown New Orleans in a building on the riverside of Camp Street one block from Canal Street. The building no longer exists. *New Orleans City Directory*, 1856.
3. After the Concordat of 1855, the Active Members of the New Orleans Supreme Council were brought in as Honorary Members of the Charleston Supreme Council. As with all Honorary Members of a Supreme Council, they held the 33° but not the active office of Sovereign Grand Inspector General (SGIG). It was at this time that the Charleston Supreme Council began elevating 32° Masons to the 33° but not including the office of SGIG in their elevation. Albert Pike was one of the first 32° in the SJ elevated to the 33° without being invested with the office of SGIG Pike would be elected an Active Member (SGIG) of the Charleston Supreme Council on March 20,1858.
4. "...*I was not the last to devise the means of placing you at the head of the order, 1st by making you a 33rd against the will of Messrs. Furman & Honour: 2nd by vacating my office of Deputy in your favor, & twice you got in the S.C. & especially twice you were unanimously elected to the Presidency, I consider myself as having done my duty, all I could do. The lifeless council of Charleston was revived; it lives now! Only now tho!*" Ladébat to Pike, Jun. 24, 1860.
5. *The New Orleans City Directories* from 1856 until 1859 show that while Pike had opened a law office in New Orleans, he did not have more than a temporary home in the city. The Minutes of the Grand Consistory also reveal that he was absent for many of the meetings of the Grand Consistory. There is no record that Pike ever moved his family to New Orleans, and it is probable that he traveled between his home in Little Rock and New Orleans. One of the many boarding houses in New Orleans would have likely been his residence during his stays in the city. Despite Pike's statement, New Orleans would never be his permanent home.
6. At the time of this address, the term *Ancient and Accepted Scottish Rite* was not in common use in the U.S. This accounts for Pike's repeated use of the older (in the U.S.) term *Ancient and Accepted Rite.*

7. Pike refers to Claude Pierre Samory. Samory was elected an Active Member of the Charleston Supreme Council on Nov. 20, 1856.

8. Charles Laffon de Ladébat.

9. Freemasonry in pre-Civil War New Orleans was reflective of the New Orleans culture of the time. Pierre Roup was the son-in-law of New Orleans Mason and Battle of New Orleans hero Dominique Youx. Roup was a member of Perseverance Lodge No. 4 and sat on the lodge's building committee. He was an African-American Creole. While it is clear that there were more than a few African-American Creoles who were members of New Orleans lodges, identifying them is difficult as a member's race was not a question asked or recorded except in notable situations. It is quite possible that there were African-American Creole members of the Grand Consistory of Louisiana present at the time of Pike's address. It is, likewise, possible that Pike used the word "race" in reference to the French Masons who were often considered part of the "Latin race".

10. On p. 249 of his *History of the Supreme Council 33°, A.&A.S.R. S.J., U.S.A (1801- 1864)* (Washington: Supreme Council, 33°, 1964) Ray Baker Harris, 33°, reproduces a letter sent by Albert Mackey to Claude Samory dated Mar. 21, 1855. The letter concerns the Southern Jurisdiction's Ritual Committee and lists its members. Claude Samory is listed as the member from New Orleans and Albert Pike the member from Little Rock. Ill. Harris writes: *"From all indications, the 'preparation of new copies' was in the hands of Albert Pike. He was then in New Orleans, and may have conferred with Samory in this work, but neither of them ever mentioned such a collaboration in their numerous letters written in this period."* Until this address by Pike was rediscovered, it was assumed by most Scottish Rite scholars that Samory was on this committee with Pike for a substantial period of time. Bro. Harris, assuming that Samory remained on the committee, logically wondered about the absence of communications between Pike and Samory concerning ritual matters. This address brings to light the fact that Samory retired from the committee shortly after his appointment to be replaced by Ladébat. The collaboration was not between Pike and Samory, but between Pike and Ladébat. This makes the degrees written by Pike and Ladébat and their communications understandable.

My Story of Discovering the Present Day
Supreme Council of Louisiana

I joined Freemasonry in New Orleans in 1975. Like most all who join, my actual knowledge of Masonry at that time was very limited and superficial. I had several family members who were Masons, but I really knew only the very basics of the nature of Freemasonry and certainly not much in the area of Masonic history. Several years later, I joined the Valley of New Orleans. I knew even less about the Scottish Rite. I did, however, know one thing very clearly — I was impressed to no end with the Masonic philosophy and ritual, especially concerning the Scottish Rite.

While I was very impressed with the Scottish Rite, there was another aspect of which I became quickly aware. The Valley of New Orleans was, for lack of a better term, an emotional place. Laughter in the valley could be quick, deep, and genuine. But at the same time, there was a cloud of hurt and anger that always seemed present and could surface almost any time. I didn't understand why at the time, but the emotion in the valley was tangible.

My craft lodge had two members who were 33rds in the New Orleans Valley. In itself, that is not such an unusual accomplishment as many lodges can boast of members who hold the 33rd degree. What was, however, very unusual about these members was the title in the Scottish Rite that they both held. They were both Past Grand Masters of Kadosh of the

Grand Consistory of Louisiana. That's a title you don't hear every day. You see, from 1811[1] until 1973 (just several years before I joined), the Valley of New Orleans was the Grand Consistory of Louisiana. The presiding officer of the grand consistory was the Grand Master of Kadosh. In 1973, Sovereign Grand Commander Henry Clausen downgraded the Grand Consistory of Louisiana (the last grand consistory under

Henry Clausen

the Southern Jurisdiction) into a statutory consistory of the Valley of New Orleans.[2] This action of abolishing the Grand Consistory can explain much (but not all) of the bad feelings in the valley at the time of my joining. There was a general feeling that much was being, and had been, unfairly taken from New Orleans.

Whenever I talk on this subject, the question often arises, "What is a grand consistory?" To give you a little background, a grand consistory is a Scottish Rite body subordinate to a supreme council but superior to lodges of perfection or other Scottish Rite bodies. In the grand lodge system, you might think of a grand consistory as something along the lines of a provincial grand lodge. Its job was to provide local supervision to bodies under the jurisdiction of the supreme council but at a considerable distance from the council itself.[3] The collective voice and vote of a grand consistory carried the same authority as a Sovereign Grand Inspector General. The Valley of New Orleans, and that includes its time as the Grand Consistory of Louisiana, is the oldest continually active high-grade body of Ancient and Accepted Scottish Rite Masonry in North or South America.

Another body that I learned about soon after joining the Valley of New Orleans was a body identified to me as the "New Orleans Supreme Council." Wow, what a collection of stories I remember learning about this body! And, what an exercise in contradiction. After reading a few of the books and documents and listening to members, I had no idea in the world who or what to believe concerning this body. When I listened to the stories told by some of the then senior members of the valley, I learned of a near-mythical body akin to a Shangri-La or Camelot where everything was done correctly. Everyone was wise & kind, and all were content. But then, the stories continued, others became jealous of this utopian paradise. Outsiders wished the New Orleans Scottish Rite harm and sought all they possessed. The New Orleans Scottish Rite Masons were tricked, lied to, and destroyed just so that everything good about them could be taken away.

Interestingly enough, there was another side to the coin and a *very* different story. When I read any of the old Scottish Rite history books, and that included the grand-daddy of all Louisiana Masonic history books, *Outline of the Rise and Progress of Freemasonry in Louisiana*, a completely different tale was told. In these accounts, it was the New Orleans Supreme Council who were the bad guys. It was not just a body of Masons who held a different view of Masonry, nor was it simply an irregular body. The New Orleans Supreme Council was a collection of morally corrupt gangsters. They were portrayed as near monsters who would steal the Masonic souls of the naive and foolish, all so that they could practice their perverted Scottish Rite abomination.

I couldn't believe what I was reading and hearing. This was not just a little difference of opinion; the stories were complete spectrum opposites. The "other guys" were not just wrong but pure evil! I was absolutely fascinated. I also found it amazing that both sides offered their arguments with an outrageous lack of evidence and always with extreme emotion. The *only* thing that both sides agreed upon was that this supreme council died off in the late 1800s.

There was no question in my mind - I *had* to do my own research into this astonishing historical puzzle. I just needed a place to start.

My first goal was to collect and study as many of the old Masonic and Scottish Rite history books as I could find. Most were long out of print. I visited used bookstores as well as Masonic, public, and university libraries. When I could not buy a book, I would find one in a library or elsewhere and photocopy it. I spent months pouring over these books. The next step was to try and locate as many of the documents mentioned in the books as possible. I contacted the then Grand Secretary of the Grand Lodge of Louisiana, RW Brother Jack Crouch, and the then Sovereign Grand Inspector General in Louisiana, Ill Brother D. Walter Jessen, and asked both for letters of introduction. Both kindly gave me wonderful letters, which allowed me to contact grand lodges and supreme councils with questions and requests for aid in my search.

As my search for documents continued, I began to realize that it was necessary for me to travel to various locations and do "boots on the ground" research (the internet did not exist in those days). I visited both the Southern Jurisdiction and Northern Masonic Jurisdiction in my quest. Both supreme council visits brought me valuable documents from which I gained insight, but my trip to the Southern Jurisdiction brought much more.

I was in communication with Dr. John Boettcher, the then Editor of the *Scottish Rite Journal*, for some time. The communications normally concerned things I had written and were published in both the *Scottish Rite Journal* and its earlier incarnation, *The New Age*. I also worked on several research projects with the then Librarian of the House of the Temple, Mrs. Inge Baum. I contacted Dr. Boettcher and made plans for a visit. I explained that I was looking for any documents relating to early Scottish Rite Masonry in Louisiana and the troubled times of the "Scottish Rite war" before and after the Concordat of 1855.[4]

Upon arriving at the House of the Temple, I was greeted by Dr. Boettcher. He gave me a tour of the massive building. As we walked into the library, I was impressed with the extensive collection of books. But really, I expected nothing less. We were greeted by a slight, elderly lady smiling from ear to ear; it was Mrs. Baum. After a few friendly words, she led me to a long, beautiful table that took up a large portion of the room. The table had chairs on both sides and at the head and foot. I noticed a large stack of papers right to the side of the head of the table. This is where Mrs. Baum was leading me. She pointed at the papers and told me that this was the collection of Louisiana documents that I had requested. There was an odd smile and look in her eyes. She then asked me if I knew why she had placed the documents in that particular spot on the table. I told her that I had no idea. She then said with a large smile that this was where the last person who requested Louisiana documents always sat when he studied them. She then asked me if I knew who she was speaking about. I told her that I did not. With an even larger smile, she said, "Mr. Clausen." With a bit of surprise, I asked her if she meant Past Sovereign Grand Commander Henry Clausen. She said yes and that he came to the library several times a week, sat in that spot, and studied anything and everything he could find concerning the Louisiana Scottish Rite and Louisiana Masonry. I was more than surprised and filed that information away for later consideration.

On the same trip, I planned on visiting the Grand Lodge of the District of Columbia. I had communicated a number of times with the then Grand Secretary, MWBro Stewart Miner, and became friendly with him. He was very interested in Masonic research and greatly assisted me in researching his grand lodge's archives. During my visit, MWBro Miner told me he wanted me to meet several young researchers with whom he had become acquainted over the last few years. He said one, in particular, had also shown great interest in researching the early history of the Scottish Rite. He was a Texas Mason by the name of Arturo de Hoyos. Over the next few years, Art and I would become good friends and make trips to the House of the Temple together in search of Scottish Rite documents. We also spent countless hours on the phone discussing the "lost history" of the Scottish Rite. Bro. de Hoyos shared my interest in the enigma of the New Orleans Supreme Council. It was an amazing academic, Masonic detective mystery.

As I began to delve deeper into the books and documents concerning the troubled Scottish Rite times of the mid-1800s and the heartbreaking war that turned Brother against Brother, an extraordinarily depressing picture started emerging. The language in the books, from both sides, was akin to spitting acid. It didn't matter if it were James Foulhouze, Albert Pike, or whoever was writing; it was all so very harsh. I felt physically ill when I would stop and realize that these were *Masons* speaking to and about other Masons. I had never read anything that reached this level of near hatred. Every possible insult, attack, and nastiness was levied against "the other guys" simply because they existed. No one would give an inch. Looking from the outside, I could see that neither side was completely right or wrong. The only thing that both sides shared was that *neither* were acting very Masonic. The heart of the problem seemed to be ego. Neither side could admit that they could be in *any way* wrong or the other in *any way* right. They both sacrificed Masonry for pride. It was truly the saddest collection of documents I had ever read. All they had to do was put their hand out and welcome the other. The fact that they were both living in glass houses and both insistent on throwing rocks seemed to escape them. Honestly, there were no winners in that war.

Some months later, on a visit to the Grand Lodge of Louisiana, I was asked by the Grand Secretary if I could take over communicating with someone who I was told was a "French Brother living in Germany." I was told that the brother had shown great interest in the early history of Louisiana Masonry but was asking questions that no one in the Grand Lodge office could answer. I was shown the last letter the brother wrote. I recognized the name immediately. It was WBrother Alain Bernheim.

Over the next few months and years, Bro. Bernheim and I became good friends. We would write to each other regularly (starting with postal mail and then e-mail), sharing information on Masonic research with special attention to the early history of Louisiana Freemasonry and its Scottish Rite. In one mail to Bro Bernheim, I wrote about how I felt it was such a shame that a body that seemed to be so very regular and Masonic in nature as the New Orleans Supreme Council could cease to exist. I lamented the loss of this historic and significant body. He wrote me back a very short e-mail. He said that he only had two questions for me. The first was why did I continually call that body the "New Orleans Supreme Council" when their correct name is "The Supreme Council of Louisiana?" The second question was, why did I continually say that they no longer existed?

I was stunned. As to the first question, I called them that because that was how I had always heard them called in New Orleans. I knew their official name but used the common term that I had repeatedly heard used. As to the second astonishing question, I told Bro. Bernheim, I assumed they no longer existed because I have never heard or read a single word to the contrary. I had never seen a scrap of evidence to suggest that they still existed. He wrote back, saying that I was in New Orleans, and he was halfway around the world. He said that if I am so sure of their non-existence, then the accounts he learned of must be incorrect.

I remember sitting in the chair at my desk, thinking about my exchange with Bro. Bernheim. How ridiculous. I had been a Mason by that time for some 20 years in New Orleans. Not once did I *ever* hear anything of the supreme council still existing. But what a resounding kick in the pants it would be if they did exist. As I was sitting there, I looked over at the telephone book on my desk. I stared at it for a time and then laughed to myself. It simply could not be possible that they were listed in the phone book. That was too easy. I could no longer help myself, I had to look. I picked up the phone book and flipped through the pages.

I cannot tell you exactly how I felt next. I imagine the best way to describe it was the old image of someone falling out of their chair in shock. There in the phone book, as big as life was listed, *"The Supreme Council of Louisiana."* What in the world was going on? Was I in an episode of *The Twilight Zone*? I just sat there for a little while, totally bewildered. Then I did the only thing I could think of doing. I picked up the phone and called the number listed. They answered the phone, *"Supreme Council of Louisiana."* I had no idea what to say. Finally, I said that I had a question to ask. I asked if they were the same supreme council that was created in 1839. The voice on the

The Supreme Council of Louisiana located at 3200 St. Bernard Ave. in New Orleans. Hurricane Katrina destroyed this building.

phone came back with, "Yes, we are." I thanked him and hung up. What in the world was going on? I had by then spent many years digging into the early history of a body that I *thought* had ceased to exist in the late 1800s. Am I now to believe that they still exist? How stupid could I be? But, in my defense, not *once* did I *ever* see, hear, or read *anything* to suggest that they still existed. And, really, what proof did I have that they did still exist? Anyone can list a phone under whatever name they like. That's no proof at all. So, I grabbed my keys, went out to the car, and drove to the address given in the phone book.

I recognized the building as I drove up. I had passed by it many times over the years, noticed the signs, but never paid much of any attention to it. I had always assumed that it was some fly-by-night Masonic self-creation. I parked the car and went inside. There were several African-American men inside, and one introduced himself as the Secretary-General. He then introduced me to the Sovereign Grand Commander, Philip Washington, Sr. I introduced myself and told them that I had been researching the early history of the Scottish Rite and Freemasonry in Louisiana. I felt a bit uncomfortable as I had no idea if this could possibly be the real deal or if they had simply found some old documents or records and created a body with an old name. In other words, I didn't know if they were frauds or not.

We talked just a little, and most of it was superficial. I then asked if they had a list of their Sovereign Grand Commanders from the time of their creation. The secretary said that he thought he had something like that around. He looked through his desk and pulled out a piece of paper. He made a photocopy of it and gave me a copy. I thanked them all and left.

When I got home, I looked at the paper I was given (See: Appendix D & E). It started with a list of names that I knew well. But, after Eugene Chassaignac, began a long list of names that I had never seen before. At that time, I noticed something that gave me reason to believe that the body I had just visited was, indeed, a self-created, fraudulent body. Following Eugene Chassaignac were 19 names listed as Sovereign Grand Commanders. 17 of the names were printed with the last two (Joseph Williams, 1987 and Philip Washington, Sr., 1993) handwritten onto the list. The last printed name was George Longe, showing that he was elected Sovereign Grand Commander in 1938. That's almost 50 years between the election of George Longe and Joseph Williams. Prior to George Longe, most Sovereign Grand Commanders served only a few years. I had no idea how long George Longe served, but it seemed likely that *maybe* he served until sometime around WWII, and then the council died off to be recreated in 1987 by Joseph Williams.

Philip Washington, Sr.

What interested me most, at the time, were the 17 printed names (some serving more than once) that followed

Eugene Chassaignac. If these names were proven to actually be Sovereign Grand Commanders of the Supreme Council of Louisiana, then it would mean that the council existed far longer than had previously been believed. I wanted to find a way to check out these names and any possible association with the council. I went to the public library.

The New Orleans Public Library has provided me with a great deal of help in the past. Their main library had a microfilm section with most all the old newspapers published in New Orleans in the 1800s. My idea was to look up the death notices in the old papers for each of the names listed and to see if I could find anything of interest. To my amazement, for each and every name I searched, I found a death notice published in the newspaper by the Supreme Council of Louisiana. The notices were announcing the death of their Sovereign Grand Commander. Every single name was accounted for, and each carried a death notice from the council. It seemed that the Supreme Council of Louisiana had existed far longer than had been known. I realized that this was a major discovery. How they could have existed all this time with no record of their existence was a question I put aside for a later time. I then came to the name of George Longe. As I began the search for his death notice, I realized that, with this information, I would likely find the actual date of the death of the Supreme Council of Louisiana.

Earlier, I mentioned a discovery that was so surprising to me that I almost fell out of my chair. Well, that was when I was in the privacy of my home, sitting at my desk. For the same

George Longe

thing to happen to me in a public library was considerably more embarrassing. I found the death notice of George Longe. Like the others, it carried a notice from the Supreme Council of Louisiana. But George Longe didn't die until late 1985. My mind was whirling. If the council died in the 30s, 40s, or 50s, how could it announce his death in 1985?[5] Does this mean that George Longe served as Sovereign Grand Commander for almost 50 years? Does this mean that the body I visited is *actually* the very same supreme council that I learned about when I joined Masonry?

There were simply too many questions for me to deal with at that time. I needed a bit of time to process everything and think about the information in a logical and structured manner. I decided to take some time off and let things sink in and only then formulate my next steps. But, sometimes, things go differently than we plan.

George Longe

In boxing, there is something known as a one-two punch. The first part of that punch came at the library with the discovery concerning George Longe. The second part of the punch came the very next day. I went early to the University of New Orleans to pick up a French-to-English translation of an old Masonic document that I had found some time back. I was able to make my way through many of the old French writings, but when I suspected something was important, I would call on a friend of mine who was a French Professor at the university. I spoke to him about some of the discoveries. He was not a Mason but was very interested in Masonic history. He told me that I really should go to the history department and speak with one of the instructors there. She had recently received her PhD, and a good part of her dissertation was on, of all things, early Louisiana Freemasonry, especially Scottish Rite Freemasonry in New Orleans. I walked over to the history department and met Dr. Caryn Cossé Bell.[6] We talked for a while, and I gave her a few names of key figures in my research. She knew them all. I then asked her if she knew of George Longe. She said she knew of him well and asked if I visited "his collection" at Tulane University. I had not and didn't even know that it existed. Dr. Bell gave me directions to the building to find the collection, and I was off like a shot.

When I arrived at Tulane, I went to find the collection. [7] If I tried to explain how I felt when I saw what was in that collection, I imagine the best way to describe it is to think of that little boy upon first arriving in Willy Wonka's candy factory. I was overwhelmed. It was not just a large collection of Scottish Rite documents; it was a large collection of *very important* Scottish Rite documents. To give just one example, I found what is today known as *The Bonseigneur Rituals* within that collection.[8] It is a collection of 18th-century New Orleans Ecossais Masonic Rituals. Upon finding them, I sent a copy of these rituals to Alain Bernheim for dating. I also sent a copy to Gerald Prinsen of the Latomia Foundation in the Netherlands for publication. The rituals are a hand-written copy of a much older collection of rituals. The copy is dated as being made about 1785 to the early 1790s, and some of the rituals look to date prior to 1750. Even with this aside, it is very possibly the lost rituals of the Grand Lodge of Louisiana, being worked by the Grand Lodge and the five French-speaking lodges that created it. This significant find was made in *their* collection. To this day, I have yet to completely explore all the collection.

The first thing I did upon entering the collection was to pull out that list of Sovereign Grand Commanders and search for each of them. I was able to find letters, documents, diplomas, and other official records for each of them signing as the Sovereign Grand Commander of the Supreme Council of Louisiana. Yep, George Longe served as Sovereign Grand Commander for almost 50 years! There was now no doubt, the body known today as the Supreme Council of Louisiana is the very same body from the 1800s. But, apart from a footnote, what does it mean? Then, years later, came 2011.

It was the 200th anniversary of the creation of the Grand Consistory of Louisiana — the one valley of high-grade Ancient and Accepted Scottish Rite Freemasonry that continued to exist when all others in the United States slumbered. A foresighted Scottish Rite Honorary Sovereign Grand Inspector General and Past Grand Master of the Grand Lodge of Louisiana, Clayton J. Borne, III, felt that a celebration was in order and appointed me to the planning committee. He obtained permission and organized a Scottish Rite symposium where the Scottish Rite could be celebrated and studied using public lectures on the Scottish Rite. I had spoken many times about the Supreme Council of Louisiana. We thought that an invitation for them to attend such a celebration was in order.

On June 1st to 4th, 2011, for the first time in history, representatives of the Supreme Council, Southern Jurisdiction, USA; the Supreme Council of Louisiana and the Grand Lodge of Louisiana joined together with the representatives of other supreme councils and Grand Lodges to meet at the Royal Sonesta Hotel on Royal Street in New Orleans ... and peace and harmony prevailed. The symposium location was just steps away from where Albert Mackey met with James Foulhouze in Mackey's failed attempt to have Foulhouze join the Southern Jurisdiction.[9] There was no ritual, no "secrets" exchanged, no compromising situations. It was a public gathering that was, in this writer's experience, the most truly Masonic gathering I have ever attended. It was beautiful.

Through knowledge, we now have an opportunity. We will own the choices we make. But what will we do? Continue a pointless "war," continue a policy of "hidden in plain sight," or respect others who do the true work of the Scottish Rite? Do we battle against ourselves or against ignorance?

The beauty of the future is that it is an open book upon which we can write whatever path we choose. We now know far more about this aspect of our Scottish Rite history than we knew not too many years ago. And, with that knowledge, we can do whatever we like. The future of the Scottish Rite is up to us. I truly hope that we can put all the pain, misinformation, ego, and nonsense aside and once again become what the creators of Freemasonry knew *as* Freemasonry. I have deep faith in the Scottish Rite.

Current Sovereign Grand Commander
of the Supreme Council of Louisiana,
Ill Eddie Gabriel, 33°

Notes:

1. The earliest known appearance of the Grand Consistory of Louisiana was in New Orleans in 1811. There are, unfortunately, no known surviving minutes or documents from this body. Most of the information that has been collected concerning the 1811 Grand Consistory is recorded in a few secondary sources. James Scot gives us, in his 1873 *Outline of the Rise and Progress of Freemasonry in Louisiana*, a piece of information concerning this body by reproducing a communication dated 20 April 1811 from the Sov. Grand Consistory of Princes of the Royal Secret of Louisiana to Etoile Polaire Lodge. The communication seeks to establish relations between the Grand Consistory and Etoile Polaire Lodge. It is issued under the name of "Des Bois, Grand Secretary." (See: James Scot, *Outline of the Rise and Progress of Freemasonry in Louisiana* 1873 [New Orleans, LA: Cornerstone Book Publishers, reprint 2008.] pp. 21-22). Also, in his 1882 "Official Bulletin V," Albert Pike tells us that on March 28, 1811, the Grand Consistory of Louisiana was granted a charter by Louis Jean Lusson and Jean Baptiste Modeste Lefebvre, both SGIGs of the Supreme Council of Kingston, Jamaica. Pike also tells us that the Grand Consistory held its first meeting on Sunday, April 7, 1811, at 5 p.m. in the hall of Perfect Union Lodge. The meeting was attended by many of the "founding fathers" of Louisiana Freemasonry, who were Members of this Grand Consistory. (See: Albert Pike, *Official Bulletin of the Supreme Council of the 33rd Degree for the Southern Jurisdiction of the United States*. Washington, D.C. 1882). For many years 1813 was given as the creation date (incorrectly) for the Grand Consistory of Louisiana. This was the year the Grand Consistory passed under the jurisdiction of the Cerneau Sovereign Grand Consistory (supreme council) in New York. The Cerneau system used different names for some of their bodies. This is why from 1813 to the early 1830s, the surviving Minutes of the Grand Consistory of Louisiana show that it was known as the Grand COUNCIL of Louisiana. It was still a body of the 32nd degree but used a different name. So strong was the attachment to Cerneau by the Louisiana Masons that they seemed to have "forgotten" the time of their existence before Cerneau. (*Minutes Book of the Grand Consistory of Louisiana* [1822-1846]). Located in the *New Orleans Scottish Rite Bodies*. New Orleans, Louisiana.) See also: Michael R. Poll, "The Early Years of the Grand Consistory of Louisiana (1811-1815)." *Heredom Vol. 8*, (Washington, D.C., The Scottish Rite Research Society, 1999-2000) pp. 39-53., Arturo de Hoyos, "The Early Years of the Grand Consistory of Louisiana (1811-1815) - A Rejoinder" & Michael R. Poll, "A Few 'Rejoinder' Comments." Both: *Heredom Vol. 9*, (Washington, D.C., The Scottish Rite Research Society, 2001) pp. 69-110.

2. "For multiple reasons, I directed that the Grand Consistory of Louisiana be converted into a statutory consistory of the Valley of New Orleans. I outlined the required procedure and our Grand Secretary General processed the necessary papers. Grand Consistories were inaugurated when communications over long distances were difficult. Later they were found to be impediment to effective administration so became outmoded. All except Louisiana had been converted into statutory consistories. There is no longer any sanction under our Statues for a Grand Consistory." -Henry C. Clausen, 33°, Sovereign Grand Commander. See: *Transactions of the Supreme Council, 33° for the Southern Jurisdiction, USA* (Washington, D.C., Supreme Council, 33° Southern Jurisdiction, USA, 1973) p. 46.

3. See: Albert Mackey, *An Encyclopedia of Freemasonry* (New York , NY, The Masonic History Company, 1925), p. 305.

4. See: Ray Baker Harris, James D. Carter, *History of the Supreme Council, 33° Southern Jurisdiction, USA (1801-1861)* (Washington, D.C., Supreme Council, 33° Southern Jurisdiction, USA, 1964) This Scottish Rite "war" centered itself on the reawakened "Charleston Supreme Council" (Supreme Council, Southern Jurisdiction, *USA*) and the "New Orleans Supreme Council" (Supreme Council of Louisiana). The two councils argued over regularity, with half of the Supreme Council of Louisiana signing a concordat in 1855 to pass under the jurisdiction of the Charleston Council and half refusing to participate. In 1856, the half of the Supreme Council of Louisiana, which refused to sign the concordat, announced that the signing of the Charleston concordat was illegal and that the Supreme Council of Louisiana continued to exist. In 1857, the powerful Past Sovereign Grand Commander, attorney, and judge, James Foulhouze, returned as Sovereign Grand Commander of the New Orleans Council. The Charleston Council answered with the young attorney, Albert Pike, being elected Sovereign Grand Commander in 1859 (the first *election* of a Grand Commander in the Charleston Council's history). The two went toe to toe in an epic battle equaling the Charleston/Cerneau battle some years earlier. See also: James Foulhouze, *Historical Inquiry into the Origins of the Ancient and Accepted Scottish Rite*, 1858, (New Orleans, LA: Cornerstone Book Publishers, reprint 2012).

5. It did not escape me that George Longe's death was in 1985, but the next Sovereign Grand Commander was not elected until 1987. I learned later that Longe was suffering from dementia for a number of years prior to his death. During this time, the Lt. Grand Commander assumed the day to day duties of the Grand Commander and continued them until the 1987 election. It seems that the council was in something of a shock. Longe had served in office for so long and had been such a massive and successful figure in the council that there was uncertainty about how to carry on after his death. The

only other time which seemed to have brought such sock to a supreme council was in the Southern Jurisdiction following the death of Albert Pike.

6. Dr. Bell's doctoral dissertation was first published (hardback) by the Louisiana State University Press in 1996. In 2004, it was released in paperback as *Revolution, Romanticism, and the Afro-Creole Protest Tradition in Louisiana, 1718-1868* (Baton Rouge, LA Louisiana State University Press, 2004).

7. The George Longe Collection is located in *The Amistad Research Center* at Tulane University in New Orleans, LA. Online, the collection can be found at: http://www.amistadresearchcenter.org.

8. *The Bonseigneur Rituals*, (The Netherlands, The Latomia Foundation, 1996. Republished in the USA by Cornerstone Book Publishers, New Orleans, LA, 2008).

9. Michael R. Poll, "James Foulhouze: Sovereign Grand Commander of the Supreme Council of Louisiana" *Heredom Vol. 6*, (Washington, D.C., The Scottish Rite Research Society, 1997) pp. 64-69.

A Final Thought

Before this book closes, there is an interesting argument that I have heard advanced on several occasions over the last few years concerning the Supreme Council of Louisiana. The argument is rather simple. While it is acknowledged that the Supreme Council of Louisiana was "most likely" a very regular and valid Supreme Council of the Ancient and Accepted Scottish Rite, the claim is that it does not matter as the original body no longer exists. It is pointed out that when the Concordat of 1855 took place, the Supreme Council of Louisiana was, with that vote, dissolved and ceased to exist. What the "former members" created was a *reorganization* (without authority and rights) of the former body. The argument continues by saying that what happened in the mid-1800s was a very unfortunate series of events that was most likely not very Masonic in nature. But what was done is done. There is simply no way to go back in time to correct what happened.

That's a very interesting and reasonable-sounding argument. The problem is that it ignores other similar events around that same time in Louisiana Masonry. The problem is also that both sides, at times, seemed to define reality by their own terms. You see, Louisiana is a very interesting state in quite a number of ways. For example, I lived in Virginia for about ten years and became a realtor. At that time, I was told that my real estate license was good in all states *except* Louisiana. I was told that Louisiana has a "strange" and different Civil Code (*The Napoleonic Code*). This was something that I had heard before, but I didn't know how far it reached or differed from other states. I then considered Masonry in Louisiana and realized why the argument relating to the present-day Supreme Council of Louisiana may not be as valid as some might believe.

We need to revisit, for a moment, the 1850 merger of the Grand Lodge of Louisiana with the Louisiana Grand Lodge. With the new Grand Lodge of Louisiana, the 1833 concordat between the Grand Lodge of Louisiana and the Grand Consistory of Louisiana was pretty much thrown out of the window. The new Grand Lodge announced that the lodges working in the Scottish Rite or French Rite rituals would be turning in their charters and would, from then on, work in the York Rite. Lodges were *very* unhappy. They felt, with good reason, tricked. Three lodges applied to the Supreme Council of Louisiana for relief. They cited the reason for doing this was because the agreement between the Grand Lodge and the Grand Consistory had been violated. It was because of that violation of the agreement that the Supreme Council of Louisiana accepted them and began controlling craft lodges. Masonry in Louisiana was in a total state of upheaval and confusion.

With the Concordat of 1855, everything again changed, and action had to be taken in regard to the craft lodges under the Supreme Council of Louisiana. The lodges were given little choice as to their future. The Supreme Council would no longer allow them under their jurisdiction. They were given the choice of returning to the Grand Lodge or closing shop. With that decision, the lodges returned to the jurisdiction of the Grand Lodge. Following the Concordat, another announcement was made. It was announced that the Supreme Council of Louisiana had never ceased to exist, was under new (former) leadership, and made the offer for the lodges to return to their jurisdiction. With that announcement, two lodges voted to return to the Supreme Council, and one did not wish to return. But we need to turn our attention to one of the two lodges that voted to return, Etoile Polaire Lodge No. 1 (Polar Star Lodge No. 1).

Following the announcement that the Supreme Council of Louisiana was still in existence and the offer to return was made, the majority of the members present at Etoile Polaire voted to pass again under its jurisdiction. One of the members of Etoile Polaire, however, had a serious problem with the lodge passing again under the Supreme Council's jurisdiction. This member was Charles Claiborne. It makes perfect sense why Claiborne did not desire to return to the jurisdiction of the Supreme Council of Louisiana. Claiborne was the Sovereign Grand Commander at the time of the signing of the Concordat of 1855 with the Southern Jurisdiction. It would be, to say the least, awkward for Claiborne to have his own craft lodge under the jurisdiction of the very body that he attempted to abolish and, according to the Grand Lodge of Louisiana, was abolished.

But the result of the vote was that the lodge passed again under the Supreme Council of Louisiana. But the Grand Lodge of Louisiana did not consider the lodge's vote or the changing of jurisdictions as legitimate. They continued to charge the lodge and members with dues and Grand Lodge assessments. The members of Etoile Polaire who voted to leave the Grand Lodge refused to pay, saying that they were no longer under the jurisdiction of the Grand Lodge. In effect, there were then two lodges with the same name (but different members), with both claiming ownership of the lodge building and all assets.

A lawsuit followed which went to the Louisiana Supreme Court. The case of "Polar Star Lodge No. 1 v. Polar Star Lodge No. 1" (16 La. Ann. 53, Louisiana Supreme Court) was decided on January 01, 1861. The Grand Lodge Etoile Polaire lodge won the lawsuit. The Supreme Council Etoile Polaire was ordered to turn over all property and assets to the

Grand Lodge Etoile Polaire. But how was that decision possible? Maybe on the night of the vote, the members voting to change jurisdictions did not actually have the majority of the votes? No, that was not it. From the court transcript of the meeting night:

> *Of the members present, 17 members voted in the affirmative; 4 voted negatively, to-wit, J. L. Tissot, Oct. Schwaner, P. Deverges, F. Levasseur; and three members left the room before the vote and opposed the measure, to-wit: Michel Meilleur, F. A. Lumsden and Ch. Claiborne. – Polar Star Lodge No. 1 v. Polar Star Lodge No. 1, 16 La. Ann. 53, 55 (La. 1861)*

You see, in Louisiana, all Masonic lodges and bodies are state corporations. As such, they must follow state law. If members of a corporation desire to leave the corporation in order to form a new corporation, they are free to do so. But their action will have no effect on the original corporation unless *all* of the members of the corporation desire for the corporation to end or dramatically change the nature of the corporation. Also, from the Supreme Court transcript:

> *The seceding members had, no doubt, a right to cease to be members of the corporation; they have made so complete an abandonment of the corporation, and such a resignation of their interest, in the charter, in declaring the dissolution of Polar Star Lodge that their acts amount to an express declaration that they would serve no longer as members of the corporation, and they must be bound by their declarations and considered and treated as not being members of the corporation any longer. But if it was in the power of the seceding members to abandon the corporation, it was not in their power either to dispose of the property of the corporation, or to destroy the charter of the corporation.*

The corporation, therefore, still existed, with all their rights, privileges and franchises unimpaired, and the members remaining faithful to the charter and contract of incorporation, were the only members of the corporation of Polar Star Lodge No. 1, and they alone formed and continued the same corporation. — Polar Star Lodge No. 1 v. Polar Star Lodge No. 1, 16 La. Ann. 53, 56 (La. 1861)

Once the members of Etoile Polaire voted to leave the jurisdiction of the Grand Lodge, they essentially created a second Etoile Polaire Lodge. The Grand Lodge did not have a legal right to charge the new lodge with dues and assessments, but the new Etoile Polaire did not have a right to the property and funds of the original Etoile Polaire. The only legal way that a Louisiana corporation could accomplish what the Etoile Polaire vote suggested is if it was a unanimous vote. If even one member objected, the vote would have no effect on the corporation. The members were free to create a second Etoile Polaire, but they could not destroy the original one nor lay claim to any of the original's property or funds. Matters such as who is entitled to vote, who is and who is not a member are, in Louisiana, ultimately decided by a court following civil law.

Now, let's look again at the Concordat of 1855. Like Etoile Polaire, the Supreme Council of Louisiana was and is a Louisiana corporation. The debate as to if they were to dissolve themselves and pass under the jurisdiction of the Charleston Supreme Council was a long, hard-fought, and highly contested debate for the New Orleans Scottish Rite Masons — long before and after the Concordat. While it does seem that most of the Active Members present on the night of the vote (and again, membership is ultimately decided by courts) acted in favor of it, it would be ridiculous to suggest that it was a unanimous vote of the membership. The events following the

Concordat clearly show the anger and disapproval of the Concordat by many of the members.

James Foulhouze stated:
From the moment I had noticed of that nameless act [the Concordat of 1855], I called upon some 33ds, whom I knew to be true to their obligations, and with them I immediately opened the Supreme Council and continued its work, in order that it might not even be said that it had slept a single instant ... (The Masonic Delta November, 1857).

Did James Foulhouze (a District Court Judge) possibly have some "inside legal information" regarding the Concordat of 1855? Polar Star Lodge No. 1 v. Polar Star Lodge No. 1 clearly shows that it is the court, not any of the parties involved, who has the final say in regard to civil law. The internal actions of any Louisiana corporation are always subject to reversal by a civil court if they are found to not follow civil law.

So, what did the Concordat of 1855 accomplish? Did it dissolve the Supreme Council of Louisiana? As shown in the Polar Star case, this would take the unanimous approval of all the membership. Was the vote taken the unanimous wish of the entire membership? Given the upset, anger, and refusal to accept the decision by so many of the New Orleans Scottish Rite Masons, this seems highly doubtful. But what was the actual vote? I have not seen a report of the vote results. It would seem that, once again, we are left with either accepting someone's word or not. We do not have the basic option of examining documentation. And then, we need to consider the statement of James Foulhouze.

Foulhouze certainly acted as if he was confident of the legal right of the Supreme Council of Louisiana to continue as if it never "slept." It is possible that he knew full well the law and that his action would, if pushed, go in his favor if it came to a lawsuit. But there is another factor that we must consider. It has to do with good faith and the reputation of Masons. There is clearly only one reason why the New Orleans Masons who voted in support of the Concordat did so — they believed what the Charleston Masons told them about the New Orleans Scottish Rite being irregular. Look at Samory's speech in the chapter on the Supreme Council Session in New Orleans. Samory clearly believed the story about the Grand Constitutions of 1786. He believed the Charleston Masons when they told him that the Supreme Council of Louisiana did not have a Masonic right to exist. He believed them when they told him the story of the Grand Constitutions. He believed them when they told him that the Charleston Council did not slumber and that it was an active supreme council when the Supreme Council of Louisiana was created. Because he was a Mason of honor, he realized (as did all the New Orleans Scottish Rite Masons who supported the Concordat) that as men of honor, they should do what they felt was right over personal considerations. They faced very harsh criticism from the members of their own council for not supporting the body in which they were in leadership. Still, they placed honor first and acted as their belief led them. How would they have acted, however, if they had the information concerning the Grand Constitutions of 1786 that we have today? How would they have acted if they knew that there was not a single scrap of evidence that the Charleston Supreme Council came out of their "slumber" and reorganized in a manner not violating the Grand Constitutions of 1786? I believe it is very fair to say that the only reason those who voted for the Concordat of 1855 did so was because they believed the information told them by the Charleston Council that we today *know to be false.*

1. We cannot say with any certainty that the Concordat

of 1855 was a unanimous vote.

2. The ones who did vote for the Concordat clearly voted as they did because they received and believed false information from the Charleston Council.

The two Active Members of the Supreme Council of Louisiana who worked the hardest and advanced the Concordat more than anyone else were Claude Samory and Charles Laffon de Ladébat. Following the Concordat of 1855, both of these Masons would be rewarded by the Southern Jurisdiction with Active Memberships. But neither would remain. After a time on the inside of the Southern Jurisdiction, both became deeply disenchanted. Ladébat attended no Supreme Council Sessions outside of New Orleans and regularly criticized the actions of the Council.[1] Ladébat would resign his Active Membership in the Southern Jurisdiction and move to France.[2] Claude Samory not only resigned his membership in the Southern Jurisdiction in 1866, but he moved to France and reportedly renounced all of Freemasonry.[3]

The truth is not for all men, but only for those who seek it.
~ Ayn Rand

It would seem that sometimes the questions we ask are equal to or more important than the answers we receive. Exactly what is it that we seek?

Notes:

1. Ray Baker Harris, James D. Carter *History of the Supreme Council, 33° Southern Jurisdiction, USA (1801-1861)* Washington, D.C.: The Supreme Council, 33° 1964), 266, 284.
2. James D. Carter *History of the Supreme Council, 33° SJ USA (1861-1891).* (Washington, D.C.: The Supreme Council 33°, 1967). 264
3. Ibid., 20, 364.

ORDO AB CHAO

DEUS MEUMQUE JUS

APPENDICES

APPENDIX A
Charter for the 1852 "Mackey/New Orleans Consistory
Page 218

APPENDIX B
Transcription of Appendix B
Page 219-220

APPENDIX C
Petition to the "Grand Consistory of the State of Louisiana"
Page 221

APPENDIX D
List of Sovereign Grand Commanders of the Supreme Council
of Louisiana
Page 222

APPENDIX E
Transcription of Appendix D
Page 223

APPENDIX A
Charter for the 1852 "Mackey/New Orleans Consistory

Error! Bookmark not defined.Error! Bookmark not defined.

APPENDIX B
Transcription of the charter for the "Mackey/New Orleans" Consistory

Universi Terrarum Orbis Architectoms per Gloriam Ingentis
ORDO AB CHAO

From the Grand East of the Supreme Council of the Most Puissant Sovereign Grand Inspectors General of the Thirty Third degree under the C\ C\ of the Zenith answering to 32° 45′ North Latitude:

To our Illustrious, Most Valiant and Sublime Princes of the Royal Secret, Knights K-H, Illustrious Princes and Knights, Grand Ineffable and Sublime Freemasons of all degrees, ancient and modern, over the surface of the two hemispheres: To all whom these Letters Patent shall come, Greeting Health, Stability and Power:

Know ye that we the undersigned Sovereign Grand Inspectors General in Supreme Council of the Thirty Third degree (which Council was lawfully established in the city of Charleston, South Carolina on the 31st day of May A.D. 1801) duly congregated this 1st day of the Hebrew month Thebet in the year of the creation 5612 corresponding to the 24th of December in the Christian Era 1851, [*not legible*] the and or of our Illustrious Princes and Knights John Gedge Thrice Illustrious Grand Commander, Henry R. W. Hill and John Pemberton Illustrious Lieutenant Grand Commanders and B. P. Voorhies, Wm M. Perkins, N.J. Pegram, Wm. Prehn, L.H. Place, William DeBuys, Geo. Arnold Holt and reposing special trust and confidence in their capacity and zeal for the Order of Freemasonry.

By these present, Do Constitute them our aforesaid Princes and Knights a regular Consistory of Sublime Princes of the Royal Secret to be holden in the city of New Orleans and state of Louisiana.

Herewith investing them with all the titles and prerogatives which anywhere throughout the globe of rights belong to Consistories of Sublime Princes of the Royal Secret; And we do hereby grant to them, their associates and successors full authority to assemble and exalt and perfect Princes of Jerusalem in all the intermediate degrees of Knight of the East and West, Prince of Rose Croix, Grand Pontiff, Master Ad Vitam, Prussian Knight, Prince of Lebanon, Chief and Prince of the Tabernacle, Prince of Mercy, Knight of the Brazen Serpent, Commander of the Temple and Knight of the Sun. _____

And we the aforesaid Supreme Council do hereby constitute and appoint the Illustrious Grand Commander and his two Lieutenant Grand Commanders in the Consistory and their legal successors, our Proxies to be and appear for us or any three of us in the said Consistory, and in our name and behalf to confer the high degrees of K-H, Knight of St. Andrew, Grand Enquiring Commander, and Sublime Prince of the Royal Secret upon such duly qualified Knights of the Sun as their

Consistory shall deem worthy; and we invest the said Proxies with all the authority in the premises which we should have if personally present. _____ And we do furthermore authorize the aforesaid as our special Deputy to open and hold, and grant Warrants for opening and holding Lodges of Perfection, Councils of Princes of Jerusalem and Chapters of Rose Croix in the State of Louisiana and agreeably to the Ancient Constitutions of the Order._____ And aforesaid Consistory is hereby empowered to do all things which Sublime Bodies have a right to do in either hemisphere agreeably to the Laws, Rules and Regulations of the Ancient and Accepted Rite, with this provision, that the aforesaid Consistory do make an annual return to this Supreme Council of all persons therein admitted; specifying what degrees the said person have received and remitting a fee of two dollars for every person admitted and the aforesaid Council shall at all times hereafter pay and care to be paid due obedience to the edits of this Supreme Council, and faithful allegiance thereto, otherwise this warrant shall be null and void. _____

In testimony whereof, that full faith and credit may be given to all the lawful acts and deeds of the aforesaid Consistory of Louisiana at New Orleans, by all regularly constituted bodies throughout both hemispheres, we have granted this Warrant, and having signed the same with our own hands; have caused thereunto to be officiated the seals of our Order on the day and year above written.

J. H. Honour

R\+\, K-H\, S\P\R\S\, S\G\I\G\ 33

M\P\ Sovereign Grand Commander

James C. Norris

R\+\, K-H\, S\P\R\S\, S\G\I\G\ 33

Illust. Treasurer of the H-E-

Albert G. Mackey,
M.D.

R\+\, K-H\, S\P\R\S\, S\G\I\G\ 33

Illust\Secretary of the H-E-

R\+\, K-H\, S\P\R\S\, S\G\I\G\ 33

Illust\Gd Master of Ceremonies

J.A. Quitman

R\+\, K-H\, S\P\R\S\,

Sov\G\I\G\ 33°

C.M. Furman

R\+\, K-H\, S\P\R\S\, S\G\I\G\ 33

APPENDIX C

Petition to the "Grand Consistory of the State of Louisiana" from the Worshipful Master of Western Star Lodge #61 signed on February 11, 1852, but interesting enough recommended by John Gedge and Edward Barnett, both of the "Mackey" Consistory in New Orleans. This suggests the confusion concerning the bodies of the time.

APPENDIX D

T∴ T∴ G∴ O∴ T∴ G∴ A∴ O∴ T∴ U∴

THE ANCIENT AND ACCEPTED SCOTTISH RITE OF FREE
MASONRY GRAND COMMANDERS OF THE SUPREME COUNCIL
OF LOUISIANA

"Freemasonry is the subjugation of the Human, that is in man, by the Divine."

ILL∴ B∴ Orazio de Attellis, Marquis de Santangelo	Oct. 27, 1839
ILL∴ B∴ Jean Jacques Conte	Jan. 29, 1842
ILL∴ B∴ Jean Francois Connonge	Sept. 20, 1845
ILL∴ B∴ James Foulhouze	Jan. 31, 1848
ILL∴ B∴ Charles Claiborne	Jan. 1, 1854
ILL∴ B∴ J. J. Massicot	Oct. 7, 1856
ILL∴ B∴ James Foulhouze	April 22, 1857
ILL∴ B∴ Eugene Chassaignac	Jan. 7, 1867
ILL∴ B∴ Edouard Marc	Jan. 3, 1872
ILL∴ B∴ Armand Bertel	Feb. 23, 1875
ILL∴ B∴ Jean Gentil	June 20, 1876
ILL∴ B∴ Armand Bertel	Feb. 27, 1877
ILL∴ B∴ M. J. Piron	Sept 17, 1887
ILL∴ B∴ A. J. Guiranovich	Sept. 17, 1889
ILL∴ B∴ Joseph N. Cheri	Sept. 4, 1891
ILL∴ B∴ R. A. Chiapella	Feb. 24, 1893
ILL∴ B∴ O. A. Giovanni	March 24, 1893
ILL∴ B∴ R. A. Chiapella	Aug. 27, 1893
ILL∴ B∴ Joseph N. Cheri	Feb. 23, 1894
ILL∴ B∴ George U. Maury	July 3, 1915
ILL∴ B∴ Rene C. Metoyer	Feb. 26, 1923
ILL∴ B∴ George U. Maury	Feb. 24, 1925
ILL∴ B∴ Rene C. Metoyer	Feb. 26, 1926
ILL∴ B∴ Charles W. Vance	Oct. 27, 1937
ILL∴ B∴ George Longe	July 21, 1938
ILL B Joseph Williams	FEB 1987
ILL B Philip Washington Sr.	FEB 1993

248

APPENDIX E
Transcription of Appendix D
T:. T:. G::. O:. T:. G:. A:. O:. T:. U:.
THE ANCIENT AND ACCEPTED SCOTTISH RITE OF FREE
MASONRY GRAND COMMANDERS OF THE SUPREME
COUNCIL
OF LOUISIANA

ILL:. B:. Orazio de Attellis, Marquis de Santangelo ... Oct. 27, 1839
ILL:. B:. Jean Jacques Conte ... Jan. 29, 1842
ILL:. B:. Jean Francois Connenge [sic][1] ... Sept. 20, 1845
ILL:. B:. James Foulhouze ... Jan. 31, 1843
ILL:. B:. Charles Claiborne ... Jan. 1, 1854
ILL:. B:. J. J. Massicot ... Oct. 7, 1856
ILL:. B:. James Foulhouze ... April 22, 1857
ILL:. B:. Eugene Chassaignac ... Jan. 7, 1867
ILL:. B:. Edouard Marc ... Jan. 2, 1872
ILL:. B:. Armand Bertel ... Feb. 23, 1875
ILL:. B:. Jean Gentil ... June 20, 1876
ILL:. B:. Armand Bertel ... Feb. 27, 1877
ILL:. B:. M. J. Piron ... Sept. 17, 1887
ILL:. B:. A. J. Guiranovich ... Sept, 17, 1889
ILL:. B:. Joseph N. Cheri ... Sept. 4, 1891
ILL:. B:. R. A. Chiapella ... Feb. 24, 1893
ILL:. B:. O. A. Giovanni ... March 24, 1893
ILL:. B:. R. A. Chiapella ... Aug. 27, 1893
ILL:. B:. Joseph N. Cheri ... Feb. 23, 1894
ILL:. B:. George U. Maury ... July 3, 1915
ILL:. B:. Rene C. Metoyer ... Feb. 26, 1926
ILL:. B:. Charles W. Vance ... Oct. 27, 1937
ILL:. B:. George Longe ... July 21, 1938
ILL:. B:. Joseph Williams   Feb. 1987
ILL:. B:. Philip Washington, Sr.   Feb. 1993

1. Correct spelling "Canonge"

(Left side text)
"Freemasonry is the subjugation of the Human,
that is in man, by the Divine."

Index

About The Author

Michael R. Poll (1954 - present) is the owner of Cornerstone Book Publishers and former editor of the *Journal of The Masonic Society*. He is a Fellow and Past President of The Masonic Society, a Fellow of the Philalethes Society, a Fellow of the Maine Lodge of Research, Member of the Society of Blue Friars, and Full Member of the Texas Lodge of Research.

A New York Times Bestselling writer and publisher, he is a prolific writer, editor, and publisher of Masonic and esoteric books. He is also the host of the YouTube channel "New Orleans Scottish Rite College." As time permits, he travels and speaks on the history of Freemasonry, with a particular focus on the early history of the Scottish Rite.

New Orleans Scottish Rite College
www.youtube.com/c/NewOrleansScottishRiteCollege

Clear, Easy to Watch
Scottish Rite and Craft Lodge
Podcast & Video Education